THE JOURNALISM BREAKDOWN:

WRITING MULTIMEDIA JOURNALISM CONTENT IN THE ERA OF CHANGING MEDIA SYSTEMS AND ECONOMIC MODELS

THE JOURNALISM BREAKDOWN:

WRITING MULTIMEDIA JOURNALISM CONTENT IN THE ERA OF CHANGING MEDIA SYSTEMS AND ECONOMIC MODELS

SHANE TILTON, PH.D.
OHIO NORTHERN UNIVERSITY

CFSC PUBLISHING

A DIVISION OF THE CENTER FOR SOCIETY AND CYBERSTUDIES

For more information, write: CFSC Publishing, ℅ The Center for Society and Cyberstudies, 4200 Regent Street, Suite #200, Columbus, OH 43219

10 9 8 7 6 5 4 3 2

LCCN: 2020913266
ISBN: 978-1-7354254-0-5 (trade paper)
ISBN: 978-1-7354254-1-2 (ebook)

Dewey Decimal Classification: 070.17 TIL
Library of Congress Call Number: PN4775

LCCO Topic 1: Journalism--Journalism. The periodical press, etc.
LCCO Topic 2: Technique, Practical journalism--General works.

Printed by KDP

ACKNOWLEDGMENTS

It always feels weird to talk or write anything about mass media or journalism. I joke that "I'm so meta even this acronym" when presenting in front of a crowd about media and communication. Being a media practitioner and educator for the past two decades would not be possible without a ton of people, especially those that helped me finalize this rather thick tome of knowledge.

Brandy Tilton needs to be recognized first for supporting me along the way, including copy-editing my 73,448-word dissertation. I decided to save her that madness by getting others to do that work. She is my biggest cheerleader and the love of my life.

I need the thank my support staff of Roscoe, Nano, Gray Eye, Juniper, Mambo, and Bitsy, as my cats are always my fiercest critics, especially when I am the only thing standing between them and dinner.

Much love needs to be sent to my mom, my dad, Becky, Jim, my aunts, my uncles, my cousins, my step-brothers, and my step-sisters, as it is fair to say most of them still don't quite understand what I do, yet they still love me.

My appreciation also goes to the Uher family and the Plummer family. Their reunions are an excellent time to see familiar faces and take a break from the world.

I would like to thank Craig Evans from CFSC Publishing, Ross Wagenhofer and Margaret Farrelly from Routledge, Lily Norton from SAGE Publishing, and the various reviewers. They helped make this book better with their thoughtful feedback and attention to detail.

Warm words of thanks also need to be given to the Worshipful Company of Stationers and Newspaper Makers, especially the Young Stationers and their Digital Media Group. Their support makes me proud to be a Freeman of the Company.

The main reason that this book has finally been published after 18 months of consistent writing and rewriting was in part due to the support I received from all of my colleagues, students, and former students from the Ohio Northern

University School of Social Sciences and Human Interaction and the Institute of Civics and Public Policy. I would especially like to thank Erin Swick, Jenny Walton, and Mark Cruea from Communication and Media Studies and Dean Holly Baumgartner of the Getty College of Arts and Science at Ohio Northern University for their encouraging words for the past two years.

I also need to thank Gary Earich, George Hiotis, and Hank Littick from WHIZ-TV and Jim Barstow from the Coshocton Tribune for giving me my first jobs in the media. It's weird to think of myself as alumni from WHIZ because that was my dream job as a kid.

My job has been made easier thanks to all journalists and staff members (both current and former) who served the Northern Review, WONB radio, and ONU-3 TV. Their pursuit of excellence has made it effortless to show off the high-quality work they produce.

It would be impossible to give enough thanks to all my former students and colleagues at the Ohio University of Zanesville, Ohio University Lancaster, Muskingum University, and the Instructional Communication & Research program at the University of Kentucky's College of Communication and Information. They made me the higher education profession I am today.

I need to thank my conference family (Emory & Melissa Daniel, Anthony & Holiday Bean, Rachel Kowert, Sarah Hays, Kelli Dunlap (and Jack), Rafael Boccamazzo, Ryan Kelly, Lea Hughes, Adam Jones, Adam Davis, Megan Connell, Jamie Madigan, Randall Hampton, Jared & Elizabeth Kilmer, Amelia Herbst, Jess Stone, Steph Orme, Arienne Ferchaud, John Savage, Emily Layne Floyd, and Alex Abrate) for always breaking me out of whatever rut I am in at the moment.

I need to thank *Borderlands*, *Overwatch*, and *Tak* for being wonderful distractions in between writing chapters. I also need to thank The Mountain Goats, Alexrainbird Music, The Tragically Hip, Winterpills, Milk Carton Kids, The Main Squeeze, Vulfpeck, Theo Katzman, Apartment Sessions, Frog Leap Studios, Walk Off The Earth, Live from Here, Postmodern Jukebox, NPR Tiny Desk Concerts, Gogol Bordello, Chillhop Radio, Dave Matthews Band & Kerrigan-Lowdermilk for producing great music to listen to while writing.

ADDITIONAL THANKS:

- *QI, The Last Leg, Taskmaster, Last Week Tonight with John Oliver, Hypothetical,* and *Have I Got News For You?* for being my rewards for finishing chapters.

- New York Times' *The Daily, The Federalist Radio Hour, Freakonomics Radio, It's All Journalism,* WNYC's *On the Media, Pod Save America,* CBC's *Spark, This American Life,* NPR's *Up First,* and VOX's *The Weeds* for being my news podcast diet throughout the day.

- *Young Nostalgia, You Look Nice Today, Welcome to Night Vale, NPR's Wait Wait… Don't Tell Me, The Underculture with James Adomian, NPR's Tiny Desk Concerts, The Thrilling Adventure Hour, Reply All, Oh, Hello: the P'dcast, WNYC's Note to Self, Live from Here, The Horne Section Podcast, The Geek Bracket, Fun City, Do By Friday, The Darkest Timeline, The Good Place: The Podcast, Conan O'Brien Needs A Friend, The Black Door,* and *Back to Work* for being the entertainment podcasts that help keep my sanity.

- Alex Tvaroch for making me wonder if the Doors were a good band.

- Connor Gillmor for making me wonder if a Pop-Tart is a sandwich.

- Austin Gammell for making me wonder about my sanity.

- Sam Ventrella for not making me wonder if I could handle being an advisor for a college newspaper.

- Rachel Doty, Brianne Mosley, and Nicki Tebbe for helping me with WONB.

As always, thank you, Nick.

Shane Tilton
July 4, 2020

TABLE OF CONTENTS

Acknowledgments...v

Preface: Journalism in the Current Media Environment 3

Part 1: The Journalism Breakdown 7

Chapter 1: Pre-writing 13

Chapter 2: Writing Progressions...24

Chapter 3: Interview Protocols 47

Chapter 4: Using Quotes in Context 67

Chapter 5: Media Enhancements...82

Chapter 6: Creating a Compelling Narrative 98

Chapter 7: Addressing the "So What" Question in the Narrative...................108

Chapter 8: Tying Up the Loose Ends of the Story 120

Chapter 9: The Five Criteria of Journalistic Content.........................131

Chapter 10: Executive and Editorial Review 154

Part 1: Conclusion 170

Part 2: Practicum Modules...173

Chapter 11: Photojournalism...176

Chapter 12: Audio Production 193

Chapter 13: Video Production 209

Chapter 14: Social Media...226

Chapter 15: Feature Writing..239

Chapter 16: Journalistic Ethics 253

Chapter 17: Math for Journalists 265

Chapter 18: Infographics 284

Chapter 19: Content Management Systems 296

Chapter 20: Crafting Executive Summaries..312

Part 2: Conclusion 325

Postscript: The Future of Journalism in Society 328

Index 330

Author's Bio...337

PREFACE: JOURNALISM IN THE CURRENT MEDIA ENVIRONMENT

Greetings,

You have in your hand (either in book form, on the phone, on a tablet, or another type of computer) something that represents almost two decades of media and journalism teaching in American higher education and an additional half-decade working in the industry. The information in this book is an encapsulation of lessons taught in both the classroom and the field to improve the quality of journalistic content my students produce. It might help to introduce myself and explain why such a primer of journalism is needed now.

My name is Shane Tilton. I am an associate professor of multimedia journalism at Ohio Northern University. My teaching career began in 2002 after several years working in television as a senior production assistant, in newspapers as a stringer, and in a video production company as a jack of all trades. This collection of experience means nearly 25 years of experience in the field of journalism. During this time, I've been awarded Advisor of the Year twice by the Society for Collegiate Journalists. The Young Stationers' awarded me their Prize in 2018 for excellence in the field of journalism and communication. I was the first American to be given this honor and only one of a select few international members to earn such acclaim in the more than 600-year history of the Worshipful Company of Stationers and Newspaper Makers. Several of my students have received national honors from the Broadcast Education Association, College Media Association, Ohio News Media Association, and other media organizations while teaching at Ohio Northern University. Where I am now as an educator made it feel like it was the right time to write down the fundamentals from my course and turn them into a book to help other journalists improve the stories' quality.

Three driving factors led to my decision to write a multimedia journalism textbook. The primary force was that I wanted to create a manual I wish I had as an undergraduate journalism major. One of the most significant issues that I felt most journalism programs and textbooks did not cover was how to incorporate a good narrative flow into our work. Crafting a tremendous journalistic narrative is vital for maintaining a better-informed public that can engage in civic discourse to improve the local community and society as a whole. The problem with that idea of journalism is that it is hard to agree on what makes:

- a better-informed public,

- thoughtful engagement between citizens,

- reasonable civic discourse, and

- community & social improvements.

The problem with those four bullet points is that they are becoming more contentious, given the changes in how journalists produce the news and how audiences receive that content. Economic pressure and other factors have dramatically changed the media landscape over the past decade. The public is becoming more splintered, using the media sources that speak to citizens' beliefs rather than their social or cultural values (Edy & Meirick, 2019). The nature of newer channels of communication has lead to less reasonable civic discourse and thoughtful engagement between citizens (Elder, 2019). It is also fair to argue that the definitions of a community and society are evolving, given the more mobile nature of people in their everyday lives (Atzori, Iera, & Morabito, 2017).

Even with all of those concerns, journalists need a good foundation for moving forward with their story. It is easy to have writer's block or simply be clueless about how to approach the story. This book's techniques should help with some of the confusion that journalists experience from time to time. Understanding the practices laid out in *The Journalism Breakdown* will provide clarity on where to proceed with the narrative.

Another consideration was that I wanted to have a more comprehensive multimedia journalism handbook during my first year as an assistant professor of multimedia journalism. The problem I ran into when looking for a textbook for "News Writing" was that most of the books I went through dealt too much with current multimedia practices, specifically the right platforms to deliver the news. My concern with those practices is that the students are more worried about formatting the reporting correctly for Facebook or Twitter audiences rather than thinking about how all of the different modes of delivering the news work together to present a clearer understanding of the components and narratives which make up the story.

The Journalism Breakdown model allows those different modes to work in concert with one another to enhance the audience's understanding of the story rather than using the social network to promote a brand or an individual journalist. This model looks at the history of journalism to provide some guidance to craft quality stories that will compel the audiences to keep reading, listening, or watching the story. Students of journalism can examine past reporters and the mediums they used to tell the stories of the day and apply some of those narrative techniques in multimedia reporting.

My last thought was that I wanted a book that my students would want to keep after taking my classes as it would be useful for their future work. I understand that most students will rent their textbooks or sell them back at the end of the semester. This book was written in a way that will allow readers to find wisdom months or even years after its initial purchase. One of the biggest continuing takeaways I want readers to have from this book is how to be an ethical journalist. Ethical journalism is difficult nowadays as the speed of news demands quick turnarounds to met publishing deadlines. *The Journalism Breakdown* allows students to maintain ethical standards while still meeting the audience's expectations for news.

I believe that the book in front of you meets those three requirements that I was looking for in a journalism textbook that I was unable to find. This textbook works well with both the current version of the *Associated Press Stylebook* and a useful grammar guide. I like Susan's Thurman's *The Only Grammar Book You'll Ever Need*, Brooks, Pinson, and Wilson's *Working with Words*, or Marda Dunsky's *Watch Your Words*. Those three guides have found a place on my syllabus at one time or another with success.

The last wisdom I give you before starting this process is the last words I put on all of my syllabi, "Don't panic; this is the way to happiness." I explain that if any part of this experience is causing your immense trouble that we need to talk about the issue and find a solution. The reason that this saying (which comes from the words of both Douglas Adams and Brian Browne Walker) is a starting point in this discussion about journalism is now (more than ever) journalists need a sound social support system to make it through the day. I would not have survived the day-to-day struggle to hit the daily deadlines without editors, journalists, and friends keeping me calm and sane.

Journalists must find their people to make it through.

WORKS CITED

Atzori, L., Iera, A., & Morabito, G. (2017). Understanding the Internet of Things: Definition, potentials, and societal role of a fast evolving paradigm. *Ad Hoc Networks, 56,* 122–140. doi: 10.1016/j.adhoc.2016.12.004

Edy, J. A., & Meirick, P. C. (2019). *A Nation Fragmented: The public agenda in the information age.* Temple University Press.

Elder, A. (2019). The Interpersonal is Political: Unfriending to promote civic discourse on social media. *Ethics and Information Technology, 22*(1), 15–24. doi: 10.1007/s10676-019-09511-4

PART 1: THE JOURNALISM BREAKDOWN

Any discussion about the journalist's development of writing and media production in the era of multimedia journalism needs to start with a "realm of the known" analysis. First of all, we need to begin with a simple description of journalism to ensure we are all on the same page from here on out. I use a four-point definition to explain the creation of editorial content that balances the past practices and interpretations of journalism with the current implementation of content creation throughout the Internet. These bullet points become part of the first class session of any course I teach related to journalism.

1. Journalism is any mediated work that explains a topic / issue / point of interest / event of current interest using a truthful, compelling narrative about a community to a given audience.

2. The created content allows the audience to understand the actors that influence that truthful, compelling narrative where the reporter acts as the voice or record of a given community.

3. The content explains why the audience should care about that topic / issue / point of interest / event within the story's flow.

4. The content follows the ethos and spirit of journalism as defined by journalistic organizations (Tilton, 2016).

This definition is an encapsulation of my experience being a freelance newspaper journalist (aka a "stringer"), a senior production assistant for a local 6 o'clock and 11 o'clock news, and educator in the fields of journalism, communication, and the media for around two decades. However, it seems fair to clarify some of the terms used in this definition, as I want to make sure that we are talking about the same aspects of journalism.

Mediated work is any produced work distributed through media channels such as a website, television channel, radio station, podcast, magazine, newspaper, or application. The mediated work includes a narrative that drives the content. Any **narrative** allows a person who reads, listens, or sees a story to start at one particular viewpoint and end with a slightly to a dramatically different understanding of the world. How the journalist should advance the story depends heavily on the situation (topic / issue / point of interest / event) that forms that narrative.

A **topic** is a story that covers an area of community knowledge that citizens talk about that represents a part of civic life for the audience. Schools within a community can serve as a topic if the story is about teaching students the history of the local community. The facts of the topic drive this type of narrative.

An **issue** is the abstraction of a core concern that impacts a community's factions in different ways to the point of causing a conflict. The tricky part of writing this type of story is making that abstraction concrete. A tax levy is an issue as there can be people for and against the levy. Conflict drives these stories.

A **point of interest** is a human-interest aspect of community life representing the spirit of that given community. A teacher teaching a school for forty years tends to be a point of interest story if the teacher is a respected member of the local area. These stories are personality-driven.

An **event** is a community action that occurs during a specific time. Homecoming is one classic example of an event article that most college journalists write about in their careers. The story is driven by how the event impacts the local community during the time of the writing of the article.

Actors are the people or groups in the narrative whose efforts to affect something in the story. These efforts add to the narrative when the journalist explains how their actions relate to other activities performed about community members. Using actors in this definition does not mean that they are fictional. Instead, this term helps journalists focus on the crucial aspects of the narrative. Actors make up one of the Elements of the story. **Elements** (when capitalized in this book) are the objects that are vital in the telling of the story.

Communities and audiences are two different groups of people that the journalist works with daily. **Communities** are the groups that journalists force their story on in the content they create. **Audiences** are the people that read, see, or listen to the work that the journalist produces. Both audiences and communities can have a more specific reason that they are a member of a given community or audience.

There seem to be four general types of these groups that journalists should be aware of when starting in a new job. The journalist will need to change the nature of communication between themselves and those various groupings. It is also important to note that there can be an extensive overlap between those two populations.

A **community of place, community of location,** or a **local audience** typically has a similar set of "shared social experiences" reflected in geography, institutions, and social structures of a given region of the world that the community or audience has some permanence or semi-permanence to that given area. Your hometown is a community of place, and the local newspaper serves the local audience (Kemmis, 1992).

A **community of convenience** or an **audience of convenience** form from an impromptu gathering of people where none of them are "bound" to the group for an extended period. Attendees of a weekend-long festival would represent a community of convenience. Those that can not attend the festival but want to know more about what is happening at the festival would be an audience of convenience (Pool, 1983).

A **community of interest** or an **audience of interest** promotes the passions, knowledge base, and mutual respect of the criteria that define a hobby or pastime. Baseball card collectors would be a community of interest. Fans of baseball that watch as much of the sport as they can represent the audience of interest (Swales, 2016).

A **professional community** or a **professional audience** formally believes in a common set the ethical standards, training, and best practices to maintain the status quo and advancement of an occupation. Medical professionals would be the community, while those reading up the specific branches of medicine would be a professional audience (Wenger, 1998).

The audience depends on journalists to craft a solid narrative that provides a new perspective about the actors, actions, places, cultures, and societies referenced in the story. Narratives like this are only successful if the journalist creates a reliable flow within the story. **Flow** allows the audience to forget they are reading a story and absorbed by the narrative within the mediated work (Rogers, 2019 July 3).

The **ethos** is the ethical standards that journalists practice and the credibility that journalists have on maintaining the audience's civic engagement with their community and other communities. Journalism without ethos is just rumor-mongering. The **spirit** of journalism is a more abstract set of criteria that allows the person practicing journalism to be recognized as a journalist by the audience and community. These criteria can include the news's aesthetic presentation to the general level of interactions that the journalist has with the community.

A **journalistic organization** or **news organization** represents a collective of journalists under one editorial system and workflow. This standard banner allows the journalists under that banner to share a common set of visual practices to present the news, a general model for organizing information in a story, and a network of sources that give clarity to what is happening in the communities highlighted by the journalistic organization.

This technical construction of journalism serves a purpose for the rest of the book. It's the rationale for a model of crafting a journalistic narrative that is the Journalism Breakdown. One of the concerns raised by colleagues, friends, and others that teaching journalism is "how do you write a book about multimedia journalism that won't be obsolete the moment it is printed?"

To be honest, this is a legitimate concern.

I created this book because I was frustrated that I couldn't find one that showed good journalistic practices and recognized that the nature of journalism was changing rapidly. My proposed solution to this obsolescence problem is not to depend on multimedia services being there by the time you read this book. This solution means focusing more on the general practice of journalism than being a series of tutorials on the tools of production. Journalists should think critically about how different services (social media, content creations, or even promotional sites) help journalists connect with audiences, communities, and sources for stories.

This understanding led to the development of the **Journalism Breakdown**. I developed this technique of training students as a means to improve their ability to craft great journalistic content. I explain throughout this book the different points of inspiration that led to its creation. This technique is a step-by-step process we go over during the first journalism course students take with me. The steps are:

- Step Zero: Pre-writing (Fundamental Research and Freewriting)

- Step One: The Writing Progression

- Step Two: Interview Protocols

- Step Three: Using Quotes in Context

- Step Four: Media Enhancements

- Step Five: Creating a Compelling Narrative

- Step Six: Addressing the "So What" Question in a Narrative

- Step Seven: Tying Up the Loose Ends of the Story

- Step Eight: The Five Criteria of Journalistic Content

- Step Nine: Executive and editorial review

Applying this method will allow journalists at their first job to have success in journalistic content creation. Also, I think this model can help all journalists find a technique that will improve their writing and communication skills regardless of the mode of communication they must use as this process is grounded in the practices of effective communication for a variety of audiences.

Journalistic content is only meaningful if the journalist can explain what is significant to the community within the context of a given story. This significance is based on the type of community it is. Journalists must find a way to communicate the crucial elements to the audience on terms they understand. Those elements must also be deemed informative based on the audience's level of need to understand broader social and cultural concerns.

WORKS CITED

Kemmis, D. (1992). *Community and the Politics of Place*. University of Oklahoma Press.

Pool, I. de S. (1983). *Technologies of Freedom*. Belknap Press.

Rogers, T. (2019, July 3). *What is a Quality Method for Writing a News Story?* Retrieved April 15, 2020, from https://web.archive.org/web/20191015225004/https://www.thoughtco.com/producing-the-perfect-news-story-2073904

Tilton, S. (2016). "Steve Jobs is Dead": iReport and the ethos of citizen journalism. In A. Davisson & P. Booth (Eds.), *Controversies in Digital Ethics*, (pp. 308-319). Bloomsbury.

Wenger, E. (2018). *Communities of Practice: Learning, meaning, and identity*. Cambridge University Press.

CHAPTER 1: PRE-WRITING

Any discussion about the process involving the development of good journalistic content must begin with a conversation about how a journalist plans out their story. It is almost second nature and an invisible part of the process for seasoned journalists.

They just start writing.

Their experiences and expertise allow them to start crafting the narrative early on in the process. It can be more difficult for others to find the underlying thread that the story should follow.

My first story as a stringer was to cover the local summer league baseball team. They played a double-header and won the first game that season during the second game of the day. I wrote a chronological play-by-play description of the game. It was a pretty dry article, and I failed the cardinal rule of journalism. There were no quotes in the story. The major problem was I spent too much time during the game worrying about the statistical accuracy of my figures that I failed to get the narrative flow of the story. My editor needed to publish it as I hit the deadline and did so. He explained to me that I got all of the facts right and still got the story wrong. I got the story wrong because I failed to do the journalist's primary role in that situation.

The journalist's primary role is to act as the in-between from the community's view of the topic / issue / point of interest / event to the audience's understanding of the reality of the world. This role forces the journalists to explain the critical factors of the story in narrative form. An in-between clearly explains the relationships between all factors within the context of the story. To do that, journalists must identify all of the factors that make up the topic / issue / point of interest / event.

A journalist must have a level of expertise in the given topic / issue / point of interest / event to present the story using the standards and practices of journalism. **Expertise** is more than having enough of the baseline knowledge about the subject matter to write the story. It means understanding the more significant social and cultural issues that drive it.

Cultural issues affect the way that an audience will read a story. Culture is the set of central characteristics that define the audience and the community that the journalist writes about in their story. Shared values, goals, and attitudes of a community or audience represent their culture (Vos, Eichholz, & Karaliova, 2019).

Social issues affect the way the audience will relate to the people referenced in the story. Society refers to the people of a group and their interactions with each other. A standard set of institutions, activities, interests, and traditions make up that community or audience's societal references (Borger, van Hoof, & Sanders, 2019).

The only way journalists can feel the confidence that they have the necessary level of expertise to cover a given story is by performing two vital pre-writing exercises, Fundamental Research & Freewriting.

FUNDAMENTAL RESEARCH

Fundamental Research is the first principle and practice that students go through before writing their first journalistic article. This technique borrows heavily from the liberal arts tradition of academic research. **Academic research** forces students to think critically about the sources they are looking at to determine if they address the central thesis of their paper or presentation (Lander, Seeho, and Foster, 2019). The student should be able to summarize the key points from their sources and know how to turn that information into knowledge that is useful for their work.

Another inspiration for the Fundamental Research comes from practicing observational reporting or traditions of the "town crier." **Observational reporting** represents the "perspective that may not be reflected by the social or educational composition of a given professional newsroom" (Clements-Housser, 2018, 40). This type of reporting is driven by explaining the story's facts using the universal language of the community where the story takes place.

Both academic research and observational reporting serve the purpose of giving the journalist a standard level of understanding of a given subject. Academic research forces the journalist to summarize the facts of a story present in sources that reflect the reality of the topic / issue / point of interest / event. Observational reporting grounds the story toward the journalist's experiences about the topic / issue / point of interest / event.

THE PRACTICE OF FUNDAMENTAL RESEARCH

Journalists start Fundamental Research (and by extension the Journalism Breakdown) by taking the time to address the **Essential Questions** of journalism (who, what, where, when, why, and how) as broadly as possible. The following six questions represent a way to ask the Essential Questions that takes advantage of academic research and observational reporting practices.

1. When are all of the significant actions happening?

2. Where are all of the central locations?

3. Who are all of the fundamental actors and organizations?

4. What are the essential documents and other materials?

5. Why should the audience care about this story?

6. How do the actors, actions, locations, documents relate to one another?

The first four questions will provide the answers to the last two questions. All of the answers to these six questions make up the critical **factors** of the narrative. It is fair to the point that this practice is the first of the two pre-writing techniques used by the journalists that come out of the Ohio Northern program. Reporters can skip this step if they feel they have enough of an understanding of those critical factors. It is also possible that the reporter will need to return to this step if their narrative dramatically shifts during the process of working on their story.

THE VALUE OF FUNDAMENTAL RESEARCH

Fundamental Research's biggest strength is that it allows the reporter to define a given story's boundaries. One of the issues that I dealt with regularly when advising students on their stories was discussing how you would if you had a completed story. The classic editor's line "it is done when it is done" was not a satisfactory answer for my students. The way I currently answer this query is "when you feel you have addressed all relevant critical factors so your audience clearly understands them."

The second valuable reason to use the Fundamental Research techniques is that it acts as a litmus test to determine if the journalist can begin writing the story. An inability to answer one of these questions entirely means that the journalist must learn the answers to work on the story. This gap of knowledge can only be resolved by working with the available resources. This practice will also give journalists direction to know what questions to ask editors about the story before taking it on.

A final point to note about Fundamental Research is that journalists who use this technique regularly for their stories will find better reliable sources in future reporting. This practice helps journalists apply the **CRAAP Standard** (Currency, Relevance, Authority, Accuracy, and Purpose) for evaluating the sources for story ideas, quotes, and embedded links. Journalists will need to make sure that:

- the information they are gathering is timely,

- the information fits the needs of the story,

- the information's author is identifiable,

- the information is correct, and

- the reasoning for the person to share that information is clearly understood (Blakeslee, 2004).

All of these central modes of assessment allow journalists to feel better about the information they include in their stories. Completing Fundamental Research means that the journalist must start putting the pieces together to form a narrative. This section of the Journalism Breakdown is where Freewriting is used.

FREEWRITING

Freewriting is the practice that allows journalists to put down everything that they know about a story in one continuous form. This practice is often confused with "stream of consciousness" writing or even mindmapping. All three of these techniques have different purposes that solve various problems associated with the practice of creating content.

Stream of consciousness writing is a non-restrictive mode of writing designed to get the "inner monologue" of the writer onto a page. Writers who use this technique are less concerned with the proper use of punctuation and more concerned with showing a self-reflective awareness of the world. With no restrictions, the subconscious mind has a free space to work. This issue that makes this type of writing a problem for journalism is that it amplifies the author's bias toward a given topic by crowding out the ignorance a writer has about the subject with a flurry of information related to the avenues of knowledge that the author has (Armstong, 2019).

The literary value of the practice of stream of consciousness is known in the world of writing (Siewert, 2019). It is used less often in all forms of journalism, excluding the "Gonzo Journalism" model practiced by Hunter S. Thompson (Kremmer, 2018). The problem occurs that the narrative in this style of writing is tough for the audience to follow. The central thesis of the work hides behind all of the elements thrown on the page. These weaknesses of the stream of consciousness style of writing can lead some journalists to use mindmapping as a means to organize their thoughts on a page.

Mindmapping allows journalists to see the connected themes of a given story. This visualization presents clear connections between the complexity that represents most aspects of society and culture. A mindmap starts with a circle in the middle of a page that describes an explorable central concept. A person will use colors, lines, pictures, and other rings to connect the different themes and ideas associated with the central idea of the mindmap.

This visual model is a relatively newer technique for understanding the relationships between people and concepts (Buzan, 1974). The graphics associated with the style of this organization technique also helps those that think better with visuals (Vigo, 2019). A primary concern with using this method regularly is that it can create a massive model of the overall story that makes it difficult to see a clear narrative that the audience will understand. This model might be useful for complex story structures that a journalist would write for a feature or data journalism story. A method that works better for the majority of stories that a journalist writes is Freewriting.

THE PRACTICE OF FREEWRITING

The purpose of Freewriting is threefold:

1. to force everything out of your brain into the real world,

2. to discover relationships between actors / locations of a story, and

3. disconnect personal emotion / bias from the topic / issue / point of interest / event.

The practice of Freewriting, when done well, develops a train of thought in the narrative rather than creates a stream of consciousness flow. Train of thought writing focuses on writing around a specific topic, building one sentence after another around that particular topic. This formatting allows the writing to be coherent and make sense as one continuous thought.

At the beginning of this practice, the writer can write down anything that is related to the specific topic of the story. There are three guiding principles in this practice that must be followed.

1. Write in complete declarative sentences.

2. The next sentence must connect to the previous sentence in some manner.

3. Stop when the hand is tired.

These three guiding principles are there to ensure that the journalist gets what's in their mind onto something physical (either on paper or in a computer file). Declarative sentences help organize complete thoughts on the page. The next sentence connecting to the previous one helps with the flow of the work. Stopping when the hand is tired is code for your brain thinking you are at an excellent place to end. Sometimes you may not think you can stop, but you can't think about a logical next sentence. There are four focusing questions/prompts that a journalist can use if such a point happens while Freewriting.

1. If you were to describe this topic in one sentence, how would you do it?

2. Why is this topic interesting?

3. What should the audience know about this topic?

4. Describe one of the actors/locations related to this story.

These focusing elements provide clarity to the journalist as they show what the audience would be most interested in for a given story.

THE VALUE OF FREEWRITING

Freewriting allows journalists to present everything they know about a given topic in a way that shows a clear narrative trend in writing. The flow within a finished piece of Freewriting will not look like a journalistic work. It will look like an informed position about the given topic. The last item to recognize is that Freewriting is a means of checking that the journalist has a story that they can write. An inability to write for a significant amount of time means that the journalist must learn more about the topic, or the story will be boring. Freewriting is a skill set based on the ability of the journalist to maintain a conversation about the subject and understand what supporting information will help enhance that conversation. These conversations are presented in journalistic articles in graf form.

PARAGRAPHS VS. GRAFS

Grafs are one of those legacy terms that I still use to teach journalism. Students come into the multimedia journalism program with a very general understanding of writing. Writing is a means to explain what the student knows about a subject so that their teacher can believe that they have at least basic competency in the subject matter. Students plug in what they know one paragraph at a time.

Paragraphs are useful structures. They present a single theme with groups of sentences that are crafted to highlight one idea. This conceptualization of the paragraph is a problem for journalism as it promotes a blocky style of writing. Students too often think (if they think of paragraphs at all) as storage units for information to be placed. The end result of their work has a similar feel anytime I enter a storage unit I own. It is crammed so full of stuff that it is hard to move around or know where anything truly is inside. They become these dense presentations of knowledge.

Journalistic writing is supported by short, clear, and concise thoughts packaged into small groups of sentences. Those sentences are best described as "fragile structures that can only support so much semantic weight.[1]" This understanding of journalistic writing leads me to use the term graf. **Grafs** are concentrated paragraphs that get to the heart of the subject quickly. The term will come up often in this book. Think of this term as a form of encouragement to write in a short, clear, and concise manner when working on an article.

CONCLUSION

The speed of the news cycle might lead journalists to believe that pre-writing a story is a by-product of **Legacy Journalism**[2] (any form of journalism whose standards and practices are influenced by the workflows introduced before the

---

[1] Credit goes to Eric Rothenbuhler

[2] I need to thank one of my former colleagues Dr. Ian Punnett for suggesting the terms Legacy and Disruptive Journalism when describing the eras of journalism being discussed in this book.

introduction of the modern Internet). Journalists might find it challenging to develop the journalistic narrative In the era of **Disruptive Journalism** (journalism after mass acceptance of the Internet as a means of distributing journalistic content). This process should not be seen as busywork before the "real work" of newsgathering but rather as a failsafe to protect the journalist's integrity and the underlying truth of the story. Knowing the information gets to that central truth prepares the journalist for the next step of the Journalistic Breakdown.

POINTS TO PONDER

- Select one news story from the past 36 hours. The story should be related to a given audience. Answer the six Fundamental Research questions about this story.

- How do we turn this Fundamental Research into a consistent flow for a news article?

- How is Freewriting different than your previous pre-writing practices?

- What is the toughest part of completing your first writing assignment?

WORKS CITED

Armstrong, J. (2019). Spatial Stream of Consciousness. *SubStance 48*(1), 5-25. https://www.muse.jhu.edu/article/719601.

Blakeslee, S. (2004). The CRAAP test. *LOEX Quarterly, 31*(3), 6-7.

Borger, M., van Hoof, A., & Sanders, J. (2019). Exploring Participatory Journalistic Content: Objectivity and diversity in five examples of participatory journalism. *Journalism, 20*(3), 444-466.

Buzan, Tony (1974). *Use Your Head.* BBC Books

Clements-Housser, K. (2018). *Welcome to Bridgetown: Bridging the Gaps Between the Worlds of Professional and Citizen Journalism.* Retrieved April 17, 2020, from https://web.archive.org/web/20190217055535/https://scholarsbank.uoregon.edu/xmlui/handle/1794/23566

Kremmer, C. (2018). Gonzo Down Under: Matthew Thompson and the Literary and Political Legacy of Hunter S. Thompson. In R. Alexander & C. Isager (Eds.), *Fear and Loathing Worldwide: Gonzo Journalism Beyond Hunter S. Thompson* (pp. 6–14). Bloomsbury.

Lander, J., Seeho, S., & Foster, K. (2019). Learning Practical Research Skills Using An Academic Paper Framework–An Innovative, Integrated Approach. *Health Professions Education, 5*(2), 136-145.

Siewert, C. (2019, August 28). *On Needing Time to Think: Consciousness, temporality, and self-expression.* Retrieved April 17, 2020, from https://doi.org/10.1007/s11097-019-09631-8

Vigo, J. (2019, July 3). *The Tech Management Of Knowledge And Thinking Intelligently.* Retrieved April 18, 2020, from https://web.archive.org/web/20190704122734/https://www.forbes.com/sites/julianvigo/2019/07/03/the-tech-management-of-knowledge-and-thinking-intelligently/

Vos, T. P., Eichholz, M., & Karaliova, T. (2019). Audiences and Journalistic Capital: Roles of journalism. *Journalism Studies, 20*(7), 1009-1027.

CHAPTER 2: WRITING PROGRESSIONS

One of the fundamental issues with modern primary and secondary education in the United States is how students learn to write. It makes sense that one of the modes of assessment that teachers in those fields would use is a written essay. It is a natural way to determine if the student knows the materials taught during a particular class. The problem is that most students associate the practice of writing with the essay format. This central focus on the essay means the students would likely believe that writing is just the means of transmitting knowledge from their brain to an expert in a field to evaluate what they know. It shows when a student tries to organize their thoughts for any writing assignment. Students refer back to how they learned to organize their writing in grade school. Language arts and English teachers use one primary method to train their students to organize their essays. It is the most basic of all organizational techniques for writing.

That method would be the outline.

An outline format makes students begin with an introductory paragraph that prepares them for the main points they will address in the essay. Body points form the next three to five parts of the outline. It forces the writer to develop those points discussed in the introductory paragraph using supporting claims and transitions to the next section of the essay. A writer finishes their outline with a concluding paragraph that reinforces the body points from the middle part of the essay. There is a redundant construction in this format. It is beneficial in showing the teacher that the students clearly understood the materials covered in the essay by having the students restate the evidence in the essay multiple ways. Journalism audiences would be bored if all articles were written in this style. Essays do not allow for narrative development, which is crucial in explaining how most topics, issues, points of interest, or events impact the reader's daily lives.

Traditional outlines fail journalists.

Journalism students needed an organizational system that allows for a narrative thread that presents the highlights of the topic, issue, point of interest, or event in a way that compels the audience to continue reading the story. The bullet-point style of the traditional outline encourages writers to create a blocky paper that is informatively dense but lacks flow. This understanding is why the inverted pyramid is the standard format for most journalistic content.

THE INVERTED PYRAMID

The **inverted pyramid** formatting is a legacy of journalism's past. A newspaper editor might need to cut two or three inches from an article to have it fit on the paper edition. Therefore, journalists would need to incorporate more critical information early on in the article. A good reason for the inverted pyramid being one of the standard practices of journalistic presentation is that it dealt with unreliable past communication between the field and the newsroom. It was an artifact of army official bulletins during the Civil War. It reinforced the "relevance principle" found in the United States' progressive era communication, and it factored in the cost-saving practices of modern media organizations (Pottker, 2003).

> There are several pros and cons of the style. The positives of the format come from how the story is newsworthy. "The conventions of the inverted pyramid require the reporter to summarize the story, to get to the heart, to the point, to sum up quickly and concisely the answer to the question: What's the news? The pyramid approach addresses the most important questions at the top of the story. It states the thesis and then provides supporting material" (Scanlan, 2003, para. 6).

This format builds in the relevance to the audience early.

As for the cons, Scanlan makes the argument that it

> is the anti-story. It tells the story backward and is at odds with the storytelling tradition that features a beginning, middle, and end. Rather than rewarding a reader with a satisfying conclusion, the pyramid loses steam and peters out, in a sense

defying readers to stay awake, let alone read on.

Journalists should be aware of the pros and cons as they relate to telling a story in the realm of multi-mediated platforms.

Journalists attending J-Schools learn to put the essential information early on in the article. The early parts of the article that addressed the Essential Questions that answered the critical questions that the audience would have about the topic, issue, point of interest, or event would often be called the **lead, lede, lead paragraph, or lede graf**. Journalists were encouraged to explain the answers to those questions with one or two paragraphs that used no more than 40 words in each paragraph.

LEDES

Ledes are the first of the three essentials grafs of journalism. There are three types of ledes that a journalist can use in this section of the article. A **boring lede** mainly addresses the wheres and whens of the story. Boring ledes are boring because they rarely represent an active part of a story. The answer to the where questions in a given story are locations that don't change. Buildings normally don't walk away from their foundation. The answers to the when questions of a story are boring because days and dates repeat. Thursday always follows Wednesday. An example of a boring lede might look like this:

> **Last Monday,** City Council met at **City Hall** for their weekly meeting.

Don't do this. Please, don't...

Informative ledes are the second type of ledes that a journalist can write. These ledes primarily address the whos and the whats of a story. Informative ledes are dramatically better than the boring ledes as they start to address the essential parts of the story, the people in the story. Answering the who questions in the lede represents the actors within a story. Whos gives the reader somebody to connect with while reading the story. It is important to note that making the audience connect with somebody in the story does not mean making the audience like that person. The audience wants to know who is significant in society and their everyday lives. They also want to know the actions of those significant people. That knowledge comes from answering the what questions. The last item to know about informative ledes is when and where information can be in an informative lede. That information must follow the answer to the whos and whats of the article. An example of an informative lede would be:

> **City Council** was **given a $25,000 donation by the ACME Company** at last night's council meeting in city hall.

The final type of ledes is **descriptive ledes**. They primarily address the how and the why questions of the story. These ledes are better than the informative ledes as they make the story more interesting. The journalist gets to the motivations that drive the people and organizations referenced in the story. How questions tend to explain the underlying actions that allow the whats to happen in the story. Proper research of the story allows for an answer to these how questions. The why questions represent the motivations of the actors within a given story. The difference between the descriptive and the informative or boring is when the questions are answered. Hows and whys must be embedded in the lede and not necessarily lead the sentence to be descriptive. An example of a descriptive lede would be:

> The ACME Company presented a $25,000 donation to Cityville **to help build a dog park** at last night's city council meeting. **The company sold special edition tins to raise the money.**

Ledes are followed by a paragraph or two that compels the audience to continue reading the story. This part of the story after lede is known as the **hook, hook paragraph,** or **the hook graf.**

HOOKS

Hooks are grafs that attract the attention of the reader using simple and clear language. These grafs tend to break the flow of the narrative through rhetoric methods. It is the point of the article that the writer grabs the reader's attention by presenting an exciting or compelling aspect of the story. Journalistic hooks borrow some of the traditions of narrative hooks with some significant differences.

Narrative hooks are typically at the beginning of the long-form piece of writing. Creative license is used in crafting this type of hook as they do not need to be grounded in the reality of the story. Authors will use a wide variety of techniques to build their hooks, such as analogies, a bold statement or command to the reader, foreshadowing future actions, onomatopoeia, rhetorical questions, or establishing the underlying thesis of the work. Journalism hooks traditionally are not crafted using those techniques.

Journalistic hooks are typically added after the beginning of the story to support the lede of the article. They usually do not use most narrative hook techniques as those methods described above find their way into more extended pieces of writing (think more than 2,500 words). Most journalistic feature articles tend to be around 1,000 to 2,000 words, with some exceptions for more detail-oriented pieces. There are five examples of hooks that journalists can pick up quickly.

The most basic, yet effective, hook that writers can craft is the **one-sentence graf**. This hook is based on the idea that the writer can find the sentence that narrows the lede but also gives you a place to go with it. The right one-sentence graf hook brings clarity and focus to the paragraphs written before it and allows the writer to focus on the next section. One of the best examples of using the one-sentence hook came from Grant Pepper in the Northern Review..

> The day we sat down for a second interview, Cody Hurley looked tired.
>
> The 23-year-old squatted with the grunt of a man twice his age, sliding his glasses up to the bridge of his nose as he looked through them with peaked eyes. In our first interview, about a week before, I opened up with a request...
>
> **'Tell me about your life.'**
>
> The conversation lasted over an hour.

The graf "Tell me about your life" quickly draws the attention of the reader. They know they will hear someone talk about their experiences and memories in an unbroken narrative form. Also, the writer now has a new direction to go with the story. They are moving from a more neutral narrative of the interview to the first-person description of a person's life.

Another hook graf technique was made popular by Walter Steigleman, a former Professor of Journalism at Iowa State University. Highlight a single fact that makes the story unique and build a paragraph around that fact. This technique is called the **whammy**. Whammies break one of the more notable conventions of journalism. Students should avoid using clauses (especially introductory clauses) when writing an article. Using introductory clauses in an article invites passive voice in the sentences the journalist is writing. The active part retreats the tail end of a typical introductory clause sentence. Whammies make the clause an active part of the sentence by introducing new knowledge to the audience. A classic example of the whammy comes from Amy King's (2008) excellent WordPress site on college journalism::

> Vern Walters, **one of Canada's last remaining maritime blacksmiths,** has put his shop in Lunenburg up for sale, closing a family-owned business begun 120 years ago by his grandfather.

Professor King rightly points out on her site that the hook's clause gets to why Vern Walters is an interesting and unique person. Walters was practicing a craft that will most likely die out when he no longer works as a blacksmith.

The third hook style that is popular with novice journalists is the **rhetorical pivot and shift**. This hook uses a definite moment of emotion, logic, or credibility as a jumping-off point to move the story towards another direction. This technique does not require the section before the hook to use ethos, pathos, or logos. Instead, this technique allows the writer to move away from a narrative thread to a new theme. Grant Pepper also provides this example.

> And when he does, he slips into the water ever-so-cleanly, an unbelievably light splash rising from the surface after such a dramatic routine.
>
> **The crowd roars.**

On this day, a Jan. 14 dual meet against Mount Union, Kuhn
would surpass the NCAA qualifying mark on the one-meter
board. The senior would do the same a week later at Oberlin...

"The crowd roars" is the perfect pathos punch that allows Pepper to break the narrative construction from the preceding paragraph, which describes the act of diving and introduces after the hook what the dive meant for the diver.

The final of the four hooks that novice journalists can use easily is the simple **drop quote**. Drop quotes traditionally use some form of visual emphasis to attract the reader's attention to focus on the quote. A drop quote follows the lede because while the quote is outstanding for the story, it does not fit the lede's context. Holly Dyer of the Northern Review provides a great example of this style of hook.

> It's no secret that the housing market has changed since the
> foreclosure epidemic of 2008. The 2008 recession
> understandably left many millennials associating buying a home
> with turmoil and financial instability.
>
> **The Bank of America says, "Remember that the bulk of the
> current 25 to 34-year-old cohort started their careers
> during the financial crisis and early stages of the recovery
> when the economy and labor market were fragile."**

The reason this hook works well for this article is that the quote allows Dyer to introduce ethos early on in her article while providing a clear fact that frames the rest of her article.

The four hooks listed above will most likely cover 75% to 80% of the stories they will write throughout their careers. A problem arises when they are dealing with local culture or an annual event that has been covered for decades. The "if all else fails model" of hook writing that I teach is a modification of Bridget Lyons' (2016) wonderful *7 Ways to Create a News Hook* webpage. Lyons created seven lines of thinking to help public relations professionals writing news hooks in press releases. Since I teach journalism and not public relations, I adopted her techniques to fit a journalistic mode of writing. These seven hook writing techniques are:

1. craft a narrative twist that the audience doesn't expect,

2. address the surprising local connection to a national story,

3. explain how a vital facet of the story goes against conventional wisdom,

4. highlight the one statistical point (using clear layman's language) that brings together the rest of the story,

5. use the hook as an acknowledgment of the repetition of the story's material to take it in a new direction,

6. drill down the novelty of the subject of the story, and

7. focus one or two sentences that hyper-personalizes the thesis of the story.

All seven of these techniques work well with the four hooks styles described earlier. Readers of this section should note that the hook suggestions are not an exhaustive nor complete list of hooks used in journalism. Instead, think of these suggestions as a good starting point. You can use these five for the rest of your career and be fine. You will find the perfect hook based on your voice, story you are creating, and the publishing platform's context.

The right hook makes a story better as it acts as the set-up for the final of the three essential grafs that journalists must master.

NUTS

The nut graf is the last of the essential grafs used in journalistic work. A **nut graf** should be the key takeaway of the story and performs a different function than the lede. Your reader should understand how the story impacts them if they read nothing more than the nut graf. Most nut grafs will lead to an engaging conversation between the community members when the section is written well. This engaging conversation about the nut graf focuses typically on what actions the audience should take, given what they know after reading the nut of the story.

A good nut graf justifies the reader's time reading the story by explaining why the reader should care about the content in the story. Nuts do this by connecting the lede to the rest of the story. The graf introduces information that makes the story timely and related to the audience's needs or wants. The nut also includes supporting content to add to the story's relevance to the audience.

Some of these supporting content pieces include an excellent quote to add to the credibility of the article and frame the takeaway. The article's takeaway also helps put the lede within the context of the broader cultural, social, or historical perspectives that the audiences and interviewees have about the topic, issue, point of interest, or event. This understanding of the nut makes it one of the denser sections.

Like the section on ledes, I teach three different types of nuts that journalists can use. This list should be considered a starting point for them in an article. All three of these styles could work depending on the thesis, purpose, and focus of the article.

The **chronological nut graf** is the first of these types of nut grafs. It is also the easiest of the nut grafs to write. A journalist must place the information discussed in the lede within the context of historical references. This graf is most effective with a descriptive lede and historical / community experts that can provide in-depth quotes about the topic, issue, point of interest, or event. Chronological nut grafs offer a transition to a more narrative-driven storyline as long as the nut addresses why was this narrative important in the past. Finally, the graf proves that the story is timely as it connects past actions to today's topic, issue, point of interest, or event.

The **institutional nut graf** is the second of these types of nut grafs. It is helpful if the journalists know the fundamental social institutions in the community (schools, churches, civic groups, etc.) and their overall connection with the story. Journalists must place the information discussed in the lede within the context of its impact on those institutions. This graf is most effective with a descriptive lede and institutional experts that can provide in-depth quotes about the connection between the topic, issue, point of interest, or event to the institutions mentioned in the nut. Chronological nut grafs break away from a specific narrative to address the broader social issues connected to the story. The nut will justify the reader's time and attention if it can explain how the narrative in the story, the institutions address in the story, and the audience connect. Finally, the graf proves that the story is timely if it discusses the day's social issues within the context of the article.

The **humanistic nut graf** is the last of these types of nut grafs. It is helpful if the journalists know how the community members define the community, how community members describe their place in the community, and how those two ideas connect with the story. These nuts only work when the article is about a small group or an individual with strong ties to the community. They become representative of the community as a whole. Journalists must place the information discussed in the lede within the context of the story's impact on the community's everyday lives. This graf is most effective with a descriptive lede and community members that can provide quotes about the topic, issue, point of interest, or event with credibility, emotion, or facts. Humanistic nut grafs connect a more significant and abstract social issue to a single person or small group of people's issues, thus making the problem more concrete. The nut will justify the reader's time and attention if it can explain why your audience should care about this person or group of people. Finally, the graf proves that the story is timely if it shows the day-to-day lives of people in the community.

Effective nut grafs become the epitaph to the narrative of the story. They act as the sharable bit that can be remembered most about the story you wrote.

All three of these essential grafs (ledes, hooks, and nuts) explain the critical details of the story and add that information to the audience's knowledge about the given topic, issue, point of interest, or event. Great journalists craft the rest of the story with a good progression that deals with the content addressed in these three essential grafs.

WRITING PROGRESSIONS

We need a short review of what's been covered in this chapter up to this point. An excellent article needs the three essential grafs to maintain the flow of the narrative. Journalistic works are more than those three grafs. There must be a sense of narrative flow to help support the article's cohesiveness to engage the audience. There needs to be some indication of the direction that the story is going. This ability to create an excellent journalistic flow requires a different mode of writing organization.

The previous paragraph is the main reason that we need a new structure that supports the story's flow while maintaining the aesthetics of journalistic writing. The method that we use in the Multimedia Journalism program at Ohio Northern is the **Writing Progression**. Next, we will focus on the history of this method, the basic format of a Writing Progression, and its overall value in journalism.

THE WRITING PROGRESSION EXERCISE

Writing Progressions became a standard practice that my students followed starting about eight years ago when I was still teaching at the Ohio University of Lancaster campus. My students were writing stories for the social media feeds of the university. They were struggling to craft well-written stories about the campus. During this time, that inspiration struck me after listening to Merlin Mann on the *Back to Work* podcast. It describes Mark Baechtel's book, *Shaping the Story*. The book laid out a plan to help fiction writers develop their narratives. I got the book and read through it carefully. After multiple readings of the book and listening to episode 36 ("Writing on the Wind") a few times, I developed this journalistic practice.

The progressive writing exercise is designed to help break from the standard way of preparing to write a story. A student begins by answering a straightforward question about the story that they are working on:

- What is the most important truth about the story that my audience needs to know to understand this story better?

The underlying concern posed by this question is related to the concept that the journalist MUST address the audience about the story. Journalists address the audience in a language and style that makes the story easily understood by those who depend on journalists to keep informed about the day's events.

The student begins to write down this fact about their story in the form of a simple declarative sentence. The simple part of the simple declarative sentence means that there are one subject and one verb in the sentence. A declarative sentence is a sentence that is making a statement. A declarative sentence example is, "It is a nice day today."

Once the student has this sentence written down, we go over:

- why this sentence is important,

- how they know it is the truth,

- why their audience needs to know this truth, and

- why does knowing this truth make their story better?

The writer has a primary truth if they can answer those four questions successfully. The next step is to use that primary truth as a jumping-off point to the secondary truth of the story. Secondary truths begin with the introductory clause "Because I know this to be true, it means…". The secondary truth starts with this phrase because it helps the writer find additional meaning to their story. The secondary truth must also be a declarative sentence and successfully answer the four bullet point questions that the primary truth answered. If that is successful, the writer creates a tertiary truth using the same introductory clause and answering the same bullet point questions.

One of the significant issues that novice journalists have with the progression after they get the format down is that some of the later truths incorporate many ideas from the primary or secondary truths. Those following truths might echo a significant amount of the language from the previous truths. This issue is known as **writing in the round**.

Another issue is the **Goldilocks' effect**. This effect happens when the journalist does not create enough "narrative distance" between the two truths. If the writer can not create a 60-word to 100-word transition between the two truths, those two sentences are too close to one another. The writer should have the "just right" amount of narrative distance between the two truths in the progression. The progression is a structure that depends on facts, quotes, and narrative transitions to make the story complete.

One solution that can create more narrative distance is underlining or highlighting the terms or themes within each of the truths. Performing this action allows the writer to find the strongest conceptual point in the sentence to jump off and create a new truth. This action also provides the journalist with clarity that there is a narrative flow in their progression.

If a journalist is writing in the round, suffering from the Goldilocks' effect or simply cannot develop a progression, that journalist needs to do more Fundamental Research to complete the progress. A five-truth sequence is typically the right size for most day-to-day stories that a journalist will write. Experienced journalists will find the correct number of truths to put in their progressions with practice. It is also fair to note that some journalists will find this practice difficult.

THE PRACTICE OF PROGRESSIVE WRITING

This practice tends to be difficult for novice writers because they aren't taught structural or modal writing before college. Structural writing forces the writer to be more aware of word selection, the placement of sentences within a paragraph, and knowing which words will have an impact on the audience. Premiums are placed on talking to the audience with the right tone. A journalist cannot speak down to them nor make the story too juvenile.

Modal writing simply means that the student should be aware that there is more than one mode of writing that people will use every day. Public relations students tend to be too promotional in their stories. Creative writing students tend to be too poetical in the crafting of the narrative. Professional and technical writing students will make the narrative too choppy with the inclusion of bullet-point facts to their articles. Journalism depends on the short, clear, and concise use of language to make the news understandable to their audiences. Both the understanding of structural and modal writing is not typically taught in the secondary education system in the United States.

Writing in high school and middle school/junior high tends to be a hybrid between rote, bullet-point-driven, and formulaic writing. As stated before, the primary function of academic writing is to evaluate students' knowledge of particular subjects in school. Most of the written work you produce in journalism should be a hybrid between functional, purpose-driven, and analytical writing.

There is value in learning a technique that promotes this style of writing.

THE VALUE OF PROGRESSIVE WRITING

Journalism, at its core, is built on creating narratives that address the necessary details and points relevant to the audience about a given news story. This central tenet of journalism means that journalists need to create clear narratives that the audience can follow. A progressive writing chain helps build in that narrative thread with essential details. When a Writing Progression is done correctly, it will note the crucial parts of the story that should be highlighted for the audience.

WRITING PROGRESSIONS FOR MULTIMEDIA JOURNALISM PLATFORMS

Writing Progressions work best on platforms that allow for structural journalistic work (such as newspaper, radio, television, digital news sites). Many journalists are using new and social media platforms to get the news out to the audience. This practice of writing a progression to organize a story is easily adaptable to a variety of newer platforms if the journalist recognizes the ways those platforms function and connect people.

COMMUNITY-DRIVEN PROGRESSIONS

A **community-driven site** (like Facebook) works best in conjunction with a digital news site to develop the audience for the digital news site. The progression tends to begin with a strong, compelling visual that acts as a focal point for dialogue on the posting. The caption of the image or video should get the audience to do three actions. The first action is that the audience clicks on the link that goes back to the organization's leading digital news site. The second action is that the audience needs to share that content with their friends. Finally, the audience should be willing to engage with others in their community civically and honestly. The nature of the Internet can make that last action a challenge. The first two actions listed are more likely to be performed by the audience if the journalist changes the primary question used to start the Writing Progression.

> What is the most important truth about the story that my audience needs to know for them to discuss the story intelligently and constructively?

This question means that the journalist will need to understand the vital truths that drive the story's narrative and present those truths in a way that reflects the audience's perception of the reality of the story. There are two additional follow-up questions that we go over before calling it a primary truth that works for this format.

1. How will the audience react to this truth?

2. How does this truth help facilitate an honest dialogue about the story?

Journalistic content for a community-driven site will typically demand a three to five truth progression that leads the audience to either the primary digital news site of the larger story or a focus question that will drive comments on the post. The latter requires moderations to maintain a reasonable discussion about the story.

MICROBLOGGING PROGRESSIONS

A **microblogging site** (like Twitter) can be a stand-alone mode of breaking stories. The best progression for this format is one that presents a series of "contextually dense" truths that use source materials from a variety of reliable sources to present a story of general interest to a broad audience quickly. Contextual denseness means that the post has layers of information that different communities pull different pieces of information or knowledge from the post (Bhatt et al., 2019). This story uses a threaded format to present the story. A thread is a series of posts that are connected by a series of replies. The individual posts might contain:

- hashtags (to find other posts that share characteristics with the one published),

- references to other users (to highlight their role in the story),

- links (to provide credibility to the story being written),

- content (to explain visually or audibly something that can not be explained textually), and

- embedded posts (to show how this story impacts the social network at large).

The progression for this type of site depends on several verifiable facts, quotes, and other content to act as the transitional components of the story. This acknowledgment of the purpose of the progression also leads to a different question to start the progression.

> What is the most important truth about the story that my audience needs to know that can provide a starting point for a long series of facts about the story?

This question means that the journalist will need to understand that a microblogging platform is less about crafting narratives and creative transitions between the truths and writing the truths in a way that makes those truths stand-alone and causes the audience to respond to that information.

Journalistic content for a microblogging site will typically demand an eight to ten truth progression that leads the audience to evaluate the merits of each of the truths on its own. The entire story crumbles if one of the truths has even a slight point of weakness.

MEDIA-DRIVEN PROGRESSIONS

A **media-driven site** (like Instagram or YouTube) depends on a sharp image, piece of audio, or video clip to tell the story. This fundamental analysis of these sites means that the crafted progression must focus on that piece of media.   The progression must also recognize that the words under the picture must be more than a simple caption explaining what's happening in the image and who took the picture. That space under the visual must be a detailed description that provides the context of the image and its social or cultural significance.

Media-driven progressions use cultural and social clues within the image to describe the connection between the actions and actors in the image to the community highlighted in the story. This understanding means that the photojournalist or reporter should be writing the progression from the vantage point of having a keen awareness of the community they are covering.

A progression written to support mediated work begins with the following question.

> What is the most important truth that my audience needs to know about the highlighted piece of media that will help them understand what is happening in this community?

This question means that the journalist will need to understand that a media-driven platform's audience might be seeing or hearing about the community highlighted in the story for the first time. Journalistic content for a media-driven site will use a two or three truth progression that leads the audience to understand how that piece of media reflects the everyday realities of the people living in that community.

40

EPHEMERAL PROGRESSIONS

An **ephemeral site** (like Snapchat) depends on a story appearing for a short period of time and then disappearing entirely from the site. Ephemeral sites are a tricky area for journalists to work with as there is not a "collective memory" of the day's issues on the site. The trends expressed on the website are typically a reflection of the users maintaining those trends (a "bottom-up" approach) as opposed to sites detailing the critical stories of the day (a "top-down" approach).

Ephemeral sites do not allow for long, detailed, or even memorial analysis of a story. Postings in this system disappear from the network, forgotten into the ether. An archive of the content happens if somebody transfers the file to another format. The content might be erased from the site, but an expertly told story in this format might remain in the minds of audience members who remember that shared content.

A progression written to support ephemeral accounts begins with the following question.

> What is the most important truth that my audience needs to know about the story that will make the story unforgettable?

This question means that the journalist will need to understand the living legacy of the story's narrative and present that narrative so that the audience easily retells it. This understanding might mean understanding what makes the story "meme-able" so that they can share a small piece of the story that retains the central narrative's truth. There are a couple of follow-up questions that can be asked to determine if the progression hits this mark.

1. Why will the audience share this truth?

2. What harm comes from this level of simplification of the story?

Journalistic content for an ephemeral site will typically demand a three to five truth progression that leads the audience to either the primary digital news site for the larger story or explain the story to their friends via social media or real-world engagement.

PROFESSIONAL NETWORK PROGRESSIONS

A professional networking site (like LinkedIn) depends on stories speaking to the professionals on the site in a way that connects their expertise with the events happening in the world. There is a premium placed on content that reflects the languages of business, innovation, and management. Journalists will need a keen insight into what makes the organizations highlighted on these sites attract the attention of the professionals that use those sites.

Professional progressions should begin with:

> What is the most important truth about this story that speaks to the professional interests of members of this site?

This question means that the journalist will need to have a clear understanding of an abstract sense of what the story is about, a firm understanding of different professions affected by the story, and a grasp of the professional language to communicate the intricacies of the story's narrative to produce a story for a professional network.

OTHER PROGRESSIONS

One of the concerns writing a book of this nature is that the content will become outdated the moment it is published. The principal defense against this concern (and the takeaway that journalists should take away from that concern) is that there needs to be an understanding of how the various sites allow journalists to communicate the news to the audiences who need it. Journalists need a foundation of media theory to apply the primary progression question to the variety of sites that organizations will use to spread the news. This foundation of media theory will allow journalists working on websites outside the scope of the ones covered in the chapter to apply a critical analysis to determine:

- how people interact on the website,

- content shared most often on the site,

- the format that can best share journalistic content on the site, and

- an excellent primary truth progression question to ask when creating content for the site.

Addressing those points clearly and concisely will give you clarity on how to approach creating content for those sites.

CONCLUSION

The Writing Progression is a reflection of journalism's legacy and history while allowing the craft to adapt to the disruptive nature of the modern media environment. It will survive the changes to the media economy if smart journalists find wisdom in the progression format.

The power of the progression comes not from understanding the flow of the story. Instead, it is that this structure allows for transitions, quotes, media, and embedded links to efficiently support the truths that form the foundation of the progression. The rest of the chapters in this part of the book will show how to turn this humble series of sentences into excellent journalistic content.

The next step that journalists, once they have a solid progression, is to fill that progression with more of the narrative, facts, and quotes that drive the story. Most of those are gathering through interviewing others. The next chapter will show how to use the Writing Progression to craft a reasonable Interview Protocol to fill in the story.

POINTS TO PONDER

- Create a five-truth progression for something that happened to you within the last two weeks.

- Create a seven-truth progression for an assignment or other writing project outside of this class. How well did it work?

- What is traditionally one barrier that prevents you from completing a writing assignment?

- Find one example of a descriptive lede graf in professional journalism that you like. What makes that lede effective?

- Pick a professionally written story and find the hook in that story. What is good or bad about the hook?

- How do we make the audience care about the narrative we are crafting?

- Find one example of a nut graf in professional journalism that you like. What makes that graf effective?

WORKS CITED

Applebee, A. N., & Langer, J. A. (2013). *Writing Instruction that Works: Proven methods for middle and high school classrooms.* Teachers College Press.

Baechtel, M. (2004). *Shaping the Story: A step-by-step guide to writing short fiction.* Longman.

Bhatt, S., Padhee, S., Sheth, A., Chen, K., Shalin, V., Doran, D., & Minnery, B. (2019). Knowledge Graph Enhanced Community Detection and Characterization. *Proceedings of the Twelfth ACM International Conference on Web Search and Data Mining.* DOI: 10.1145/3289600.3291031

Dyer, H. (2019, Apr. 12). *Why We Won't be Buying Houses Anytime Soon.* Retrieved April 14, 2020, from https://web.archive.org/web/20200414153001/https://nr.onu.edu/node/6870

King, A. (2008, July 23). *Just the Facts, Ma'am?* Retrieved April 13, 2020, from https://web.archive.org/web/20111009043821/https://collegejournalism.wordpress.com/2008/07/23/just-the-facts-maam/

Lyons, B. (2015, November 6). *7 Ways to Create A News Hook That A Reporter Can't Resist.* Retrieved April 13, 2020, from https://web.archive.org/web/20190222075433/https://www.brigittelyons.com/news-hook/

Mann, M., & Benjamin, D. (2011, October 11). *Back to Work #36: Writing on the wind.* Retrieved April 14, 2020, from http://5by5.tv/b2w/36

Pepper, G. (2018, March 1). *Braden Kuhn, Calm and Collected, Gears up for National Run.* Retrieved April 14, 2020, from https://web.archive.org/web/20200414152745/https://nr.onu.edu/node/6225

Pepper, G. (2018, May 11). *Cody Hurley and the Art of Never Giving Up.* Retrieved April 14, 2020, from https://web.archive.org/web/20200414152221/https://nr.onu.edu/node/6413

Pottker, H. (2003). News and its Communicative Quality: the inverted pyramid —when and why did it appear?. *Journalism Studies, 4*(4), 501-511.

Scanlan, C. (2003). Writing from the Top Down: Pros and cons of the inverted pyramid. Retrieved June, 15, 2019 from: https://web.archive.org/web/20160520211339/http://www.poynter.org/2003/writing-from-the-top-down-pros-and-cons-of-the-inverted-pyramid/12754/

CHAPTER 3: INTERVIEW PROTOCOLS

The area that distinct journalistic work from other forms of communication is the ability of journalists to incorporate their discussions with experts about the central points of a story and add that information to the overall narrative. A story without engaging good quotes is nothing more than an opinion piece, encyclopedia article, or a dry monologue. Journalists use interviews to find intelligent, persuasive, emotional, or community-centering quotes that connect the truths from the Writing Progression together into one overall journalistic narrative (Liebelson, 2018).

Interviews are conversations that people engage in to get to the truth about a given subject. This process is used in a variety of fields to gain an understanding of the world. Scholars use an academic interview to gather themes related to a given research question or hypothesis. Employers will use hiring interviews to determine a person is a good fit for a job. A psychologist might use a behavioral interview to establish the mental state of a person. There are many other interviews that people can use to understand the world and people through questions and answers. This chapter will focus on one type of interview that is vital to journalism.

Journalistic interviews are conversations that fill the blanks in using questions both the journalists and the audience have regarding the story. Great journalistic interviews depend on:

- knowing whom to interview,

- knowing how to ask for the interview,

- knowing the right questions to ask,

- knowing how to ask those questions,

- knowing how to follow-up on an answer, and

- knowing the perfect time to end the interview.

These pieces of knowledge will allow a journalist to craft an Interview Protocol that addresses the holes in their Writing Progression and explain the story's critical details to the audience.

Interview Protocols are the plans used by the journalist to get the right person and interview them successfully. Unlike the Writing Progression, there is no specific template that journalists will use to ensure a great interview. Instead, journalists depend on a series of guidelines that help them develop the conversation. There are three phases in the Interview Protocol to help build this conversation. The next section of this chapter will focus on the first stage, namely the "behind-the-scenes" preparation for the interview.

CRAFTING THE INTERVIEW PROTOCOL

There are three priorities that journalists must address before going out for an interview. Figuring out precisely what you want to find out from the interview is the first of these priorities. The interview should address the "gaps of knowledge" from the Writing Progression if that progression was carefully created.

A progression with no gaps gives no room for transitions, quotes, or style. It merely is the reporter reflecting on the state of the story. There should be enough narrative distance between the truths to frame some questions about the unknowns within the progression. Those questions form the foundation of the Interview Protocol. There should be one less question than truths in this protocol. The nature of these questions should also give a sense of who would be the appropriate people to ask those questions. Fundamental Research should help you know who to interview.

SELECTING INTERVIEWEES

There tend to be four groups of people to select for a Journalistic Interview and one consideration in the selection process. Stories that involve either government action or civic response should focus on the highest level of official that can address the questions from the progression and are accessible to the journalist. Those people should explain what the government response is for the topic / issue / point of interest / event, what resources it will take to address the topic / issue / point of interest / event, and how the community and audience should respond to the subject at hand.

Content that relates the information that the average person would not know requires an expert to make the complicated nature of the subject simple enough for the audience to understand. These interviewees are credible if they have the proper credentials for a given story. For example, I am an Associate Professor of Multimedia Journalism. There are no reasons to interview me on a story about Norwegian Death Metal. I have not written books or papers on the history of the genre. There are zero presentations or research projects I have done on the characteristics of that form of music.

Straight up, don't interview me on that.

The third type of interviewees is related to issues with two or more positions that are dividing the community. Journalists need people who can express REASONABLE opposing views that clearly show the division lines in the community. These interviews can be tricky to do well. The purpose of conducting these types of conversations is that the format allows the journalist to get to the deeper truths affecting the community and diffuse toxic narratives that are unnecessarily harmful to the community. Usually, the perfect interviewees are the leaders of groups that support a particular position.

Complicating the narrative around the issue is a useful technique that helps clarify positions. Amanda Ripley (2019) focused on six techniques that lead to a more accurate description of the issue, make the content more meaningful to the audience, and allows the viewer to be "more curious and less closed off to new information."

1. Amplifying the contradictions reminds the audience that "life is not as coherent as we'd like."

2. Widening the lens: allow for a bigger conversation of the broader questions this issue poses for the community.

3. Asking questions that get to people's motivations: the questions need to address a person's sense of caring, fairness, liberty, loyalty, authority, and sanctity. More liberal-minded people and progressive positions focus on the first three. Conservative-minded people and regressive positions will focus on the last three. All six are central to how any community defines itself (Haidt, 2013).

4. Listening more and better: this comes from clarifying the metaphors that people use to describe their world, learning to listen for what the interviewee isn't saying, and picking up on the "subtle cues" that come up in the interview. This level of active listening helps build a level of trust between interview and interviewee.

5. Exposing people to the other tribe: it leads to fewer caricatures of others and a comprehensive reflection of the issue's impact on the entire community.

6. Countering confirmation bias: using a wide range of sources with graphical information that does not repeat false information and includes solutions to the issue is a useful means of getting the story's central community truth.

Ripley suggests some types of questions that are useful for this type of interview.

- What is oversimplified about this issue?

- How has this conflict affected your life?

- What do you think the other side wants?

- What's the question nobody is asking?

- What do you and your supporters need to learn about the other side to understand them better?

- What do you think the other community thinks of you?

- What do you think of the other community?

- What do you want the other community to know about you?

- What do you want to know about the other community?

This interviewing style is more resource-intensive as it requires a more thoughtful approach in addressing the central issues to the story.

The fourth group of interviewees is those directly impacted by a particular topic / issue / point of interest / event. Impacted is not the same as negatively affected. These interviewees have some experience (positive, negative, a mixture of the previous two, or neutral) regarding the story's subject. They can share that experience with the audience. The interviews can be boring if it is an **evergreen** subject (something that happens annually or regularly). In this situation, journalists can try to use how it is different this year or focus on the changes that have occurred in the immediate past with regards to the story's subject. The questions are easier to construct if it is a **novel** subject (something new that is happening to the community).

Journalists must have a diversity of interviewees in their stories. The problem arises that the typical newsroom might not reflect the variety of communities or audiences that they serve. This problem means that the journalist would not have the trust of either population as it could fail to reveal the truths experienced by both groups. Journalists need a "deep knowledge of this nation's communities and constituents' by race, gender, class, region, and religion, among other factors" (Chideya, 2018, para. 9) to expose the correct narratives in their stories. Failure to do so makes the story incomplete. It is the journalist's responsibility to do their homework in the process of gathering interviews, which is the second priority of the journalist planning out their interviews.

DOING YOUR HOMEWORK

This preparation is one of the areas that newer journalists overlook or do not spend enough time on because of the rush to get an interview quickly. A baseline understanding of the interviewee helps the journalist prepare the best questions to ask them based on the subject at hand. The primary area that preparation can help the journalist with for their interview is doing some homework on the interviewee before the interview.

Gathering background information about the interviewee allows the journalist to understand what themes the interviewee can speak about freely, honestly, and thoroughly. There might be people that understand the subject of the story well. Still, they are unable to talk openly about the question because of conflicts of interest, fear of speaking on the record, or just plain useless as an interviewee. Some interviewees will consistently lie to the press or be less than truthful in their answers to the general public. Finally, some interviewees are better able to explain some parts of the story, but only know or can talk limitedly about other parts of the story. Looking for past interviews with the interviewee or talking to others in your organization might give you clarity about how much help your interviewee can provide you.

The best reason to research the interviewee is that they may have already talked about the story before, and the quotes are already in the public record somewhere else. People hate repeating the same information over and over to the press. A journalist will either need to find different questions based on their progression, approach the premise of the question differently, or use the quote in the public record and give credit to the original story and reporter that published the quote.

If you are sure that the interviewee is the best person to answer the questions from the progression and the background research tells you they have not addressed them before, the next step is to structure the interview questions.

THE INTERVIEW QUESTIONS

The next step of the Interview Protocol is crafting the questions for the interview. The key to structuring the interview questions is to try to make it a conversation rather than a cross-examination. A conversation depends on long and flowing answers from the interviewee that give you and your audience a better understanding of the facts, background information, and narratives that form your story. **Cross-examining** the interviewee happens when the interview is built around leading questions instead of probing or clarifying questions.

Leading questions have a structure that suggests the answer within the question. It is also known as a loaded question as the premise of the question locks the interviewee only to answer the question with a limited number of responses. The classic example is, "when did you stop beating your wife?" The nature of this type of engagement can put the interviewee on the defensive.

The major problem with the leading question is that they are mostly modified versions of closed-ended questions. **Closed-ended questions** usually are questions whose answers are a version of yes, no, or maybe. These questions tend to brake up good quotes and better narratives. At worse, too many closed-ended questions stop an interview cold. Asking **open-ended questions** (questions that require a long-form answer) that allows for a wide variety of responses will make the interview smoother.

Another example of a leading question is a technique that I call the **60 Minutes Echo.** This technique (otherwise known as **mirroring**) happens when the question's structure prompts a specific phrase from the interviewee, so the interviewee produces the exact soundbite the journalist needs. "60 Minutes" interviewers would use this technique enough to be almost a clique of their work.

> Interviewee: he's a notorious tunnel manufacturer...
>
> Interview: The tunnel king?
>
> Interviewee: The tunnel king

The problem with this technique is that the words spoken are not the "natural thoughts" of the interviewee. Avoid this technique and type of questioning in your interviews. It is too forced. It is better to frame probing questions that can achieve the same level of soundbyte that one would get using the mirroring questions.

Probing questions help the interviewee think more deeply about the issue at hand. By their nature, probing questions are open-ended and directly connected with the interviewer's understanding of the story's reality. These questions tend to open up the interviewee and allow them to address the central premise of the question more broadly. Some examples of probing questions are:

- What do you think would happen if the event was held later this year?

- What impact does this event have on this community?

- How did you determine the budget for the upcoming year?

- How did you come to that conclusion?

- What is the connection between the event and the community?

- What if the opposite were true? Then what?

Probing questions allows for practical deliberation of the central theme of the story. It is helpful to keep these type of questions in mind when crafting an interview.

Finally, be straightforward when crafting questions. The interviewer should not be making a speech with their questions unless you are following the Maddow Method. Interviewers use the Maddow Method to make sure that they and the interviewee are on the same page regarding the topic at hand. The **Maddow Method** is when the interviewer explains their current understanding of the state of the subject to the interviewee. The follow-up question is, "Is there anything I got about that wrong?" I find this style of question useful as it can prevent misunderstanding about the subject at hand as long as the interviewer recognizes their potential bias in the examination and presentation of the facts.

Once the interviewer is comfortable with this part of the Interview Protocol, the next step is to schedule the interview with the interviewee.

SETTING UP THE INTERVIEW

The most crucial element to remember regarding setting up an interview with someone is to NEVER, EVER call it an interview. Interviews tend to be a nerve-racking experience for members of the general public. People in the public sphere will also manage to get defensive if they know a member of the press is interviewing them. The phrase that works better in setting up the interview is, "Would you have some time to have a conversation with me about..?" A conversation works better than an interview. People have a more positive view of the term conversation than an interview (McIntyre & Gyldensted, 2017).

The next part of setting up the interview is explaining an overview of what you plan to talk about during the interview. Treat this part of the set up as the agenda for the interview. These agenda points are broad bullet points that allow the interviewee to see if they are the right person to be interviewed. If they are not, what typically happens next is that they suggest someone else to talk to who is better suited for the subject of the story.

NEVER EVER give the interviewee all of the exact wordings of the questions for the interview. The problem with that information is the interview becomes nothing more than public relations professionals, press agents, and communication directors feeding the interviewee the word for word answers to give. It is no longer an interview with the interviewee. Instead, it is a series of bullet points that the organization wants you to know.

If the interviewee believes they can handle the nature of the interview, the final step is traditionally addressing the time and type of interview. The type tends to be discussed first. There are two categories that you can discuss with the interviewee, which will determine the third category. The first category is the **medium of the interview**. There are four choices an interviewer can give the interviewee. **Telephone interviews** tend to be the most common method of doing a journalistic interview (Kassel, 2019). Sometimes the interviewee is ready to do the interview the moment they confirm the agenda. Other times, the interviewee might need a couple of days to make sure that they are prepared. Both are fine.

Face-to-face interviews are traditionally the more popular form of interviewing. The rationale for using this style of interviewing is that the interviewer will get more information from the interviewee using this method. The most information an interviewer will get is from the non-verbals of the interviewee. Watch body language and pay attention to how a question is answered. It can sometimes tell you more than the answer the subject gave you. Is the interviewee calm or fidgety? Are they trying to look away from you? Those actions are worth noting when you are attempting to understand the value of the quotes in the interview.

Video conferencing is also an excellent way to interview someone. They allow the ability to see the person and judge some of the non-verbals a person would give. There is one more useful technique that works (for both video conferencing and face-to-face) to get more information from your interviewee.

Silence.

Silence is effective in both of these mediums as people are uncomfortable with silence. If I need to have the person continue their thought and give more information without being prompted, silence is productive.

The last of the four mediums for interviewing is **email**. It seems that email is the "worse case scenario" when it comes to interviewing. There are no natural follow-ups that can be asked within the flow of the interview. It is a jarring method of getting information from someone. However, it can be useful to get a quote from a hard-to-reach person to get their side of the story or input about the story.

Along with the medium of the interview, the **interview format** is useful to discuss as well. Journalists use three formats. The most common is the **individual interview**. It's a one-on-one format that allows the person to explain what they know without others to interrupt or provide external clarity to the interviewee's quotes. **Panel interviews** enable a group of experts to drill more in-depth on the questions being posed by the interviewers. The panelist will speak with some sense of order. Finally, the **group interview** is more of a free-form discussion that allows for more reactions to the statements being made. The individual is the easiest to transcribe, with the group being the hardest (Fisher, 2019).

The final point that must be addressed in the **scheduling of the interview** is the time and location. The interviewer must be polite when asking the interviewee the best place, date, and time to hold the interview. The two basic questions to ask the interviewee would be, "What time works best?" and "Where is the best place to conduct the interview?"

Once you know the interviewee(s), medium, format, time, and location, the interviewer has left to decide the kind of interview. A **Structured Interview** controls every question asked in the interview from start to finish with a minimum amount of follow-up. This kind of interview is useful because there is a short amount of time available to the interviewee, and the interviewer wants to be efficient with the question selection. Most of the interviews tend to be **Semi-Structured Interviews** as it allows for the flexibility to approach the prepared questions in a way that makes the most sense given the flow of the conversation. **Unstructured Interviews** are the most difficult to maintain some control of as they are a "free-form" discussion with some grounding related to the topic.

INTERVIEWEE HAS NOT RETURNED MY MESSAGES

The final point of wisdom to offer in the section about setting up the interview is when the interviewee has not responded to multiple requests for an interview. The two common statements I get from reporters are things along the lines: "I emailed him two weeks ago, and he hasn't emailed me back." & "I left a message for him, and he hasn't called me back."

It is important to remember that a potential interviewee ignoring the request for an interview is not the same as "no comment." Journalists should keep digging and chasing until they make contact with that person. It amazes me how few of my students think about going to that person's office or business. The office door can give the reporter time that the person is in the office or other ways to contact them. It's allowed and encouraged to visit their place of work. Going to a person's home is not encouraged or allowed.

Once the primaries are worked out, the journalist has one final checklist before conducting the interview.

BEFORE LEAVING FOR THE INTERVIEW

The final checklist reporters complete before meeting the interviewee or going to the interview location is a final self-check. Journalists need to make sure that they are prepared with the right equipment for the interview and the proper physical appearance. I still go over understanding the dress code for the location one is going to and the people that they are meeting. Journalists need to dress appropriately for both. Journalists needed to be seen as young professionals and not college kids who just got out of class.

The equipment kit has gotten more compact over the past twenty years. I have a small bag that contains:

- at least three pens

- at least two pencils

- two notebooks

- hand sanitizer

- a small garbage bag with rubber bands wrapped around it

- a small bottle of mouthwash

- fully-charged USB battery

- cords for my phone

- small bills and change

- granola bar

Some form of this equipment lineup has been in my bag for more than a decade. I find that knowing I have that equipment lineup in my bag (plus a phone and tablet) charged up and ready to go allows me to feel comfortable that I have everything I need to be on the road. Of course, if you are just doing a phone, email, or video interview, the requirement might simply have a quiet place to do the interview for an hour or so.

The last part of the checklist is one final run-through of all of the questions being asked. Ensure that the questions are reasonable, and there is a reason they are being posed to the interviewee. Partly I do this step to look for flaws in the questions. Mostly, it is to calm my nerves before talking to the interviewee. I will test my phone or recorder during this time to help me feel relaxed, and it also allows me to make sure that all of my equipment is working before the start of the interview. I will hit record, talk for a minute, stop, and playback to make sure I can hear it. The worst feeling you can have is playing back an interview, and nothing comes out.

Completion of this final checklist means the journalist should be ready for the interview.

GROUND RULES FOR THE INTERVIEW

Regardless of the medium, kind, and format, the interviewer must be on time for the meeting. Face-to-face interviewers should arrive at the location of the interview about fifteen minutes before the interview. The rationale for being there that early is that it allows for most traffic issues one would have arriving at a location. Also, there might be set up problems that need to be addressed before the interview begins. Finally, it would be essential to review the **Ground Rules** of the conversation.

The biggest of these rules is that everything spoken during the interview is **on the record.** This reminder is essential even if the person has done several interviews before. That declaration clears the air about how this interview could be used. It is a fair warning to the interviewee. The extension of that statement addresses the idea that the entire interview may be used for the journalistic piece. Once again, the purpose of this acknowledgment is that the interviewee should not be surprised how their words might be used.

The second set of Ground Rules addresses how much knowledge the interviewee has about the story. Simply put, interviewees should not be provided a list of the questions being asked in the story, nor do they get final review rights to the story. Allowing these two conditions negatively affect the narrative of the story. When a journalist no longer controls those aspects of the story, bias becomes a problem as control of the story has been shifted.

Finally, common courtesy should be part of the process of the interview. Interviewers should use more please and thank yous then they would typically use on a day-to-day basis. It shows a level of appreciation for getting the interview. Finally, do not speed through the interview. Everyone is busy. Rushing the interview and the write-up is terrible journalistic practice.

Don't.

Now, you are ready for the interview / conversation.

THE INTERVIEW

The essential first interview questions are:

- "Do I have your permission to record this conversation?"

- "May I have the correct spelling of your first and last names?"

- "What is your current job title and company you represent?"

- "How long have you served in that role and with the company?"

- "May I have your phone number and email so I may call or message you later if I have more questions?"

These five questions are the foundations for any interview I give. They serve two purposes. The first being that I am sure that I have the vital information before asking the real interview questions. We have permission, correct spelling of the name and title of the person, and the means to contact the person for follow-ups. The second and more personal reason that I start with those questions is that it puts me in the right mental state to give the interview. It's almost a mantra that I say to allow me to focus on the interview and the interviewee. You might find different ways to approach those five questions. Do whatever works as long as you get the information those questions typically give you.

Once those questions are out of the way, the journalist must determine the most critical question to ask at that moment and ask it first. The reasoning is if you only have the chance to ask one question because the interviewee needed to leave suddenly, you want to make sure you got the most relevant answers you needed. Journalists need to actively listen to that answer and feel comfortable about the direction the conversation is going with the interviewee.

A combination of continuing with the prepared questions and clarifying questions comes next. **Clarifying questions** are straightforward questions of fact based on the answers given in previous questions. They help clarify the information being provided by the interviewee and help the interviewer better understand the connection between the answers given by the interviewee and the truths from the Writing Progression. Examples of clarifying questions are:

- "What resources were used for that project?"

- "What criteria did you use to evaluate that decision?"

- "What's another way you might state that?"

- "Did I hear you correctly when you said...?"

- "Did I paraphrase what you said correctly?"

These questions reduce misunderstandings during the interview and allow for the precision of language in the story.

There will be a time that a journalist will need to ask embarrassing questions based on the topic at hand. The interviewee should get a heads-up that the matter would come up in the interview when discussing the interview's agenda. There are several things to remember when approaching embarrassing questions. The conversation should be tasteful in the way they approach the questions. This approach means no prying or snooping for personal information not related to the topic at hand.

Interviewers must be polite in their interactions with interviewees. Hostile, leading questions are not acceptable at this time. The final wisdom is that the interviewer will need to get to the truth even if the interviewee wishes not to. Ask the question again if the interviewee does not give you an answer.

There is one older piece of wisdom to mention at this point. If the interview is not producing useful information, and the journalist wants to salvage something useful for the conversation, they might need to apply the GOSS Questions to the interview. **GOSS Questions** (Gilleland, 1971) is a traditional technique that journalists use to get one or two quotes that might help frame the story. The four parts of GOSS Questions are:

1. Goals (What do you hope to accomplish with this?)

2. Obstacles (What stands in the way of this?)

3. Solutions (How can you overcome these obstacles?

4. Start (How did this all begin? Whose ideas was it?)

The four parts are generic enough that they can be applied in most situations. The problem with this technique is that the quotes provided might be less of an accurate and objective expert view of the topic and more anecdotal wisdom about the story's subject (Jackson, 1974). Still, I will use this method to get one or two more quotes that potentially can move the narrative and conversation forward.

Before the interview ends, the last question that should be used to wrap-up the conversation is, "Is there anything else I need to know?" Most experienced interviewees will know this question is coming. It allows them to provide a detailed quote about the topic that might have been outside the scope of the interview but related to the topic. This information might lead to more questions, and that's fine.

Continue the conversation if that happens.

IF THE INTERVIEW BREAKS THE PROGRESSION

One of the final concerns I've heard over the past decade has been whether the interview does not align with the truths from the Writing Progression. I usually tell my students that it is okay. There are three directions to go when this happens.

The first possibility that the interviewee is misinformed about the truths surrounding the story. This situation can be resolved by interviewing somebody else within a similar group of interviewees discussed earlier in this chapter (government official, experts, representing a position, or community member impacted by the story) that can speak intelligently about the given story. If the second interviewee's information is in line with the first interviewee, there is a second possibility.

The second possibility is there's a red flag in the progression. **Red flags** are misconceptions that the reporter has about the story. It is fair to argue that it is an important lesson to know. If the journalist is getting this fundamental truth wrong about a story after doing the pre-writing exercises, the audience would most likely be misinformed about the basic tenets of the story. It might be essential to highlight that misconception. It is also crucial to check with colleagues to see if they had this misconception as well. If you are the only one with those misconceptions, there is a third possibility you need to consider.

The third possibility that you don't understand the relationship between yourself, your community, and your audience. It is vital to understand this relationship, or you can't cover that community in your stories. My suggestion is simply to step away from the newsroom or your home and visit the community not as a reporter but as somebody trying to understand that community better.

Go in with an open mind and a willingness to learn.

CONCLUSION

A successful interview depends on having the right person addressing the story to provide clarity to the audience about the underlying facts of the narrative. This situation does not happen by accident. Journalists must develop a plan to ensure that their interviews run smoothly. Selecting the best interviewee, questions, medium, format, kind, time, and location make the odds better that the conversation will hit all of the marks for the story.

The next chapter of this book focuses on getting the best quotes from the interview and using them effectively in the story. This ability is grounded in the idea quotes should be kept in the context in which they were spoken.

POINTS TO PONDER

- Watch two or three interviews on television. Describe the key takeaways from those interviews. How do you suppose that the interviewers got those takeaways from the interviewee?

- What makes an interview compelling? How does the interviewer get the audience to watch the interview?

- Read two or three news stories, either online or in your local paper. Look for the quotes in the stories. What question do you imagine the journalist used to get those answers?

- Craft four questions based on the five truth progression you wrote in the last chapter.

WORKS CITED

Chideya, F. (2018, May 22). *'This Deepening Division is not Inevitable': The failing diversity efforts of newsrooms.* Retrieved April 19, 2020, from https://web.archive.org/web/20191223074716/https://www.cjr.org/analysis/newsroom-diversity-failing-efforts.php

Fisher, A. (2019, August 21). *16 Different Media Interview Formats and how to Handle Them.* Retrieved April 19, 2020, from https://web.archive.org/web/20200419174116/https://www.mediafirst.co.uk/blog/16-different-media-interview-formats-and-how-to-handle-them/

Gilleland, L. W. (1971). Simple Formula Proves Helpful to Interviewers. *The Journalism Educator, 26*(2), 19-20.

Haidt, J. (2013). *The Righteous Mind: Why good people are divided by politics and religion.* Vintage Books.

Harro-Loit, H., & Ugur, K. (2018). Training Methods of Listening-Based Journalistic Questioning. *Journalism Practice, 12*(7), 918-934.

Jackson, K. M. (1974). Goss Formula May Handicap Reporter if Misapplied. *The Journalism Educator, 29*(1), 31-32.

Kassel, M. (2019, March 18). *For the Record: 18 journalists on how-or whether-they use tape recorders.* Retrieved April 19, 2020, from https://web.archive.org/web/20191222025618/https://www.cjr.org/analysis/journalists-tape-recorders.php

Liebelson, D. (2018, February 22). *5 Interview Tips Every Journalist Needs.* Retrieved April 19, 2020, from https://web.archive.org/web/20191224153454/https://ijnet.org/en/resource/5-interview-tips-every-journalist-needs

McIntyre, K., & Gyldensted, C. (2017). Constructive Journalism: An introduction and practical guide for applying positive psychology techniques to news production. *The Journal of Media Innovations, 4*(2), 20-34.

Pollock, T. (2019, June 13). *The Difference Between Structured, Unstructured & Semi-Structured Interviews*. Retrieved April 19, 2020, from https://web.archive.org/web/20200419173304/https://www.oliverparks.com/blog-news/the-difference-between-structured-unstructured-amp-semi-structured-interviews

Ripley, A. (2019, January 11). *Complicating the Narratives*. Retrieved April 19, 2020, from https://web.archive.org/web/20190213001255/https://thewholestory.solutionsjournalism.org/complicating-the-narratives-b91ea06ddf63?gi=4a65a9c9046

CHAPTER 4: USING QUOTES IN CONTEXT

Quotes are sacred. Interviewees' words should be maintained throughout the editing process. Journalists must not manipulate others' words to echo a pre-written description of the events within the story. All quotes used by a journalist must add to the story's overall telling, or else they are just words or sounds on a screen. This chapter will focus on effectively weaving the quotes into the story's overall narrative while maintaining the ethos of the story.

There tends to be an acronym that I teach that helps students place the quotes in their stories in an impactful way while maintaining the integrity of the quote as the speaker intended. The acronym is **LETTER**.

- Logging Important Quotes,

- Evaluating Quality of the Quote,

- Transcribing the Quote Verbatim,

- Truth-to-Quote Connection,

- Editing the Quote Honestly in the Story, and

- Review if Placement in the Story Matches the Quote's Original Context.

This technique borrows from the more traditional method of transcribing the full interview to place quotes into the article (Jeppesen, 2017). There is value in transcribing the interview. For speed's sake, I encourage the journalist to note the time an interesting quote was spoken discretely. I still want the journalist to listen to the whole interview after its completion. After completing the interview, reporters must focus on useful quotes. A journalist must understand which quotes are meaningful during the interview and catch others during the playback of the conversation.

All of the quotes that were either deemed meaningful during the interview or caught during the playback session should be written verbatim to ensure they are word-for-word correct. Incorrect quoting of the interviewee will damage the credibility of the journalist. It is worth the time to complete this step.

After transcription, the journalists must determine where that quote fits into the Writing Progression. It should be useful as either a transition between truths or as supporting evidence of a truth in the progression. This matching up process strengthens the overall quality by showing the reality presented in the progression matches the facts experienced by the community members and others involved in the story.

The next step involves editing the quote to fit into the structure of the story. This process means maintaining the meaning of the quote through any edits. The journalist should read over the quote multiple times to check that the original message has not been lost in translation.

The last step happens after the quote is placed in the story. You read at least one paragraph before the quote appears, the paragraph(s) that the quote is used, and at least one paragraph after it is used. The journalist must then address if the meaning of the quote in the context of that writing matched the speaker's purpose when they spoke that quote. If so, you have successfully placed the quote in the proper context.

The rationale of spending this much effort on individual quotes is based on the power of recording quotes correctly.

RATIONAL QUOTES IN CONTEXT

Using quotes in the context in which they were spoken takes a keen understanding of two parallel factors that impact how the audience reads the story. Both factors are present in what makes for a successful journalist. Steve Jackson (2019), a famous game designer, described the value of a quality journalist for most professions.

> First, of course, you should learn to write quickly and clearly. Courses in journalism are usually better for this than any type of "creative writing" class. If you cannot write quickly, you'll starve. If you cannot write clearly, somebody else will get the

job. While it is possible to be a genius creative talent who cannot write a grammatical sentence, we try to avoid them. There are lots of creative talents out there who can write clear sentences, and we like them better.

This quote speaks to the ability of great journalists to get to the central themes of the story. **Themes** refer to the information about the story that is not directly spoken about the subject matter. Themes are often confused with bias. **Bias** are internal factors (both internal to the reporter and the organization) that affect the telling of the story. Themes are external elements away from the reporter and organization that speak to the story's central truth. Themes separate themselves from bias when they use the central tenets of journalism (public interest, honesty, accuracy, verification, fairness, distinguishing fact from comment, accountability, independence, transparency, restraint, & originality) to help craft the story.

Successful journalists expanded themes that speak to the truth of the story while minimizing bias that impacts the audience's trust in the journalist and journalism as a whole.

The remaining sections of this chapter will dig into more theoretical elements of journalistic interviewing and applying quotes within a story. It is fair to say if the only wisdom you get from this chapter is LETTER and why it is crucial to follow that process when adding quotes to a story, it would be a good start. You can move on to chapter five of this book and learn how to apply media to your stories.

If you want a deeper dive into the theory behind why quotes are the magic sauce that makes journalism a powerful force for society in the era of Disruptive Journalism, read on.

THEMATIC CONSTRUCTION OF QUOTES IN A STORY

We need a more concrete grounding of using quotes in the story to get to better themes and less bias in journalistic content. This grounding means knowing how to work with the themes of the story concerning:

- what is happening within the community you are covering,

- the audience that reads/watches/listens to the work you are creating,

- all of the cultural influences surrounding the story, and

- society at large.

Thematics in journalistic content comes in two flavors: the internalized constructions of themes within a given piece of content in the form of ideologies and the externalized performances of those themes in the form of analysis.

Ideologies are not directly expressed within the story. They are either hidden constructions that form the basic understanding of the story or more an unspoken code to inform the audience how to understand the story. **Performances** are more significant than the story itself. They represent the subtle presentation of the news to the audience at large. Both ideologies and performances have three levels, and those levels are all connected.

NARRATIVE IDEOLOGY

The first of the ideologies worth examining is the narrative ideology. **Narrative ideology** is a series of characteristics that define a person, place, event, or anything else newsworthy related to the location, time, cultural influences, and social institutions established within a single story. Narrative ideology allows the person to develop and explains that development through one cohesive personal story. It is fair to say this definition of narrative ideology is influenced by Joseph Campbell's (2008) *The Hero with a Thousand Faces*. The narrative stands alone in this ideology as it acts as a reflection of more significant social and cultural issues analyzed through the journalistic tenets described earlier in this chapter.

The central question answered by an examination of narrative ideology is, "How is that Element defined in the media?" When answering that question, it is essential to explain that media organizations do not act as one collective whole. This definition is an aggregation of all news stories about the Element as understood by the audience.

70

The extension of this ideology is the modern development of narrative journalism. **Narrative journalism** is the genre of journalism that takes the techniques of fiction and applies them to nonfiction. The narrative form requires in-depth and sophisticated reporting, an appreciation for storytelling, a departure from daily news' structural conventions, and imaginative use of language. One of the more popular types of narrative journalism is the "True Crime" shows like *Serial* or *Tiger King*. The format is based on Legacy Journalism as it is the reporting of a crime that happened. The narrative elements are the producers' editorial additions to the story. It is important to remember that narrative journalism is a journalism style, while narratives are the content that drives journalism.

Narrative ideology is vital for a journalist to remember is every additional quote about a newsworthy Element will influence the audience's perception of that Element. We must make sure that the quote portrays an honest representation of that Element, or it will leave a black mark on the Element and journalism.

FRAMING IDEOLOGY

The second level of ideology is framing ideology. **Framing ideology** places the narrative threads of one story into a larger picture. The larger picture model means that the more focus an element of a story has in public, the more likely the public will have a similar perception of that Element. Michael Roberts (2002), a former Training Editor from The Cincinnati Enquirer, explained that stories could be framed in the broader social and cultural issues in four ways.

1. Updating adds new information and essential facts that enhance the audience's understanding of the Element within the story.

2. Context explains the story's background and history concerning the Element's connection to other factors in the news. "It tells readers what's normal, surprising, or how similar things are dealt with elsewhere."

3. Impact tells readers how the Element benefits the audience, can cause the audience suffering, or what actions the audience should take regarding the Element.

4. Human dimension illustrates or portrays the effects the Element has on the lives of members of the community in the form of "details, textures, emotions, and colors to convey the experiences of an individual."

Framing is a double-edged sword as the framing of an Element is a "shared social understanding" that connects community members to themselves and the audience members to the audience as a whole and can be reduced to a stereotype of the Element. Framing ideology is vital for a journalist to remember is that every story about a newsworthy Element will influence the audience's perception of that Element.

The central question answered by an examination of framing ideology is, "How does this story change the audience's overall perception of the Element?" It is essential to explain that the audience does not act as one collective. Instead, it is viewed through the same mediated structure that allows journalists to send out their stories and engage with the audience.

AGENDAS AS AN IDEOLOGY

The final of the ideologies to examine are agendas. **Agendas** are the construction of frames that influence the audience's perceptions on a given topic, issue, point of interest, or event. The idea of an agenda is grounded in that different members of the audience will have levels of care about various issues that affect the audience member's community. Amplification or reduction of that care becomes based on which platforms or public figures use to address those issues (Wanta & Alkazemi, 2018). Individual stories shift agendas in two ways.

Agenda setting is the process of transferring a media organization's agenda to the general public or a specific audience (Dearing & Rogers, 1996). This type of agenda control happens when the media organization controls the overall construction of the story. Journalists should be aware of this concept as the media organization publishing the story could alter the fundamentals of a story if it affects their ability to set the agenda. It is easy for media organizations to set the agenda as they control the means of delivering content to the audience about different communities. Journalists can be unwittingly supporting an agenda that they don't natively support based on the way they tell a story. Words have power, and audiences are becoming more aware of this concept.

Agenda building means that the audience plays a role in constructing the news (Lang & Lang, 1981). Journalists should be aware of this concept as interviewees are becoming savvier on framing their quotes to push a ground-up agenda. Like agenda setting, agenda building can allow journalists to promote an agenda they do not agree with if they are unaware of the power of the quotes expressed by the interviewee.

Both agenda setting and agenda building require the journalist to examine their stories critically. A journalist's credibility is at stake every time they produce a story. A good review and analysis of the final story is a useful technique to help present the reality of a story without others' bias influencing the underlying narrative.

INTERNAL IDEOLOGIES

These three ideologies build off of one another. Journalists control the creation of an Element's narrative in the story, whether that subconsciously through the journalist's tone or consciously through narratives within an article. Multiple narratives related to a topic, issue, point of interest, or event creates the foundation for framing news stories. A series of frames connected to a topic, issue, point of interest, or event potentially represents the beginning of an agenda. These are the three areas that are under the control of the journalist. Performances are outside the control of an individual journalist. Media organizations and platforms are solely responsible for the aesthetics, construction, and distribution of news to audiences.

TRENDS AS A PERFORMANCE OF THE NEWS

Stories make their way to the audience. Audiences, in turn, share the content journalists create with others. The increase of one specific term on a given social network or online platform will lead to that term or phrase being highlighted by the system or platform. This highlighting of words and phrases is the foundation of trending online. A **trend** is an ability to synthesize an Element into a summary, headline, #hashtag, meme, or a combination of those and create a critical level of awareness through a mediated network. Most social networks and online platforms have a list of the ten to twenty trends in a highly visible area. There are multiple lists of trends divided by users' locations, general categories, or other means that are important to the users, admins, or executives of the site.

Trends can be a positive addition to any social network or media site as that network or site can act as a gateway for exposing the relevant stories of the day to their broader community of users. This exposure allows for events across the world and the local community of the audience to gain some context of why that story is essential to understand via other people's posts. Connecting a given trend with posts from a person's friends about it can humanize a story. Post can provide critical details about the underlying Element that can provide people with clarity regarding the events of the day. The problem is that this description is an ideal case of how most websites work. There's a reason that "don't read the comments" is the standard operating procedure for some people online (Searles, Spencer, & Duru, 2018).

Two of the most significant issues associated with trends is the hijacking of trends by bad actors and the oversimplification of complex Elements in the public sphere. It is effortless for trends to be taken over by spammers, trolls, corporations, and activists. Sometimes that takeover is required as it can expose the reality of the story that has mostly been covered up by powerful factions online (Gilkerson & Berg, 2017).

The oversimplification of Elements is one of the reasons commercial takeover of trends works. Oversimplification allows a single phrase, piece of media content, or headline frame people's understanding of the story. The story is so simplified and flatten in the course of turning into a trend that others can recontextualize this Element to fit any agenda (Reese, 2010).

Journalists should be aware of the influences that trends have on the construction of the story as more and more media organizations are trying to tie their stories and rundown to trending topics. Those organizations can see trends lists on websites as a direct access point to new audiences. Stories, images, and headlines can and will get manipulated in the same spirit that organizations currently use Search Engine Optimization (SEO) techniques to get audience share (Newman, 2018).

Journalists should also be aware that quotes in a story can potentially influence trends. One twist of a phrase can make the Element a viral sensation in a moment's notice. This power of words should not be taken lightly.

THE RHETORICAL CONSTRUCTION OF NEWS AS A PERFORMANCE

Journalism is more than the flat delivery of information related to the issues of the day. The vital facts of the story interwoven with a journalistic narrative and mediated content that forms the foundation of journalistic work. Audiences will tend to understand content as being journalistic in nature if the content maintains an expected level of emotional connection between the journalist and the audience (Lecheler, 2020), and the journalist presents information about a given story in a style and format that is familiar to the audience (Deuze and Witschge, 2017). The form and composition of the news speak to the rhetorical construction of journalistic content.

The **rhetorical construction of news** refers to all aspects of the composition of journalistic content. This composition includes the optics of news programming, the structure of news packages, and the language used when reporting the news (including AP Style, the regional performance of news, & the platform requirements when presenting the story). These visual and grammatical elements inform the audience how to read the information journalists present and how it relates to the knowledge the audience already has about a given story (Hall, 2012).

One of the more influential positive aspects of the rhetorical construction of news is that the audience knows how to read journalistic content. It takes limited to no training to tell the audience that the work is journalistic in nature. This understanding of the audience's reading of editorial work means that if audience members trust journalists, the content will be respected. The journalist should not assume this trust. Journalists earn this trust every time they write a story that presents the community's reality to the audience in story form.

A dominant negative aspect of the rhetorical construction of news is how headlines feed into the clickbait nature of Disruptive Journalism. **Clickbait** is the use of attention-grabbing headlines that contains vague language to confuse the reader and emotionally-driven images to drive the audience to click on the story (Chen and Rubin, 2017). These headlines perform one of the rhetorical functions of a standard headline (i.e., provide a top-line understanding of the story) to manipulate the other content within the article. The logical extension of clickbait headlines is the creation of Lego journalism articles.

Lego journalism refers to an Element within a story reduced to nothing more than a managed component of news that loses all connection to the reality of the situation. For the reporter, Lego journalism is a style construction of the story that involves short bits of information intertwined with gifs or memetic content. The issue with this type of construction is that it leads to a "non-sequitur" interpretation and presentation of the critical Elements within the story (C. Medina, personal communication, Sept. 17, 2014).

Awareness of the rhetorical construction means the journalist understands that the audience is consistently judging the reporter to see if they are presenting newsworthy information and if that reporter should be trusted.

EDITORIAL CONTENT AS THE PERFORMANCE OF THE NEWS

The final performance that journalists must be aware of is how editorial content impacts the stories that the journalist produces for the organization. **Editorial content** refers to the editors, executives, and owners of a platform creating journalistic works to set the tone and direction of the platform. Editorial influence on the platform comes typically in the form of gatekeeping. Editorial staff members perform the function of **gatekeeping** when they decide which story and pieces of content are worth publishing on their platform. Gatekeeping also generally keeps citizen journalists off of professional journalism platforms (Lindner, 2016). Editorial content is more than simple gatekeeping, however.

Editorial content, when done well, provides both the community and the audience several benefits. The editors of a platform should be able to clarify the positions that a community holds and explain those positions to the audience. Those positions should respect the diversity of opinions and voices within the community. Clearly defined positions can evoke a sense of pathos in the audience regarding the community's feelings, which in turn fosters interaction between community members and between the community and the audience. Finally, by providing the audience with the information they need, editorial content can focus on immediate issues that both the community and the viewers face and encourage changes required to maintain both groups' connectedness.

When done poorly, editorial content is nothing more than the organization ramming down a specific agenda to an audience that isn't interested in it. It becomes another example in the mind of particular audience members that "The Media" using their platform to spread lies about the community to the audience at large. Journalists need to be wary when they see this happening in their organization. That perception can impact the journalist's credibility to the audience and the community.

PERFORMING THE NEWS

These externalized performances of those themes are typically outside the control of an individual writer. Every journalist works in an editorial workflow that controls aspects of the distribution of news to the audience. However, it is important to note how the general public can receive the words and mediated content you create. Writing stories to fit the current trending topic can oversimplify critical stories within the community. The perceptions of journalists can impact if the audience trusts the story you are creating. Editorial content can manipulate the underlying narrative of your story. At the same time, this Performance can significantly enhance the audience's understanding of the day-to-day actions of the communities you cover.

CONCLUSION

The purpose of this chapter was to explain the power of quotes within journalistic work. Both professors and editors would demand a minimum of two quotes from two sources to have a story. This mandate is more than just a way to get the narrative out of the reporter's mind and into the community. There are deeper considerations when approaching the value of quotes to help tell the more vibrant stories about communities. Quotes help minimize bias and expose the central themes to the audience.

The use of quotes that express the experiences of the community is vital as journalists will tend to have a 360-degree view of the Elements and must decide which Elements are worth including into a given story. That selection process narrows the audience's view of the community. Journalists must also recognize there is no one perfect version of reality that everybody in the community has about their communities and potentially the audiences that read about their community. Instead, there is a wide array of experiences that make up a spectrum of realities within the community. This understanding is why journalists must present quotes in their proper context to show that spectrum of realities within the community. Otherwise, the story is nothing more than an encyclopedic representation of the data and information related to a given story.

Journalists must recognize that the ideologies associated with the various Elements within the story connect with the performance of news for the audience. Those ideologies also affect the use of quotes within the story. A single narrative becomes a trending topic on social media. Elements' framing becomes the rhetoric found in the public sphere. The presentation of editorial content on the organization's platforms supports the media organization's agendas that publish the work.

It is all tied together.

Journalists must stay true to what they believe is the truth of the story and explain the community's view of the world. The best way to do that is with good media content. The next chapter focuses on describing how to connect that type of content to the structure of the story.

POINTS TO PONDER

- Pick a journalistic website you are very familiar with.

    - What are the trending topics to be presented on your site?

    - What is the rhetorical construction of your site's journalistic content?

    - How is this content being packaged?

- How does understanding the ideologies and performances in the media help us effectively present quotes in our stories?

- How does understanding the ideologies and performances that exist in the media help us evaluate journalistic content?

- How do we create mediated content that reflects the reality of the story and the larger truths in society?

WORKS CITED

Campbell, J. (2008). *The Hero with a Thousand Faces* (3rd ed.). New World Library.

Chen, Y. and Rubin V. L. (2017). Perceptions of Clickbait: A Q-methodology approach. In the *Proceedings of the 45th Annual Conference of The Canadian Association for Information Science/L'Association canadienne des sciences de l'information* (CAIS/ACSI2017), Ryerson University, Toronto, May 31 - June 2, 2017

Dearing, J. W., & Rogers, E. (1996). *Agenda-setting.* Sage Publications.

Deuze, M., & Witschge, T. (2017). Beyond Journalism: Theorizing the transformation of journalism. *Journalism: Theory, Practice & Criticism, 19*(2), 165–181. doi: 10.1177/1464884916688550

Gilkerson, N., & Berg, K. T. (2017). Social Media, Hashtag Hijacking, and the Evolution of an Activist Group Strategy. In L. L. Austin & Y. Jin (Eds.), *Social Media and Crisis Communication* (pp. 141–155). Taylor & Francis.

Hall, S. (2012). Encoding/decoding. In M. G. Durham & D. M. Kellner (Eds.), *Media and Cultural Studies: Keyworks* (pp. 137–144). Wiley-Blackwell.

Jackson, S. (2019, September 9). *Job Opportunities.* Retrieved April 22, 2020, from https://web.archive.org/web/20191016050806/http://www.sjgames.com/general/jobs.html

Jeppesen, J. (2017, January 17). *From Interview to Transcript to Story: The construction of journalistic narrative as qualitative research.* Retrieved April 22, 2020, from https://nsuworks.nova.edu/tqrc/eighth/day3/35/

Lang, G.E., & Lang, K. (1991). Watergate: An exploration of the agenda building process. In: D.L. Protess and M. McComb's (Eds.) *Agenda Setting: Readings on Media, Public Opinion and Policy Making* (pp. 277–289). Routledge.

Lecheler, S. (2020). The Emotional Turn in Journalism Needs to be About Audience Perceptions. *Digital Journalism, 8*(2), 287–291. doi: 10.1080/21670811.2019.1708766

Lindner, A. M. (2016). Editorial Gatekeeping in Citizen Journalism. *New Media & Society, 19*(8), 1177–1193. doi: 10.1177/1461444816631506

Newman, N. (2018, January 10). *Journalism, Media and Technology Trends and Predictions 2018*. Retrieved April 23, 2020, from https://ora.ox.ac.uk/objects/uuid:45381ce5-19d7-4d1c-ba5e-3f2d0e923b32

Reese, S. D. (2010). Finding Frames in a Web of Culture: The Case of the War on Terror. In P.D'Angeloo & J. A. Kuypers (Eds.), *Doing News Framing Analysis: Empirical and Theoretical Perspectives* (pp. 17–33). Taylor & Francis.

Roberts, M. (2002, August 22). *Story Framing: Four vital ingredients*. Retrieved April 22, 2020, from https://web.archive.org/web/20200422172032/https://www.poynter.org/archive/2002/story-framing-four-vital-ingredients/

Searles, K., Spencer, S., & Duru, A. (2018). Don't read the comments: the effects of abusive comments on perceptions of women author's credibility. *Information, Communication & Society*, (pp. 1–16). doi: 10.1080/1369118x.2018.1534985

Wanta, W., & Alkazemi, M. (2018). Journalism as Agenda Setting. In T. P. Vo's (ed.), *Journalism* (pp. 189–204). De Gruyter Mouton.

CHAPTER 5: MEDIA ENHANCEMENTS

A story typically tells a single narrative that captures an aspect of a community against a more extensive cultural and social set of influences and factors. This story is supposed to represent the community's reality around specific narrative Elements and present that reality to an audience. The crafting of such a story depends on the journalists having mastery of a wide variety of mediums.

A **medium** is a communication system representing how a message gets from one person or group to another. News organizations will use one or more modes of communication to deliver content to their audience. For example, the *New York Times* publishes a print edition of their newspaper. They also have websites, social media accounts, and applications that the audience can use to get the news. Each of those modes is a **platform** that the *New York Times* publishes (Phelps & Consalvo, 2020). Collective platforms, content, journalists, and the way the New York Times produce their stories represent their **brand**. Newspapers, websites, communication applications, and social media services generically speaking are the **channels** of communication that a brand like the New York Times uses to deliver the news. Finally, **media** is when a variety of mediums present one coherent message within the context of a given story (Coman & Rothenbuhler, 2005).

It is important to remember that multimedia journalism platforms require a variety of mediums to work in concert to flesh out a given story for an audience fully. This interweaving of mediums means having more than just proficiency in all of the mediums that comprise a piece of multimedia journalism. Pictures and text are the absolute bear medium needed to explain the story to an audience in the era of immersive journalism.

IMMERSIVE TECHNOLOGIES

One of the strengths that allow multimedia journalists to expand the audience's view of a given story is that they can use immersive technologies to present the news. **Immersive technologies** (such as the fully immersive digital environment of virtual reality (VR), tying digital information on top of a real view of the user's world in augmented reality (AR), or the merging of the digital and the real in one virtual space in mixed reality (MR)) allow audiences to have a more detailed understanding of the Elements through the visual presentation of an enhanced narrative. This enhanced narrative is information about the story popping up in the user's environment. It is crafted by the journalist to explain more details about the story (Soper, 2017).

This enhanced narrative also gives the audience a sense of "being there" by offering them the opportunity to personally engage with a story. Immersive journalism puts an audience member directly into the event. Through this technology, the audience has fantastic access to sights, sounds, and even emotions related to the Elements in the story. This storytelling style adds more pathos and ethos to the logos, which should be naturally present in any journalistic work.

As this technique is a work-in-progress, it is crucial to recognize that content used in creating immersive journalism comes for traditional and electronic work that journalists produce regularly. This recognition means that journalists need to be more than proficient in the various forms of media that make up journalists' work to be skilled multimedia journalists. Immersive journalism demands expertise in all forms. Various mediums' strengths and weaknesses make up the rest of the sections of this chapter. It should help multimedia journalists understand how mediated content frames the story for the audience.

MEDIUMS OF COMMUNICATION

The rest of this chapter will explain the value of all forms of media by framing those mediums by describing how they help fulfill journalism's role in society. The rest of the chapter will not teach basic media production practices. These practical training sessions are in the second part of this book called "Practicum Modules." The assumption is that readers have at least a proficient level of knowledge about the various media production techniques that a multimedia journalist needs. Readers without those skills should turn to the second part of this book and do the exercises found in those pages before continuing to read the rest of this chapter.

Storytelling is more than just the textual content, especially as it relates to journalism. Journalists' ability to combine text, graphics, audio, video, and interactive elements allows for a complete telling of the story of the event, issue, point of interest, or topic to the community. Any good telling of a story needs the right media content to enhance the audience's understanding of a given subject.

A journalism student must recognize that modern storytelling means placing the right content within the structure of a story so that content enhances the person's understanding of a given story. To piece the various pieces of content within the story, the reporter must assess the strengths and weaknesses of different communication channels as they relate to the underlying narrative of the story. Journalists use their experience and expertise in a given subject to tell the story to the audience via communication mediums. Great multimedia journalists recognize which channel is most useful for telling their stories.

All mediums allow for the translation of Elements into a work of journalistic content. This translation of the experiences and knowledge about the story only happens when the journalist understands how the medium enhances the transmission of community experiences and the expression of expert knowledge. We will be focusing on the two types of mediums in the next section of the chapter to aid in the clear transmission of experiences and expertise.

The two types of mediums that we will focus on for the rest of the chapter will be traditional and electronic mediums. **Traditional mediums** (text, graphics, and photography) are the mediums that represent all of the content found in the print-first platforms of newspapers and magazines. Platforms that use traditional medium do not require electronic systems to publish (but mostly all now use electronic and digital systems to get out their content).

Electronic mediums (audio, video, and interactive content) depend exclusively on electronic means to be produced and distributed to the audience. Audio and video content is central to the broadcast-first organizations associated with television or radio. Interactive content is exclusive to new multimedia online platforms. New multimedia online platforms are not usually grounded in Legacy Journalism traditions in terms of the means that they use to produce the news. Print-first, broadcast-first, and new multimedia online platforms usually have fundamentally different workflows, journalistic standards & practices, and views of their relationships with their communities and audiences (Tilton and Fleck,

2018). The only way to understand these differences between the types of platforms is to examine the medium's strengths and weaknesses.

TRADITIONAL MEDIUMS OF COMMUNICATION

These traditional mediums are the easiest for a multimedia journalist to create and place into a story. **Text** is the primary mode of mass communication. It usually represents the most contextually concrete means of delivering information to an audience. Graphics are crafted representations of the given reality of a topic / issue / point of interest / event seen from a graphic designer's vantage point. Photography presents reality as it exists in the lens of the camera and the view of the photographer. These first three mediums require a keen awareness of the power of text and images to deliver a strong narrative that tells the community's story to the broader audience.

TEXT

The first of the six mediums is text. Text tends to lay out the groundwork of that narrative for journalistic work. This concept is why the first four chapters of this book focused on crafting a solid textual work explaining the reality of a given story in a narrative form for an audience to read. Words capture the essence of a given situation to transmit the Elements' feelings, knowledge, and experiences to the broader population. All factors that make the story a focus of a given community get laid out, word-by-word, in the narrative structure. However, text alone is not sufficient to address all Elements.

For simplicity's sake, it is fair to argue that text better serves a story when information needs to be presented with a sense of either "semi-permanence" or easy accessibility. The printed word has this reverence as it is the record of a real-world history or thoughts in the author's mind. Local newspapers have the legacy of being the "paper of record" for the cities that they covered due to the papers being a textual presentation of the day's events that define the culture of those communities. Social interactions are part of the text's legacy as past newspaper articles, government records, and various authors' writing tells the day-to-day actions that drove societies of the past.

Text fits the idea of a semi-permanent medium even in the digital age as audiences can refer back to a textual presentation of information at any time. The textual function of the Internet is to act as an archive of the world's writing. Anything online can be printed on paper and stored for later. One of the working metaphors I use for the Internet is that it is the place that files and folders are stored and can mostly be easily accessed. These backed-up text files stored in folders online explain the world as we see it. These files show the real day-to-day actions of others and our imagined ideal world created by digital citizens.

A significant weakness of text is based on how people process text. There is not a lot of information embedded in a single word of text. Sometimes a word can have a deeper meaning behind it if there is enough cultural training. McDonald's is one such word. The McDonald's corporation as spent billions of dollars around the globe to ensure that "most children recognize the McDonald's golden arches, influencing their taste and preference for McDonald's and possibly increasing demand for McDonald's products" (Bennett, 2017, para. 3). Not every word has the advertising budget or brand awareness of McDonald's. Therefore, most words have a simple meaning.

The other processing issue associated with text is that there is only so much text that a person can absorb in a single sitting. Textual content demands the focus of the audience to be understood clearly. If too much text is presented to the audience, they will not be able to remember (let alone understand) all of the words in the presentation. This inability to process leads to "death by PowerPoint" in most business meetings and classroom lectures (Tufte, 2016).

Both of the processing weaknesses should limit its use in digital content if the presentation is dynamic. Static displays allow for more text with the trade-off that staring at text on a screen for long periods of time can cause physical and mental discomfort. Textual content should always be supplemented with other mediums whenever possible[3].

---

[3] I recognize the irony or the hypocrisy of this section as it is primarily text. Textbooks, by definition, are a textual format. Therefore, I can live with it.

GRAPHICS

Graphics are a valuable resource as a means of presenting the relationship between actors within a given story. It tends to be the medium used for complex relationships as it is easier for the audience to interpret visual information than textual information. Visuals can clearly explain the various components of a story when they provide a different vantage point of those components to the audience.

One technique that journalists can use to present those different vantage points is through a **sketch** of the Elements. This technique is used in situations where cameras are either not allowed or were not available. One of the common examples of sketches used in journalistic work would be courtroom sketches. Judges typically do not allow cameras in the courtroom. Journalists need to show the room in a way that provides clarity. Courtroom sketches show the mood of the room and the placements of crucial figures in the case.

Sketches can also be an aesthetic decision of the brand. One of the more well-known examples of a brand using sketches is the Wall Street Journal using images for their bylines of reporters and prominent figures referenced in their stories. The term that the Wall Street Journal uses for this technique is a **hedcut drawing.** These pencil sketches add a sense of character to both the story and the person shown in the drawing.

Another example of graphics used for journalistic work is **comics**. Comics combine words and drawn images to become a form of visual storytelling that brings forth the story's underlying narrative to the forefront. These graphics are either found in the entertainment section of a paper (funnies) or the opinion and editorials section (editorial cartoons). Both of these newspaper trademarks tend to be **syndicated works** (content sold to hundreds of platforms throughout the United States and the world).

Comic journalism can explain the essential Elements of a story using illustrated actions to show relationships that words and other types of images can fail to express. Lukas Plank (2014) explained some key factors that make comic journalism an efficient mode of reporting the news. The journalist must be more transparent about what sources they are using to create the story.

Readers will often be confused if they are looking at work of fact instead of a work of fiction without proper citations accompanying the comic. Journalists should provide context to the reader to help them use what sources were used to create the composite of the story they are reading. Sources can include other media, scientific papers, first-hand experiences, undocumented experiences, interviews, or a symbolic representation of the Elements being portrayed.

Infographics are the third type of graphics used in journalistic works. An infographic is a single graphic that incorporates crucial data points in the graphics to explain complexity in the world. The classic example is a weather map. It often has color bars to indicate temperatures, icons to show the type of weather happening the various cities on the map, and possibly one or two other pieces of information to inform the audience how to prepare for the day.

Infographics should explain clearly what information shows in the graphic and who provided the information for the graphic. Beyond those two key considerations, the designer should also recognize what information is being left out and why it is left out. A designer that fails to acknowledge the last point will make critical mistakes crafting the infographic. The typical error that occurs in this graphic style is presenting a correlation between two Elements as one of the Elements causing the other to occur. Alberto Cairo, the Knight Chair of Visual Journalism at the University of Miami, denotes multiple examples (Jacobson, 2019) in which the data is either misinterpreted or manipulated. Text still plays a vital role in explaining the narrative within an infographic. "If you really want to emphasize something, emphasize it, so people will not miss it. If there's a particular pattern, or a particular data point or a particular fact that should not be missed, just show it."

The takeaways in understanding the use of graphics in journalistic works come down to three points. First, the visual presentation of the elements of the story can help a segment of the audience to understand its thread better. Second, graphics can clutter the story if they are overused or used ineffectively. Finally, the graphic can misrepresent the nature of the story if it is not labeled correctly or selectively manipulated. Journalists must be careful to present the reality of the narrative in the graphic, or else they harm the story.

PHOTOGRAPHY

Photojournalism has been central to journalism since the invention of the camera. Photojournalists serve an essential role in society. They tell stories that document the reality of situations in locations that may not be accessible to the general public. These stories shared by photojournalists are only part of the service that they provide. At its best, photojournalists' work leads to conversations about the issues of the day and creates a more informed public. An informed public can better understand what is happening in the world, country, state, or even down the street when images taken by talented photojournalists are available. A well-shot picture compels the public to want to know more.

Photos used for journalistic work must include a clearly written caption that performs three actions. There must be a precise and accurate description of the location, actors, and activities in the image. The caption must place the image in the context with the rest of the story. Finally, who took the picture has to be identified in the caption alongside the organization the photographer represents.

A still image's strength comes from balancing the emotion portrayed in the photo, the part of the action that was important to capture, and the overall nature of the visual elements incorporated in the photo. Emotion in journalistic work must be reserved to ensure that the story's facts are not lost to the emotional narratives that are natively present in everyday life. Emotions drive humans to act. Those actions make for the most compelling images in journalism. We feel for the people we see on television, in the newspaper, and the vibrant colors of a magazine. Those images help the audience better understand why the people in the story act in the context of the story.

Photojournalism becomes a story's weakness when the image's context is lost due to misinterpretation or misrepresentation. Misrepresentation happens when the caption of the image does not accurately match the image's real situation, or the image is staged for the benefit of the photojournalist. The earliest example of this type of staging happened in 1855 when Roger Fenton staged pictures of a destroyed Ukraine during the Crimean War (Mallonee, 2015). Journalists must be careful using other's work in their story as one false piece of information, or a doctored image will impact the overall credibility of the story and the journalist.

ELECTRONIC MEDIUMS OF COMMUNICATION

Digital and electronic mediums take a good ear for sound and a better eye for the visual to be incorporated effectively into the journalistic narrative. Audio should be included in all stories as it can be used to fill the area where a quote can be used and adds emotional complexity to the story. Video gives the audience a better view and understanding of a given area related to the given subject. Interactive media works well presenting a complex issue with supporting strong visuals and other connective elements. The means to create content and put those pieces together to enhance the audience's understanding of a story is made more accessible through the democratization of media production. The last three mediums require electronic means to create them with the technical understanding of the medium needed to tell the story well.

AUDIO

The most natural place to start this discussion of the strengths and weaknesses of audio is by stating that audio is the most foundational medium in the electronic and digital category of mediums. **Audio** is arranging sounds to be placed in a computer file, embedded on analog magnetic tape, or pressed on a vinyl recording medium. All modes of recording audio depend on translating the waves of sound produced by the human voice or instruments. Those analog waves are placed on a recording medium, or a computer records the wave by plotting an approximation of the sound in a digital format. There are four types of audio projects that journalists will use to produce a news story.

Raw interviews tend to be the least production-heavy audio content a story can use. It is merely the audio file of the interview unedited. The purpose of using this audio project is to show credibility for the quotes in the story and to prove to the audience that the interview took place. They are typically placed at the end of the article as a reference point. Edited quotes from the raw interview are **soundbytes.** These audio clips take the place of textual quotes in the article. Soundbytes are useful as they add an emotional context that would be missing for a textual transcription of the quote.

Another typical piece of audio content used for a multimedia story would be a podcast. **Podcasts** are audio programs that are typically in episodic form hosted by an individual or standard group of hosts. There are no time length requirements for the show as the frequency and format of the show will vary based on the topic the podcast is covering (Gray, 2020). Podcasts are often used in conjunction with the article to provide more details than found in a standalone article. Podcast also helps maintain a consistent style between stories that a brand would publish. One benefit of a journalist's incorporation of a podcast into their story is that the journalist can be part of the podcast. Including the journalist who covered the story can add additional information and evidence that didn't fit the story's original progression or overall narrative.

The third and fourth types of audio content are directly related to radio content. **Radio packages** are short pieces of content (typically around one to four minutes in length) that focuses on one story. These pieces of content are traditionally broadcasted on the radio first as part of a **newscast** or **a news show.** Packages have one reporter covering the story. There are quotes from three to six people addressing critical items related to the story. Sometimes, the package includes natural sounds that help the audience better understand the location of the story or the normal sounds associated with the Elements of the story.

Adding audio to a multimedia journalism work enhances the story in a few ways. The first rationale for adding audio is that audio helps set the tone of the story. Natural sounds and the tone of the interviewee make it easy for the audience to react to the story being presented. Emotions come across through tone of the voice, which allows the listener to understand the context of the story better than the basic text. Another strong reason to add audio is that natural sounds give the audience a sense of actually being in the story. Compelling audio allows audiences to close their eyes and imagine being in the location reference in the story. Finally, background information is easily included using audio. A reporter can use key sound cues to help the audience understand what is happening in the story.

The critical weakness of audio is directly related to the audience's perception of the content. Overproduced audio pieces can sound artificial and make the audience question the legitimacy of the information being presented in the piece. Using too much raw content removes clear narratives for the piece. It becomes an antidotal telling of the story instead of a vetted piece of journalistic work. The takeaway from this section of the chapter should be that audio production affects the reporter's credibility.

VIDEO

Video is one of the first mediums that can be called multimedia. It is a robust hybrid of moving visuals that tell most of the story supported by audio and text to give the audience a clear understanding of the story on the screen. This construction of the medium is why video is the most contextually heavy of the primary forms of communication. Moving images easily attract the attention of the audience. The sounds invite the audience to listen to what is happening on the screen. Text on the screen provides context to the action within the video. It is this combination of mediums that makes the video one of the more compelling mediums a journalist can use to tell the story's narrative.

Like audio, there are several types of videos that journalists will use to tell the story. **Raw videos** are unedited to show the audience the events of the story as they happened without any production technique used to manipulate the content. These types of videos add credibility to the story. An **explainer** is any video that attempts to define and explain a topic, issue, point of interest, or event. Explainers help the audience better understand the subject. A **broadcast clip** is a video package that was shown on cable or broadcast television. A broadcast clip provides the broader media context to the story. A **feature video** is a short video that focuses on a single person, a short period of time, or location. Finally, there is a **documentary video**, a longer video with voice-over narration, a complex topic, and multiple interviews. Both features and documentaries can place a spotlight on the critical cultural and social issues behind the story. Each of these videos can be effective, given the topic being covered in the story. A journalist should be familiar with these types of videos because they provide different levels of support to the story (Tu, 2015).

Journalists who primarily work in this media need to balance the various factors that make-up a solid piece of video, or the message gets lost in the production of the work. Too much care for the framing of the shot loses the spontaneity that happens when covering live events. Focusing too much on the screen means the journalist might fail to consider the quality of the audio. This balance ensures that the journalist is not leaving out any critical details from the story.

At the same time, the selective nature of video is its primary weakness.

An unremembered element of videography is that the camera is the eye and the ear of the viewer. There is a narrow viewing angle that the lens of the camera can pick up. The **depth of field** (how far back the camera can see) is also fixed. The limitations control how much of the story the journalists can show. The videographer must make the conscious effort to represent the area they are visiting and reporting on fairly.

Remember, the camera lies when it is told untruths.

INTERACTIVE

The final medium is truly a media construction. **Interactive content** is a composite of the previous five mediums with the additional elements of some user interface that allows the audience to control the flow of the narrative. How viewers managed the flow of the story has evolved over the past 40 years. The QUBE system introduced in the late 1970s was one of the first interactive news sources. It used a cable system to give the audience a chance to customize how the news was delivered to them. The interactivity was more of the audience's control and less the mediums used to present the news[4] (Tonn, 2018). As of now, interactive controls are built into more web platforms thanks to technologies like HTML5 (coding), CSS3 (style), and embedded content (Cohen & Kenny, 2020).

Most systems found online have the foundation to create interactive control. An example of an interactive system that more journalists are using is Google Maps. Google Maps is a **geographic information system (GIS)** that allows the user to place mediated content on top of the structure, which is Google's construction of the world's shape. Google Maps allows for layers of content and context to be placed on top of their maps (Napoli, 2019). This combination of "an Earth canvas," mediated content, and interactive data points allows journalists to craft a variety of stories around location and place.

---

[4] It was exclusively a textual presentation of the news.

GISs are one of several examples that shows that interactive content is the most layered mediated construction applied to a story. Journalists who delve into this style of journalism are not only balancing between the strengths and weaknesses of the various mediums used to comprise the overall final interactive artifact. Journalists must not allow the user interface and experience to be too complicated. The media and interface should virtually disappear so the audience can be engaged with the flow of the story. This understanding of engagement is the last bit of advice regarding interactive journalism.

Journalists should recognize that because a piece of the story is interactive does not mean the audience will automatically be engaged with the Elements. Removing all of the media and interactivity from the story should still leave a strong narrative that the audience can follow. If the narrative is weak, no amount of media is going to save it. A journalist should determine from their progression if the amount of work and planning it is going to take to produce an interactive story is worth it in the long run.

CONCLUSION

Explaining the strengths and weaknesses of the various mediums in the journalistic content realm is a necessary discussion to better place the right information within the correct mediation. Multimedia journalists must recognize the most effective means and modes of telling a story via communication channels to compose a clear narrative to the audience. A completed piece of multimedia journalism should allow the narrative to flow between the various form of media that tell the story and enhance the audience's understanding of the story's overall impact on the community.

The other takeaway is that the asset used for the story does not need to be perfect. Crystal-clear images, high-quality soundbytes, and high definition videos that capture the essence of the story happen enough with professionals who are at the right place and the right time. Most of the time, media assets work if they perfectly fit into the story's context and advance the overall narrative. The next two chapters get to the heart of the characteristics that define great journalistic work. The first characteristic is crafting a truthful, compelling narrative about a subject happening in a community for a given audience. The second part explains to the audience why they should care about that topic / issue / point of interest / event that is happening within the given community.

POINTS TO PONDER

- Find an example of a work of interactive journalism. How does the journalist balance the narrative, media, and interactivity in the story?

- How does this knowledge about the different modes of communication help us tell better stories?

- When is a piece of content "good enough" to be added to our story?

- How do we create mediated content that reflects the reality of the story and the larger truths in society?

WORKS CITED

Bennett, J. N. (2017, April). *Advertising: Dollars and decisions*. Retrieved April 25, 2020, from https://research.stlouisfed.org/publications/page1-econ/2017-04-03/advertising-dollars-and-decisions/

Cohen, J., & Kenny, T. (2020). *Producing New and Digital Media: Your guide to savvy use of the web*. Routledge.

Coman, M., & Rothenbuhler, E. W. (2005). The Promise of Media Anthropology. *Media Anthropology*, (pp. 1–12). doi: 10.4135/9781452233819.n1

Gray, C. (2020, January 29). *What is a Podcast? An explanation in plain English*. Retrieved April 27, 2020, from https://web.archive.org/web/20200427170929/https://www.thepodcasthost.com/listening/what-is-a-podcast/

Jacobson, S. (2019, October 17). *Beware of the Infographic*. Retrieved April 26, 2020, from https://web.archive.org/web/20191222050121/https://www.cjr.org/the_media_today/alberto-cairo-infographics.php

Mallonee, L. (2015, July 29). *Infamously Altered Photos, Before and After Their Edits*. Retrieved April 26, 2020, from https://web.archive.org/web/20181221050740/https://www.wired.com/2015/07/bronx-documentary-center-infamously-altered-photos-edits/

Napoli, P. M. (2019). Place/Space and the Challenges Facing Local Journalism and Local Journalism Research. *Journalism & Communication Monographs, 21*(2), (pp. 147-151).

Phelps, A., & Consalvo, M. (2020, January). Laboring Artists: Art streaming on the videogame platform Twitch. In *Proceedings of the 53rd Hawaii International Conference on System Sciences*.

Plank, L. (2014). *Drawn Truth*. Retrieved April 25, 2020, from https://web.archive.org/web/20150909022426/http://drawntruth.tumblr.com/

Soper, J. (2017, April). *Jump Right In: 7 ways immersive technology can transform business.* Retrieved April 24, 2020, from https://web.archive.org/web/20200424150819/https://cmo.adobe.com/articles/2017/4/immersive-technology-.html

Tilton, S., & Fleck, K. (2019). Accelerating the Photojournalist: An analysis of how media brands use Instagram for brand promotion. In *Carolinas Communication Association 2018 Annual Conference.* Retrieved from https://www.researchgate.net/publication/331413389_Accelerating_the_Photojournalist_An_Analysis_of_How_Media_Brands_use_Instagram_for_Brand_Promotion

Tonn, C. (2018, June 26). *That '70s Interactive TV.* Retrieved April 28, 2020, from https://web.archive.org/web/20190927063604/https://tedium.co/2018/06/26/qube-cable-television-history/

Tu, D. L. (2015). *Feature and Narrative Storytelling for Multimedia Journalists.* Burlington, MA: Focal Press.

Tufte, E. R. (2016). *The Cognitive Style of PowerPoint: Pitching out corrupts within.* Cheshire: Graphics Press.

CHAPTER 6: CREATING A COMPELLING NARRATIVE

One of the defining characteristics that distinguish journalistic work from other forms of communication is that those pieces of content should explain a topic, issue, point of interest, or event using a truthful, compelling narrative about a community to a given audience. Journalism presents this truthful, informative, and compelling narrative on a variety of mediums and platforms to a select audience that recognizes the story existing in some version of reality.

This essential characteristic means that journalists must be comfortable understanding the differences between a topic, an issue, a point of interest, and an event in terms of writing the narrative for each of them. This definition also means identifying what type of community is the focus of the story. Finally, a journalist must explain all of the Elements to the correct type of audience that is reading, listening to, or watching the story they have created. The final demand of the journalist based on this defining characteristic is the first focus of this chapter.

We will begin by discussing what makes a narrative compelling.

THE COMPELLING NARRATIVE

Compelling is creating a narrative that evokes the interest of the audience so that their attention does not waiver for the work. Narratives in journalistic work are compelling if they do more than have the audience read the story from beginning to end. A narrative must present information that is novel to the audience in a way that allows them to process the information as they are following the narrative (McChesney & Nichols, 2011). The conflict that is driving the narrative should also be clearly explained without exaggeration or embellishment. Journalists should tell the story from the audience's vantage point without any bias, over-emotional language, or manipulation.

In a compelling narrative, the media represents a dynamic method of telling the story that uses the natural strengths of the different mediums to amplify critical points of the story. Audio brings out the story's emotion, the action of the story comes through the video, a graphic can clarify relationships in the story, and photographs bring out the spirit of the community for the audience to see. The permanent record of the events is part of the textual presentation of the story. All forms of media must work in concert to make the narrative compelling (Mabrook & Singer, 2019).

Compelling narratives are vital to maintaining an audience in the era of Disruptive Journalism. Many of the practices that led to compelling narrative come from the traditions of Legacy Journalism. Specifically, journalists can look at past journalistic works and examples to help shape the quality of journalistic content today and in the future. The best practice of ensuring high-quality content is to work with other journalists and train with professionals regularly. Strong feedback given to improve journalist's content helps everybody out. The best place to find strong feedback would be a journalism professional development organization. Journalists who belong to professional development organizations like the Poynter, Investigative Reporters & Editors, Society for Professional Journalists, National Association of Black Journalists, the Online News Association, and many others can use their resources to find a better way to present their stories to the audience.

The area that most of my students need help with the building of the story to create a compelling narrative.

BUILDING THE STORY

It would be a good time to address a term that been used repetitively[5] with no real attempt to provide a definition. The term in question is a story. Story is one of those words that I refer to as a smurf term. A **smurf term** is any word that has so many meanings that the term itself can become meaningless as it is used to infinitum. The reason it's been used so often is that a story is the coin of the realm in journalism. A **story** is a record of how actions that affect community members are told in a manner that benefits an audience unfamiliar with those Elements. Stories are how members of the community talk about those actions. It is also the by-product of the journalist covering those actions, which is to say

---

[5] The word story was used 427 times before this spot in the book.

it's the journalist's understanding of the situation's reality. All of these definitions fit into that central characteristic that started this chapter. However, the next few paragraphs will focus on that last definition and how to form a good piece of mediated work that explains the actions that happened in a community.

Journalists understand that the story must consist of a sequence of actions that occur when a sympathetic actor encounters a complicated situation that they confront and solve. There are several terms we need to go over. A definition of actors appears in the first chapter. Still, the idea that someone is sympathetic is new ground for this book. **Sympathy** is allowing the audience to feel an emotional connection with the person in the article. It is easier to make this connection with a person as opposed to an empathic connection. **Empathy** means that the audience has been in the position that the person in the story is in, and the audience can understand that person's motivations and emotions. Journalists can create sympathy in the story by introducing key quotes and interactions with others that allow the viewer to see the person's humanity. Empathy happens when the audience is immersed in the flow of the story and sees they are "one in the same" as the person in the story (Laws, 2017).

A **complicated situation** in this characteristic refers not just to the actors within the story having to make at least two decisions with a variety of choices. This complication reflects in a broader sense of what those choices mean for the community. Every action that happens will have some impact on the overall community. Acknowledging this complexity within the story does not mean making the conflict "overly dramatic" but rather explain the various factors with clarity, so the audience understands with some certainty how the Elements are affecting the story (Lowrey, Sherrill, & Broussard, 2019).

The last part of the compelling narrative should show how the actor confronts and solves the complicated situation.

Confronting means the journalist explains the actor's connection to the situation, the actions between actor and situation, and what motivates them to resolve the situation. Journalists should also note how the actor's role in the community influences their ability to act. The **solving** of the complicated situation happens when the actions put forth by the actor resolve within the community. How the actor addresses the situation can be the first part of a longer story.

Journalists should recognize that the actors' actions in the story should lead to reactions of others in the community. These reactions can be as simple as basic support from the community to the complexity of a community-wide protest. Compelling narratives come about when the members of the community deal with decisions and the ramification of those decisions.

For example, the mayor of Townsville could decide to start a beautification project to clean up the city. A boring story would present the project's bullet points from the mayor's office and repeat the information found in the press release about the project. This presentation of the project is a basic story that any reporter could write. Let's apply the definition of a story to improve its quality.

First, we need a sympathetic actor. The mayor is as good of a place to start as any. The reporter should get to the heart of what inspired them to start this project, what Townsville means to the mayor regarding this project, and what they believe will benefit Townsville. Most mayors I have ever worked with should be able to give three quality answers to those prompts. If not, talk to the public works director or even a city employee responsible for this type of project. To continue developing this compelling narrative, the reporter must think about the next part of the story's definition.

A good reporter should ask, "What makes a city beautification project a complicated situation?" If the reporter can not think of an answer, it either means this isn't a newsworthy story (it's possible), or they haven't done enough pre-writing to answer that question (also reasonable). Let's add the complication. Through researching the story, our reporter discovers that Townsville does not have enough money to beautify the entire town and plans on cleaning up a select few areas. The report can now focus on the process that led to the selection of the regions for beautification. The decisions are what neighborhood could have potentially been selected, the type of work chosen for the neighborhood, and the time table for the cleanup effort. Those questions might be addressed to members of the city council, the city treasurer, or somebody responsible for the decision-making process. Having this information will allow the reporter to develop the third part of the definition of a story.

The reporter is most likely going to go back to the mayor to address how they will confront and solve the issue of limited funds for this project. It is vital to not position anybody as a hero or a villain in this construction. Reporters need to go where the facts and the story takes them. Hopefully, they would be able to incorporate the sympathetic actor questions into the confront and solve questions if the reporter did the Pre-writing section of the Journalism Breakdown before scheduling the interview. The confront and solve questions should be along the lines of:

- What issues arise by not cleaning up the neighborhoods left out of the beautification project?

- Why is it important to work on the neighborhood selected for this project?

- How would you explain to the citizens of Townsville the reasoning behind the selection process?

Those questions force the mayor to confront the issues created by their decision and an opportunity to solve them. This line of questioning provides the reporter with one final element necessary for a good, compelling narrative.

If the compelling narrative is genuinely effective, the reporter must focus on the momentum of the story. In this case, **momentum** is how the reporter explains where the story will end up after all of the actors in the story perform their actions. Reporters capture the story's momentum by allowing the actors in the story to reflect on their actions (either current or future). Reflection added effectively to the story makes the story more exciting and a better read for the audience. It also gets to an underlying truth about journalism.

> The human condition is messy. Explaining community members to an audience is not a simple process. We tell complicated stories.

Having the information provided in the example allows the reporter to craft a compelling narrative.

CRAFTING THE COMPELLING NARRATIVE

The elements described earlier in this chapter provide the underlying components that will drive the narrative. It is up to the reporter to turn those raw elements into a piece of journalistic content. Forming those pieces into a narrative means the reporter must understand what the audience needed to be addressed. In every good story, a reader starts in one place and ends up in another place, changed and enlightened somehow through the power of the story. It is up to the journalist to determine where the audience begins with the story, where they end after reading the story, and how the Elements enlighten them. The content will determine those three points that the journalist uses to craft the story and how they craft the flow of the narrative.

A compelling narrative starts by connecting the truths from the Writing Progression with the needs of the audience. This connection occurs when a journalist can answer enough hypothetical questions that the audience would have about the story by giving them information and quotes that address their concerns. Once the information and quotes fit into the structure of the story, the next step is to craft a descriptive lede that addresses at least two central questions that the audience would have about the story. Having this graf nailed down is vital for a compelling narrative. Using a boring lede will drain all of the energy for the story and the audience's curiosity. An informative lede is slightly better but makes it difficult to start a compelling narrative. The first two or three grafs of the story must address the six Essential Questions the audience would have about the story. Answering the six Essential Questions presents the Elements of the story to the audience. The next step in crafting the narrative after answering the question is placing a hook graf into the story.

Depending on the nature of the information gathered in the interview that any hooks described in chapter two of this book should work just fine. My suggestions are based on how I shape most stories.

- If you feel that you have a great sympathetic actor, the audience will strongly identify with the drop quote hook exceptionally well. The rationale is that if the audience has an emotional connection with the person giving the quote that they will continue to have that emotional connection and want to continue reading the story to see more of what they say about the subject the reporter is writing about.

- The whammy will make the most sense to use if you know that the story is going to a unique telling of a story that the audience might generally be familiar with. The whammy puts a strong emphasis on the Elements that should attract the audience's attention and what they would find interesting.

- The rhetorical pivot and shift is a sharp hook when there are two compelling rhetorical threads in the story that focus on different artistic points (logic, emotion, or the community). This style of the hook allows the reporter to juxtapose the two threads and create a good sense of discord that breaks the audience's mental flow.

- The one-sentence graf is reasonable if the first three conditions do not apply well to the story. It works exceptionally well if the grafs before the hook are reasonably dense.

These hooks described above work well if the way those hooks are written engage the audience's curiosity and interest in the subject matter. The hook graf provides an opportunity to address the three artistic rhetorical elements found in most compelling narratives.

After placing the lede and the hook into the story, the journalist must write a logical flow into the story that the audience can comprehend following the story's hook. This logical flow must do two essential functions within the story. The first being that the journalist must present all of the relevant facts related to the story that helps the audience be fully aware of the nature of the story. Secondly, those facts must seem to be right in the audience's mind and reflective of the everyday reality that the audience experiences. Both of those functional elements of the story help maintain the credibility and ethos of the journalist. This credibility and ethos are vital as it allows them to present new information farther into the story. The ability to introduce additional facts of the story through the narrative expands the audience's knowledge and makes the narrative more appealing. A good logical flow finally allows the journalist to inject more emotion into the story in the form of quotes and mediated content that can be persuasive for the audience to continue down the narrative path. All of this flow should give the audience a payoff in the form of the nut graf.

The only way a narrative becomes compelling is if the journalist has crafted a solid Writing Progression that moves the story in a definite direction forward while fitting into the audience's reality. It must take all of the information gathered for this point and place those critical pieces of content in a way that allows the viewer to gain knowledge after reading the story.

CONCLUSION

Dustin Grinnell (2019) noted in an article for *Writer's Digest* that using some literary techniques makes for compelling narratives in journalistic works. Beyond picking the right story for the medium, the journalist must recognize several vital factors that enhance the story. Grinnell points to structure, point of view, and mood as literary elements that help advance the narrative. If the story has a "clear and satisfying beginning, middle, and end" (para. 7) along with keeping the journalist "out of the story" (para. 8) and controlling the mood of the story with careful word selection makes a fundamental difference in how the audience reads the story. This example is not to say that the journalist should present the narrative in the literary style. Instead, the journalist should be willing to borrow techniques for other writers that they find useful and use to develop their personal voice in journalism.

This chapter should clarify that the compelling narrative is the glue that holds the audience to the Elements of the story. Journalists that can master this technique will find that the story becomes more than a simple regurgitation of facts about a topic, an issue, a point of interest, or an event. Compelling narratives are what makes journalism a service to the community. It tells the narrative beyond the facts of the story. It explains how the people referenced in the story, and the events listed impact the average community members' daily lives.

The final point to note about the compelling narrative's power is that an outstanding, compelling narrative helps the audience understand that society is a complex series of interactions between members of that society. The audience should have a better understanding of how they fit into those complex series of interactions after they finish reading the compelling narrative. The logical extension of acknowledging that point is the audience's discussions with others about the Elements might be framed by the story you produced. The journalist can help the audience make sense of the day-to-day actions in their community and have more meaningful connections with others through a compelling narrative (Krieken & Sanders, 2019).

The next chapter will focus on the second characteristic that makes for strong multimedia journalism content, which addresses why the audience should care about the story.

POINTS TO PONDER

- Pick a story published by a professional journalist. How do they make the key person in the story a sympathetic actor?

- How should a journalist avoid turning a complicated situation into an over-dramatic story?

- Pick another story and re-write the lede to turn it into a descriptive lede that leads into the beginning of a compelling narrative.

- Pick still another story and pick a spot in the story to add one or two of the hooks referenced in this chapter.

- What helps a story have the "clear and satisfying beginning, middle, and end" described in the conclusion of this chapter?

WORKS CITED

Grinnell, D. (2019, January 31). *Using Literary Techniques in Narrative Journalism.* Retrieved May 2, 2020, from https://web.archive.org/web/20190201020434/ https://www.writersdigest.com/editor-blogs/writers-perspective/journalism/ using-literary-techniques-in-narrative-journalism

Krieken, K. V., & Sanders, J. (2019). What is Narrative Journalism? A systematic review and an empirical agenda. *Journalism,* (pp. 1–20). doi: 10.1177/1464884919862056

Laws, A. L. S. (2017). Can Immersive Journalism Enhance Empathy? *Digital Journalism, 8*(2), 213–228. doi: 10.1080/21670811.2017.1389286

Lowrey, W., Sherrill, L., & Broussard, R. (2019). Field and Ecology Approaches to Journalism Innovation: The role of ancillary organizations. *Journalism Studies, 20*(15), 2131–2149. doi: 10.1080/1461670x.2019.1568904

Mabrook, R., & Singer, J. B. (2019). Virtual Reality, 360° Video, and Journalism Studies: Conceptual approaches to immersive technologies. *Journalism Studies, 20*(14), 2096–2112. doi: 10.1080/1461670x.2019.1568203

McChesney, R. W., & Nichols, J. (2011). *The Death and Life of American Journalism: The media revolution that will begin the world again.* Nation Books.

CHAPTER 7: ADDRESSING THE "SO WHAT" QUESTION IN THE NARRATIVE

What makes journalistic works different from other forms of content is the ability to invoke a rationale for the audience to pay attention to a given subject. Journalists use a combination of logic, emotion, and ethos using a style of delivery that identifies those topics, issues, points of interest, and events of current importance. The journalists must also explain the more profound social-psychological implications of those subject to their audience. The idea of exploring the social-psychological elements of the narrative isn't for the journalist to wax philosophical about the underlying story, but rather explore why the audience should care about the story. This exploration happens when the journalist addresses the "so what" question.

Journalists should not treat the **"so what" question** as a flippant remark about the story, nor treat it as a satirical response to the topic at hand. Instead, this question gets to the core of what makes the story meaningful and relevant to the audience. A journalist should have a simple understanding of why the audience cares about the community they cover. Some audience members are also members of the community. Others can be affected by the actions taken by that community. Many additional reasons can explain the connection between the audience and the community. Only one thing matters regardless of the reasoning; the journalist is the bridge between the audience and the community.

Focusing on why the audience should care forces the journalist to narrow the narrative towards the defining characteristics of their relationship with their audience. The rest of the story is set based on the actions taken in the previous six chapters of this book. The conclusion of the story is grounded in applying those defining characteristics toward the subject of the story. The journalist builds up to this point by providing credible facts about the story, quotes that reveal others' humanity, and a presentation of the story's reality that the audience feels is a truthful telling of the narrative. Getting the audience to care about the narrative you have created means knowing which parts of the story are most meaningful to them.

Capturing the meaningfulness of a story in the minds of the audience is a continuously moving target as the audience's taste evolves as other media tastes evolve. Audiences do not exist in stasis. Topics, issues, points of interest, and events are important to the audience when they first reach a tipping point of at least 10% of a given population believing that the topic, issue, point of interest, or event is of the utmost importance within the population (Xie et al., 2011). The next step is when the topic, issue, point of interest, or event reaches a critical mass of people that believe that the subject in question either represents a collective action of public good or potential harm to the overall stability of the collective whole (Oliver, Marwell, & Teixeira, 1985). Understanding this process allows the journalist to craft the story that reflects the objects of audience concern. This self-reflection also means that the journalist should recognize that they have a few options for answering the "so what" question. These options should also take into account the relationship that the reporter has with the audience, the community, and the Elements. In particular, four roles can help the journalist answer the "so what" question with clarity and focus.

JOURNALIST AS A ROLE PLAYER

In the next four roles, the journalist is mainly "playing the part" of the four roles listed. It is not to say that they aren't subject-level experts, members of the community, observed things as they happened, or even expected to document all of the significant actions for history's sake. Instead, the journalist should approach answering the "so what" with the mindset of an expert, community member, observer, or scribe. This type of mindset allows the reporter to be concise with the conclusion of the story and address the remaining issues left out of the earlier narrative components. Understanding these next four roles helps get to the heart of what the audience should take away from the story and how the community is reacting to the Elements.

JOURNALIST AS EXPERT

The journalist's first role is when the journalist is presenting from the vantage point of an expert. Experts tend to address the overwhelming consensus of evidence related to the subject at hand. There will be peer-reviewed studies and scholarly works that will help address their talking points. They will often speak in analogies to help the listener understand the complexity of their given field. In short, they attempt to make the complicated simple with good narratives and better empirical data to back up their claims (Letzter, 2016).

An **expert** would be a person that possesses sufficient knowledge in a specialized field whose knowledge is useful to help the audience better understand the Elements. When they do their role well, experts provide clarity on "conflicting claims or conclusions" (Lubet & Boals, 2020, p. 2). Most of the time, experts interpret the actions that happen in the community and explain their impact on the community and the audience as a whole. Professors, scholars, and practitioners of their fields are often thought of as the first line of experts to interview. As Lubet & Boals note, a letter carrier is an expert in postal delivery. Athletes can speak about the nature of their given sport, or high school students can talk about high school life with a level of expertise.

Journalists taking the expert role in the story will address the "so what" question by highlighting the facts and assets that an expert in the field of the story would find interesting and relevant. This highlighting happens naturally in the nut graf of the article. A chronological, expert nut graf allows the journalist to place what's changed in the field in historical context or crafts an explanation of the significance of those changes to the community's or audience's future. Institutional, expert nut grafs provide clarity on how social institutions impact the story's subject in relationship to the community. While a humanistic, expert nut graf allows the journalist to explain how the motivation of the actors in the story is a reflection of their interactions with the expert's field of study.

Regardless of the form that the nut graf takes, journalists will maintain the expert's position within the story if they can speak to the theory of the story. A narrative that speaks to the **theory of the story** hits three key points. First, it must use peer-reviewed articles or expert interviews to build up a version of reality supported by substantial evidence. Second, it must use mediated content to clarify Elements that would confuse a layman reader of the story. Finally, the journalist must avoid absolutes in the presentation of the story. These three points do not mean that the journalist should write in the language of the academy. Journalists must still use short, clear, and concise language to construct their narrative and make the story accessible to the audience.

JOURNALIST AS COMMUNITY MEMBER

The journalist's second role is when the journalist is presenting from the vantage point of being a community member. Community members present the narrative with a strong sense of the voice of the community. This role means that community leaders will tend to impact how the narrative is shaped. Those community influencers will speak in a conventional style while reflecting on how the actors and Elements impact the overall community. They will use the legacy and legends of the community to attempt to express a single voice, respected by all that consider themselves a member of that community (Tanner, 2019).

A **community member** would be a person that understands enough of the history and interactions of the community that they have credibility when discussing what the community is doing and what is relevant to a given story. Journalists can play the role of the community member when they can communicate how the community views a given story's reality in a voice that seems authentic for the given situation (Robinson, 2017). Community members talk in the mode of living experiences. They will express their day-to-day realities as part of an overall picture of what it means to be a member of that community. This individual construction of the community also means that members of the community can have different mental models of their community based more on personal experiences and less on the polished mediated image of their community.

Addressing the "so what" question as a community member forces the journalist to frame the nut graf so that the community members would find that paragraph truthful and speaking to the everyday realities of the community. These types of nut grafs are going to be grounded more in the quotes from the community. A chronological, community-based nut graf allows the journalist to explain how the community's position about the story has evolved. Institutional, community-based nut grafs show how social institutions support the community with this topic, issue, point of interest, or event and why those social institutions are central to the community. Finally, the humanistic, community-based nut graf highlights one or two of the community leaders to reveal the community's humanity through the framework of the story.

Journalists can maintain the community position if they speak to the reality of the story. The trick of this role is not to be too native to the community. A journalist should allow for some objective distancing when writing the story. At the same time, the journalist should not write the story as if they were dropshipped directly in the middle of the story.

Dropshipping is a Legacy Journalism term that refers to a reporter coming from a large city when an important breaking news story happens in some other part of the country. They arrive in the small town or community that would otherwise be considered a news desert. **News Deserts** are counties with no local newspapers, radio stations, television stations, or any other journalistic organization covering local topics, issues, points of interest, or events. Journalists will then report the news without taking the time to understand the community and its members (Jensen, 2020). The issue with that journalism style is that the community becomes nothing more than a series of simple characteristics and stereotypes instead of an area of cultural diversity that shows the complexity of the community's existence (Reese, 2010).

The sweet spot for this nut graf occurs when the journalist is familiar enough about the community to speak knowledgeably about it while maintaining an objective view that checks personal bias in the writing of the story.

JOURNALIST AS OBSERVER

The journalist's third role is when the journalist is presenting from the vantage point of witnessing the actions that happened in the course of the story. Observers present the narrative grounded in the time and the place of the actions as they were happening. Journalists playing the role of the observer must attempt to focus on the sensory experiences of a person observing the actions at the given place and time. This focus means that the journalist would explain the actions using a more conversational language than the previous two roles. They would not be speaking from the expert's logical position or at the credibility level of a community member. Instead, there would be a more emotional tone drawing from the excitement or other dynamic tone based on the nature of the story (Marchi, 2019).

There are three levels of observation that the reporter can pursue:

1. as a casual observer of the story,

2. an active observer of the story, and

3. a witness to the story.

The **casual observer** is passively examining the scene to look for details for future reference or to aid in telling the story while remaining in one static place at the scene of the action. The **active observer** is more reflective of what those actions mean for those at the scene of the action. The **witness** is more engaged with the actors and the actions and can clarify the actor's motivations in the story.

For example, a car crash happens. The casual observer hears the crash from their house and looks outside to see what happened. They remember some of the details of the crash but are more aware of the personal experiences than others' experiences involved with the crash. The active observer leaves the house to get closer to the crash to see if anybody is injured. They will get a better sense of the overall severity of the crash. They could tell the first responder who needs to go to the hospital. The witness would talk to one of the drivers in the crash to see if they were okay and find out what happened. This level of observation might allow that person to explain what could have caused the crash to first responders. All three types of observers play a different role in telling the story of the crash to others.

Journalists can maintain the observer's role if they are aware of the environment that the story is happening in and filter down those actions based on the order of importance. This order of importance will vary based on what type of observer the audience would expect to tell them about the story. This role requires the journalist to be aware of their bias that can prevent important information from becoming part of the story. The journalist must balance those experiences within the progression of the story.

Writing this style of nut graf requires the journalist to speak to the reality on the ground. The takeaway is simply the Elements that can be easily shared with others that explain to the audience the full scope of the story from the observer's perspective. This paragraph should include a reason why this information is vital for the audience to know.

JOURNALIST AS SCRIBE

The journalist's final role that they can take on when addressing the so what question is merely documenting all of the relevant facts that the audience should take away clearly and concisely. It also allows the audience to make their determination of what are the critical Elements. This journalistic role is the simplest as there is no underlying narrative within the nut graf. It is a flat presentation of facts within the structure of the story. Journalists playing the role of the scribe must attempt to focus on the truth as the vital element of the story. It is fair to argue that this method of addressing the nut graf of the story is the weakest method of concluding the story.

The scribe represents three key social functions. Scribes must be able be to:

1. present an aggregation of voices within the story,

2. record the experiences of the the people within the story, and

3. document both types of information in a way that future readers can understand what was happening (Taylor, 2017).

There is a lot of context and knowledge removed from this style of nut graf. First of all, the social and cultural context is removed from this presentation of the takeaway. If journalists accept that the functional difference between information and knowledge is that information is simply knowledge without any contextual clues, audiences will not understand why the information is presented in the nut graf (Ackoff, 1989). The second issue with the scribe method is that there's no weight on the quality of voices or experiences put into this crafting of the nut. Lastly, the scribe's documentation for future readers often simplifies or flatten the narrative surrounding conflict in the story to the point that future audience might not realize the underlying conflict that drove the actions that the actors in the story took (Reese, 2010). This understanding of the role's weaknesses means that journalists that find this role as the only way to connect with the story should do more work to minimize the concerns raised by this role.

Journalists can be a successful scribe if they both document everything relevant to a given story for the benefit of future audiences, and they create content that is native to the environment of the story. The nut graf should feel like a natural conclusion to the direction the story took in the Writing Progression. All of this flow should give the audience a payoff in the form of the nut graf.

THE "SO WHAT" GRAF

The last essential graf that a great piece of journalistic work must have is explaining the most important takeaway for the audience in the form of a nut graf. The nut graf is the "payoff" for the audience for reading the work. Several techniques discussed in this chapter should help address why the audience should care about the story, otherwise known as addressing the "so what" question.

Even if the journalist has a tough time defining their role within a given story, they must provide a reasonable nut graf. Nut grafs in a compelling narrative must sufficiently summarize all of the Elements into one to three grafs. The journalist should do this step so the audience can share what they learned about the story with others. In turn, the audience will explain to others why the story is essential for them to read. This writing style is not the same as giving the audience a reason to care about the narrative they just read. A good nut graf is the perfect combination of logic and ethos. The chronological nut graf presents a logical tie-in to the history of the story and what the future might hold for the Elements. Institutional nut graf connects the more significant social organizations that the audience is familiar with and clearly explains how the story that they just read fits into the agenda of those organizations. The humanity of the community related to the narrative is the crux of the humanistic nut graf.

CONCLUSION

After reading the last two chapters of this book, it should be clear that both a compelling narrative and answering the "so what" question are vital to journalism, as both help explain a story to a given audience and help keep the audience informed. If the narrative is the path that the audience goes through to read the story, answering the "so what" question is the finish line that rewards them for making it to the conclusion of the work. This understanding means that the conclusion should be as rewarding for the journalist to write as it is for the audience to read.

The previous two chapters should clarify that journalism is an essential practice designed to present a truthful, informative, and compelling narrative on a variety of mediums and platforms to a select audience that will recognize the story existing in some version of reality. The reality that the audience will see is judged based on how realistic the nut graf is in context with the rest of the narrative. This reality is also based on how much trust the audience put in the journalist, the journalistic platform, and journalism in general (Grosser, Hase, & Blöbaum, 2016). Addressing the "so what" using clear and concise language so the audience understands how the story impacts them builds trust and credibility in the system.

The next chapter will act as a final checklist to go over the story before a critical analysis of that story and a full executive and editorial review.

POINTS TO PONDER

- Pick a story published by a professional journalist. How would that journalist craft the nut graf based on the four roles that a journalist can play in this chapter?

- What are some other ways that a person can be an expert of a story?

- Pick a community that you have written about, what are some of the ways that a person can show they are a member of that community?

- In what ways are the observer and the scribe different in the ways that they craft the nut graf?

- What makes the scribe the weakest of the four roles that a journalist can use to craft the nut graf of the story?

WORKS CITED

Ackoff, R. L. (1989). From Data to Wisdom. *Journal of Applied Systems Analysis, 16*(1), 3-9.

Grosser, K. M., Hase, V., & Blöbaum, B. (2016). Trust in Online Journalism. In B. Blöbaum (Ed.), *Trust and Communication in a Digitized World* (pp. 53–73). Springer. doi: 10.1007/978-3-319-28059-2

Jensen, E. (2020, March 6). *Working Together To Alleviate 'News Deserts'*. Retrieved May 4, 2020, from https://web.archive.org/web/20200504100326/https://www.npr.org/sections/publiceditor/2020/03/06/812096584/working-together-to-alleviate-news-deserts

Letzter, R. (2016, August 31). *There's an Easy Way to Tell if You're Talking to an Expert or a Faker*. Retrieved May 4, 2020, from https://web.archive.org/web/20190104112452/https://www.businessinsider.com/how-to-tell-experts-from-fakers-2016-8

Lubet, S., & Boals, E. I. (2020). *Expert Testimony: A guide for expert witnesses and the lawyers who examine them.* Wolters Kluwer.

Marchi, A. (2019). *Self-reflexive Journalism: A corpus study of journalistic culture and community in The Guardian.* Routledge.

Oliver, P.; Marwell, G.; Teixeira, R. (1985). A Theory of Critical Mass: Interdependence, group heterogeneity, and the production of collective action. *American Journal of Sociology. 9*(3), 552–56.

Reese, S. D. (2010). Finding Frames in a Web of Culture: The case of the war on terror. In P.D'Angeloo & J. A. Kuypers (Eds.), *Doing News Framing Analysis: Empirical and theoretical perspectives* (pp. 17–33). Taylor & Francis.

Robinson, S. (2017). Teaching Journalism for Better Community. *Journalism & Mass Communication Quarterly, 94*(1), 303–317. doi: 10.1177/1077699016681986

Tanner, S. (2019, May). *Community Journalism: A study on the Mountain Times Publications.* Retrieved May 4, 2020, from https://libres.uncg.edu/ir/asu/f/ Tanner_Savanna_2019_Thesis.pdf

Taylor, J. (2017). Sociology as a Love Story: Confessions of a movement scribe. *Canadian Review of Sociology/Revue Canadienne De Sociologie, 54*(3), 378–381. doi: 10.1111/cars.12161

Xie, J., Sreenivasan, S., Korniss, G., Zhang, W., Lim, C., & Szymanski, B. K. (2011). Social Consensus through the Influence of Committed Minorities. *Physical Review E, 84*(1), 1–8. doi: 10.1103/physreve.84.011130

CHAPTER 8: TYING UP THE LOOSE ENDS OF THE STORY

One of the toughest lessons to learn early on in one's journalism career is taking the time to review one's work before submitting it down the road to the editor or the next person in the workflow. Journalists feel the pressure of the deadline, and it can affect when the journalist thinks that the story is ready for publication. This need to rush affects the overall quality of the work the journalist produces. In turn, this quick submission instinct lowers the tone and essence of the published content platform. These next two chapters will go over the last set of steps needed before the journalist can feel that their work is ready for the world.

This chapter will go over the last series of questions that should be answered in the story before going through the work evaluation. Journalists need to examine if all of the pieces used in their story fit the story's overall narrative. The overall narrative still must be short, clear, and concise to give the audience a reasonable understanding of the story. The journalist must fact-check the story again to ensure the accuracy of the words and the quotes in the story. This fact-checking means following up with sources as part of the final review of the story. The result of completing this personal checklist is that the journalist should feel that the information presented in the story is correct and accessible to the audience.

The six overarching questions posed in this chapter are meant to make the journalists think critically about their own stories. Thoughtful analysis of the narrative suggests the journalist can take some comfort in the fact that they have studied their article for fundamental flaws in the narrative. They either found no flaws or addressed those flaws before an editor caught them. This first level of a final, personal review also means that they can feel confident in the Writing Progression as the truths from the progression should have found their way into the story's overall narrative. These last six questions will form the rest of the sections of this chapter, starting with one of the more fundamental points to review on a given article.

DO ALL OF THE PIECES FIT WITHIN THE STORY?

I often call this the "jigsaw puzzle" question. A multimedia journalist must examine all of the pieces that they used to craft the story and determine if the story's various components present a clear image to the audience of a truthful, overall narrative about the story. The pieces of the story go beyond meditation. Media used in journalistic content are the digital artifacts that add to the public memory of the actions within the story (Tilton, 2014). These pieces include the quotes, embedded links of the story, and other forms of content that help the audience better understand its nature.

One of the follow-up questions that I will ask students in this section of the review is, "Did the progression refer to all of the essential points of the story?" The Writing Progression is still fundamental to the story as it presents the thread of truth that the audience follows throughout the story. This thread means that the audience must have essential information to make the best judgment of the story's context.

Another critical question is, "Were those points represented honestly in the story?" At this point in the review, I will encourage the journalist to either review the quotes with the interviewee for accuracy's sake or that the journalist should playback the audio one more time to ensure a faithful transcription of the quote in the story. I guarantee somebody will fact-check if there is a questionable quote in the story. **Fact-checking** refers to the process in which an editor will typically talk to a source to confirm the accuracy of the information included in a story. Fact-checkers were a stand-alone position in the era of Legacy Journalism. In Disruptive Journalism, somebody in the editorial staff takes on this role.

One of the final questions we examine is, "Do the supporting mediated elements connect with the essential points of the story?" This question comes up solely for considering the emphasis of the story. While the text on the screen has some staying power in the audience (Ackerman & Goldsmith, 2011), other forms of media allow the audience to remember key elements from the article better (Casero-Ripolés, Marcos-García, & Alonso-Muñoz, 2020).

Addressing these questions allows the journalist to evaluate the narrative's quality before giving it to an editor.

IS THE STORY AN AUTHENTIC TELLING OF THE EVENTS AS THEY HAPPENED?

The next series of questions force the journalist to define the reality of the story. It would be an excellent time to explain another of the smurf terms used a considerable amount of times before this point in the book[6]. The word in question is reality. The reason that the term has not been defined before this point is that it takes a theoretical and metaphysical discussion to apply the concept of reality within journalism properly. **Reality** is the presentation of facts that can be objectively proven to be the truth by sources that have the credibility to speak about the subject at hand. This idea of reality is also a form of agreement between the journalist, the actors within the story, the community who is the focus of the story, and the audience reading the story. Those four entities must agree not only on the actions within the story but also must come to some form of consensus about the meaning of those actions to the community and the audience (Boesman & Meijer, 2018). It is this consensus that forms the foundation of the first follow-up question for this section.

I tend to start this section of the review by asking, "Are you able to pick one moment of the story that the audience can connect with?" This question is useful as it not only looks for areas within the story that will connect with the audience. It also helps present the reality of the story through these connective points. Narratives that show the reality of the story present the community's humanity within that same story.

Another useful question in this review is, "Are you letting the people within the story say what they know?" It is essential for the journalist not to do too much paraphrasing of quotes or summarize community positions within the story. The actors' voices must be evident in the story to explain the motivations of those actions to the audience in the actor's voice. A journalist's narrative works best in

---

[6] 35 times before this point in the book

the story when it raises a point of clarity or removes misinformation within the context of the story.

Otherwise, let the people in the story.

The final question to address that very point is, "Does the story speak in the voice of the community?" This question addresses the broader issue if the journalist is merely glossing out the impact the community has within the story. It is effortless for the journalist to stereotype the community for narrative flattening purposes or to simplify the narrative if the journalist does not take the time to learn about the community (Reese, 2010).

Journalistic reality only exists if the narrative speaks to the reporters' experiences as they relate to the actors, community, and audience within the construction of the story. This level of journalistic reality is referenced in the third major question of this review.

CAN WE VERIFY THE STORY?

Verification of the story goes beyond the fact-checking practice mentioned earlier in this chapter. In this case, **verification** is a form of external fact-checking that allows the audience to judge the quality of the sources. Audiences must have some access to critical sources to be assured that the narrative is not just in the journalist's mind. Quotes and embedded links make up most of this form of access. The access does not require the audience to talk or interact with the sources. They should be able to judge if the information represents the truth based on the content and the credibility of the source. This judgment is grounded in the first follow-up question.

A quality journalist should be able to answer "Are you showing your work?" with a positive response when examining their story. This question approaches the idea if the audience understands where the information presented in the story is sourced. Quotes should be logical in the minds of the audience based on the source and the context of the story. Embedded links need to be accessible to the audience to see if the summary of the information matches what information is actually published on the site. The next question focuses on if the audience knows what the information given in the quotes and embedded links means.

The next question asks, "Can the audience reasonably verify this story?" It is crucial to assess if the audience can understand the information being presented in the story. This point of analysis means that the quotes and sites use language with a lay audience in mind. If there is a lot of jargon or hyper-technical writing, the journalist might want to consider looking for more precise references with more straightforward communication.

The last two follow-up questions address the issue of bias in the reporting of the story. "Are you referencing neutral parties in the story?" and "Are you referencing credible sources?" both focus on if the audience can trust the source used in the story. The first question focuses on the bias that the sources can bring into the story. Journalist's bias came up in chapter four of this book and how journalists deal with those issues to speak to the themes of the story. Non-neutral parties can add bias without the journalist knowing about it. Non-credible sources damage the story as they have a higher platform to spread misinformation and opinions presented as fact. A story with non-credible sources being presented as experts in a field makes the audience trust journalism and journalists less.

ARE WE FOLLOWING THE BASICS OF COMMUNICATION?

This fourth question places journalism as a mode of communication. Journalism is a specialized form of communication, but should still operate under that discipline. **Communication**, as a discipline, is the careful examination of how people and organizations find meaning in the information and interactions that they share (Eldridge et al., 2019). This central question is useful to answer as having a shared social meaning about critical concepts in society leads to better civic dialogue among community members. Reporters need to be effective communicators to be capable journalists.

This effective communicator can be addressed in, "Are you using language that your audience understands?" An audience will not care about the story if they don't understand what is happening. Language is always central to the craft of journalism. J-schools train their students to write in a short, clear, and concise manner to the point simplify the story to an elementary level. However, the journalist must not correspond to the audience as if they were children. That level of writing fails the second follow-up question of this section, "Are you treating the audience with respect?" The audience will also stop reading the story if they feel like they are being talked down to in the narrative.

The final question in this section of the review comes back to one of the fundamentals of a multimedia journalist. "Are you accounting for the strengths and weaknesses of the various media in the story?" approaches the long analysis from chapter five in a different way. Specifically, the journalist should examine each piece of media used in the story to see if anything is lost in the translation of the story by using that particular piece of media. The media used in an article should amplify the narrative and provide clarity to the overall story. Media should not be used for the sake of using media. Amplification of the narrative and giving clarity is also addressed in the fifth question of this review.

ARE WE APPLYING PROPER TECHNIQUES TO TELL THE STORY?

Proper techniques come from the Legacy Journalism's traditions of constructing the story. This question gets to the root of ethical journalism while presenting the news to make it clear that the content is part of these journalistic traditions. There are five key areas that the journalist should examine when answering this question.

It is fair to begin by looking at the claims made in the story and see if there is good evidence to support them. A journalist must not publish a story based on information that does not hold up to strict scrutiny. The story is only as strong as the weakest detail in the story. Ensure there are no questionable pieces of information by rechecking critical aspects of the story one more time.

This rechecking process will mean that the journalist has confidence that the story's sources are the best ones to address the essential details. Those sources that the journalist select might be the best ones that the journalist has access to and can present a clear message relevant to the story.

Those clear messages must also explain how the story fits into the audience's overall understanding of the community being covered in the story. This "big picture" discussion point was discussed in chapter four. Still, it is reasonable to bring it up once more here as the way the community is described has ramifications beyond one story. Journalists must make sure that the story being told is putting the community in the proper context within the story. Holding one of the actors of the story as a community representative might create a stereotypical representation in the audience's mind. Referencing a community too much in a story that reflects social harm or social good within the story will imprint on the audience that the community as a whole is part of that social harm or social good (Gulyas et al., 2018). This balancing act of how much to reference the community comes up in the next point of reviewing the story.

All of the Elements (especially the community) must be explained reasonably to the audience to clarify the story's central points. The journalist has a responsibility to use their journalistic judgment to determine the critical Elements highlighted in the story. Journalists must determine if they are stereotyping the community or actors by over-highlighting points within the story. Anytime Elements are highlighted in the story, those Elements become altered from what they are in reality due to the journalist amplifying or removing critical aspects from the Elements. The journalist puts their narrative filter on the Element to make it fit the story they are writing. **Narrative filters** are literary devices that remove some characteristics of an Element, enhance others, and magnify personality traits to make the Elements easier to understand in the audience's mind.

A classic example is when your friends talk about "Fun Max." They explain that he is a blast to be around at parties, knows lots of magic tricks, has interesting stories, and knows everybody. You meet Fun Max in a cafe, and he seems nice but relatively normal. Your friends used narrative filters to explain Max. Your friends presented Max using the standard conventions of informal dialogue. Using journalistic conventions is the last area to examine within the context of the story.

Journalistic conventions can be understood in the same way that the aesthetics of journalism are understood. People assume they are reading a newspaper if it has the look and feel of a newspaper. A local newscast has many visual characteristics that help the audience know what they are watching and understand that it is different from a national broadcast or cable news. The **essential aesthetics** of journalism come down primarily to how the different brands and journalism platforms presented themselves as credible news sources to the general public. Stories created for those brands and platforms must match those essential aesthetics or risk being rejected by the audience and the brand. Analyzing the brand and platform's essential aesthetics will be discussed in more detail in the next chapter.

IS THIS STORY A FAIR AND HONEST REPRESENTATION OF THE TOPIC, ISSUE, POINT OF INTEREST, OR EVENT?

The final of the six review questions refers back to one of the central points of the definition of journalism discussed in the introduction to the first part of this book. Answering this question means understanding these four fundamental types of journalistic stories. A fair and honest representation of a topical story indicates that the journalist must express in their accounting of the subject the impact the narrative has had on civic life in the community. Also, the journalist must clearly explain all of the facts that form the community's knowledge about the topic. Presenting an issue-driven story means making the abstract core concern that underlies the issue concrete based on the everyday experiences that the community members have regarding the issue. Point of interest stories should present a respectable narrative of how the point of interest is central to daily life in the community. Event-driven stories must allow a non-local audience to understand why the event is a part of the community's expression of itself.

Understanding which of the four fundamental journalistic stories you have will allow you to present the reality of the story better and clarify which Elements are worth the audience's focus. The journalistic focus is critical, as it is easy to get overwhelmed by all of the details that can be included in a story. The Writing Progression helps the journalist maintain their focus throughout the story, which allows the audience to concentrate on a clear narrative. Proper meditation highlights the Elements by presenting them as a dynamic part of the story in video content, emotional audio content, snapshots of reality in photographs, or exposing definite relationships with other Elements in the graphics of the story. Multimedia journalists without compelling media are simply storytellers.

CONCLUSION

This first part of the personal review focused on fine-tuning a story to connect the audience to the community's reality by crafting a narrative that explains actions in the story. A journalist must faithfully follow the standards and practices used by those past reporters. They upheld this noble profession by seeking truth and honestly reporting stories. Journalists in the era of Disruptive Journalism must maintain this central tenet of the trade or risk the whole field by losing credibility in the eyes of the general public.

Journalists must ensure that all of the necessary pieces of the story are present in the narrative to give the audience a clear picture of the actors and actions that influence the story. The actors within the story must be given clearance to tell their stories with honesty, emotion, and credibility, or the journalist risks introducing bias into the story. Audiences need to be able to check the fundamental facts to believe that the journalist is transparent with them. This transparency also means that the journalist is effectively communicating the story to the audience so they can gain meaning from the Elements. The audience will believe that the story will be fair and honest in the topic, issue, point of interest, or event if the journalist addresses all of the points listed above while using the essential aesthetics of journalistic work in the story.

The second part of the personal review goes beyond journalism. It seeks to make the work that journalists produce better by examining their work under the Five Criteria of Journalistic Content. The next chapter's five criteria allow a journalist to convert a good piece of journalism into excellent (and potentially award-winning) journalistic content by examining what makes any piece of media compelling content that the audience wants to read, listen to, or watch.

POINTS TO PONDER

- When does supporting media detract from a narrative instead of helping the audience understand what is happening?

- Watch any news program. What are the essential aesthetics that help the audience know that the program is a journalistic show?

- What are some ways that journalists can help the viewer verify the content in a story?

- When should narrative filters be used in a journalistic work?

- Why should a journalist be concerned with giving the audience a fair and honest representation of the topic, issue, point of interest, or event being covered in the story?

WORKS CITED

Ackerman, R., & Goldsmith, M. (2011). Metacognitive Regulation of Text Learning: On screen versus on paper. *Journal of Experimental Psychology: Applied*, *17*(1), 18-32. https://doi.org/10.1037/a0022086

Boesman, J., & Meijer, I. C. (2018). Nothing but the Facts? *Journalism Practice*, *12*(8), 997-1007. https://doi.org/10.1080/17512786.2018.1493947

Casero-Ripolés, A., Marcos-García, S., & Alonso-Muñoz, L. (2020). Formats for Local Journalism in the Era of Social Media and Big Data: From transmedia to storytelling. In J. Vazquez-Herrero, S. Direito-Rebollal, A. Silva-Rodriguez, & X. L. García (Eds.), *Journalistic Metamorphosis: Media transformation in the digital age* (Vol. 70, Ser. Studies in Big Data, pp. 69-83). essay, Springer.

Eldridge, S. A., Hess, K., Tandoc, E., & Westlund, O. (2019). Editorial: Digital journalism (studies) - defining the field. *Digital Journalism*, *7*(3), 315-319. https://doi.org/10.1080/21670811.2019.1587308

Gulyas, A., O'Hara, S., & Eilenberg, J. (2018). Experiencing Local News Online: Audience practices and perceptions. *Journalism Studies*, *20*(13), 1846-1863. https://doi.org/10.1080/1461670x.2018.1539345

Reese, S. D. (2010). Journalism and Globalization. *Sociology Compass*, *4*(6), 344-353. https://doi.org/10.1111/j.1751-9020.2010.00282.x

Tilton, S. (2014). Mobile Public Memory. *SAGE Open*, *4*(3), 1-9. https://doi.org/10.1177/2158244014547324

CHAPTER 9: THE FIVE CRITERIA OF JOURNALISTIC CONTENT

The Five Criteria of Journalistic Content is the encapsulation of the entire Journalism Breakdown system. Every step before this chapter was leading up to this point. Journalists need to be self-reflective when it comes to their work as it helps them examine the quality of their finalized works carefully. This practice also provides editors and other journalists a means to give useful feedback to their colleagues. It grants the journalism practice a common technique to improve the overall quality of the field of multimedia journalists.

We must keep improving journalists' work if we accept journalism as an essential practice designed to present truthful, informative, and compelling narratives on a variety of mediums and platforms to a select audience that will recognize the story existing in some version of reality. The reasoning for this improvement is the basis of the last eight chapters of this book. This reasoning is also grounded in the differences between journalism and other forms of communication.

What makes journalistic works different from other forms of content is the ability to invoke a rationale for the audience to pay attention to a given topic, issue, point of interest, or event. Journalists make the audience pay attention by crafting a story using a combination of logic, emotion, and ethos. That style of delivery present in journalistic works identifies those topics, issues, points of interest, and events of current importance while explaining their social-psychological implications to those given audiences.

One of the significant concerns with journalism is the inability of journalists to receive quality feedback and critiques in a manner that improves the whole journalist as opposed to an individual story that the journalist creates (Kabutakapua, 2012). This chapter aims to discuss a beginning place for analyzing journalistic works and expand on what makes good journalistic content. The hope is that students of journalism will feel more comfortable in requesting feedback from mentors, advisors, professionals in the fields, and peers they trust. This chapter also creates a training template for professionals, professors, and media organizations. Without proper training and feedback, the industry risks the inability of the general public to accept the credible work of trained journalists in the field (Tilton, 2016).

This method provides a reasonable rubric regardless of the mediated platforms that journalists use to publish their work. A clear discussion defining journalism beyond the simple construction of practices and formatting is required to shape this rubric. This discussion should begin with an examination of the breakdown for producing editorial content. It helps evaluate others' (and personal) works to meet an assessment based on the general characteristics of journalism.

JOURNALISM BEYOND THE WORKFLOW

One of the major conflicts within journalism is a lack of a standard set of practices, definitions, and expectations for those going into the field. Mark Deuze (2005, p. 442) understood this problem as a lack of conventional historical and theoretical training among journalists. "Although the conceptualization of journalism as a professional ideology can be traced throughout the literature on journalism studies, scholars tend to take the building blocks of such an ideology more or less for granted." This older quote speaks to a current issue that journalists face. That issue is while there is some form of journalism education throughout the world, there is no straightforward training on how a journalist could seek improvement in their field.

The nature of Disruptive Journalism means that it is hard to gain any meaningful feedback short of the journalistic analytics in the form of clicks, shares, comments, unique users, incoming audiences, and time spent on a story (Moran, 2019). We should also be concerned with the more significant issues surrounding the quality of journalism or risk pushing journalism headfirst into a field of disinformation (Ireton & Posetti, 2018) and trivial knowledge about the world (Press et al., 2015). The problem is the lack of academic and professional studies in those areas when dealing with these significant issues.

The International Communication Association (ICA) Journalism Studies interest division states that the focus of journalism studies is:

to explicate what we recognize intuitively but has become increasingly vague within both the academy and the profession: What is news? Who are the people responsible for making decisions about what news is, and how do their backgrounds, education, attitudes, and beliefs influence these decisions (International Communication Association, 2020, para. 1).

The Association for Education in Journalism and Mass Communication (AEJMC) describes its mission as:

> to promote the highest possible standards for journalism and mass communication education, to encourage the widest possible range of communication research, to encourage the implementation of a multi-cultural society in the classroom and curriculum, and to defend and maintain freedom of communication in an effort to achieve better professional practice, a better informed public, and wider human understanding (Association for Education in Journalism and Mass Communication, 2020, para. 1).

Academically, it is fair to argue that journalism is a nebulous construction.

The organizations that support the practitioners of journalism do a slightly better job in explaining the role of journalism in modern society. One of the major organizations concerned with the wellbeing of the journalism profession is the Poynter Institute. The organization tries to:

> teach those who manage, edit, produce, program, report, write, blog, photograph and design, whether they belong to news organizations or work as independent entrepreneurs. We teach those who teach, as well as students in middle school, high school and college - the journalists of tomorrow. And we teach members of the public, helping them better understand how journalism is produced and how to tell for themselves whether it's credible (Poynter, 2020, para. 4).

Another organization that is considered a leader in journalism is the Society for Professional Journalists (SPJ). SPJ helps maintain the future of journalism by promoting:

the free flow of information vital to a well-informed citizenry through the daily work of its nearly 7,500 members; works to inspire and educate current and future journalists through professional development; and protects First Amendment guarantees of freedom of speech and press through its advocacy efforts.

This focus on an informed public and maintaining the free flow of information is a good starting point. Still, it must be expanded upon to discuss multimedia journalism (and journalism in general) and avoid the relativism argument that "everything is journalism."

There needs to be a clear set of characteristics that define journalism to discuss how to help young journalists work on their craft. These characteristics should be broad enough to handle newer platforms of distribution but sufficient to articulate the expectations of journalists currently in the field. The definition given in the introduction is a reasonable start. Still, it should be placed in the actual context of the industry.

Bill Kovach and Tom Rosenstiel (2014) produced one of the keyworks for the field of journalism. *The Elements of Journalism: What Newspeople Should Know and the Public Should Expect* is one of the books that I keep on a shelf for easy reference. It is a foundational work as it provides a list of journalism guidelines. This list includes:

> journalism's first obligation is to the truth, its first loyalty is to citizens, its essence is a discipline of verification, its practitioners must maintain independence from those they cover, it must serve as an independent monitor of power, it must provide a forum for public criticism and compromise, it must strive to make the significant interesting and relevant, it must keep the news comprehensive and proportional, & its practitioners must be allowed to exercise their personal conscience. (pgs. 98-99).

The book you are currently reading is not designed to replace that work but rather give journalists the tools to ensure they are following the mandates given by Kovach and Rosenstiel. The way to ensure these mandates are followed is by having an editorial process that reporters can use to prepare high-quality journalistic works.

THE JOURNALISTIC PROCESS

Defining journalism with a series of characteristics is the first step in understanding how to produce good multimedia journalistic content. The next step in the development of a journalist is understanding and following a good process that will lead to well-constructed stories. Any process must be a checklist of followable steps with a clearly defined end-goal and helpful tips embedded in the list. The end-goal of this process should be the creation of a well-formed inverted pyramid within the context of their story. This end-goal should not be taken as the only format that journalists should write. Still, it tends to be the style that best fits the compelling narrative found in most well-constructed journalistic work. This format forces the journalist to address the "so what" question early on in the narrative. The Journalism Breakdown addressed throughout this book is the process that makes the most sense to craft the compelling narrative that addresses the "so what" question for the audience.

THE JOURNALISM BREAKDOWN

The concept of the Journalism Breakdown is that it is a checklist of the journalist's actions to produce high-quality journalistic content (Gawande, 2014). The focus, for now, is to review the Journalism Breakdown to set up the more substantial part of this chapter, which will explain the Five Criteria.

Two optional pre-steps can be performed by the journalists, followed by a seven-step process for writing a story, concluding with a final review. Pre-writing steps involve Fundamental Research on the part of the journalists to ensure they know enough about the story to talk or write intelligently about the story they are trying to cover. After the Fundamental Research, journalists can Freewrite based on the given story. Typically, Freewriting means that the person meditates and thinks about the topic from 15 minutes to an hour.

The seven-step process begins with a Writing Procession exercise that starts with a declarative statement that the author thinks is the most crucial truth about a given story that can be answered by addressing "What is the most important truth about the story that my audience needs to know to understand this story better?" The progression builds off of this primary truth with a series of statements with the prompt "Because I know this to be true, it means this…" This progression forces the journalist to create a well-connected, solid narrative throughout the story.

The second part is knowing whom to interview, knowing the right questions to ask those people, and know how to ask for the interview.

Once the interview is completed, the journalist must take out the essential quotes and relevant information from the conversation and add them to the story in an appropriate location.

Pictures, audio, graphics, videos, and interactive elements must be gathered next and placed in the story.

After all the pieces are placed in the story, the journalist must make sure there's a compelling narrative (as opposed to a series of facts or a series of bullet points). The story must then address the "so what" question.

Sixth, the journalist must make sure that they are tying up all of the story elements to ensure there are no unintentional questions left in the mind of the audience.

Finally, the journalist must review the five criteria of journalistic content, which will be addressed in this chapter.

The final review of the story usually should come in the form of an editorial review. Editorial reviews can be formal or informal, depending on the platform's size, mission, and purpose. The editorial review of the article comes typically from the editorial staff. This final step will be discussed in more detail in the next chapter.

Journalists must perform one final, personal review before meeting with the editor about their story. The more issues you correct now, the less time it will take to get the story published. Also, editors will trust your writing ability more if you present them with a nearly flawless story. This final, personal review is assessing your story based on the Five Criteria of Journalistic Content.

FIVE CRITERIA OF JOURNALISTIC CONTENT

The **Five Criteria of Journalistic Content**, as described in the earlier section, is a primary starting point to analyze the journalistic merit of a given story. All five criteria were developed over several years and implemented as part of class rubrics in the various media and journalism classes taught at my university. They were developed by a content analysis of professional works in journalism over five years and consistently reappraised based on the students' work in the classroom and the field.

The first three of the five criteria are the mechanical, rhetorical, and mediation criteria for editorial content. They are the foundations of excellent multimedia journalistic writing. Rhetorical and mechanical criteria find their way into most communication rubrics in some way, shape, or form. The mediation criteria should be considered part of the "digital literacy" for the modern informed public (Ng, 2012). The last two of the criteria are higher level points of analysis. A study of the contextual components of the story helps the journalist examine their platform. In contrast, the voice examines the journalist's style. The following five sections will discuss the five criteria' conceptualization, along with questions for evaluation related to each of the parts. These criteria typically work in conjunction with ethical feedback from an editor or another journalist.

ETHICAL FEEDBACK MODEL

Part of the analysis of the Five Criteria of Journalistic Content involves an ethical feedback review of the elements of the story (Kercsmar & Kaufmann, 2012, pg. 35). The **ethical feedback model** means that the reviewer of the story must give both positive and negative feedback focused on the story or piece of content. The reviewer must also use "I language" (e.g., "I thought the intro paragraph was too long") as opposed to "you language" (e.g., "Your intro paragraph is too long"). Each piece of feedback must be supported with a specific example from the story (e.g. "For example, the first sentence of the intro is 20 words long"). The final part of the ethical feedback model is that the reviewer must provide a specific rationale on why they focused on that particular example (e.g., "it helps to shorten the first sentence and let the reader get into the story"). I teach all of my editors this model of feedback because it provides the journalist with some level of understanding about the corrections being offered in the story and helps them improve overall. Points of positive feedback are the areas that the journalist should continue doing in their writing. Negative feedback provides areas of improvement for the journalist. The rationales can come directly from the Five Criteria of Journalistic Content listed below.

MECHANICAL

The mechanical criteria are the most fundamental aspect of the review. Creators and editors must check the story for spelling, grammatical, or syntax errors at the work's textual level. Photos and other graphics must be checked for potential manipulation and quality issues that can alter the story's interpretation. Any audio or video elements added to the story must maintain a basic quality throughout the story. Better production practices for mediated content will be discussed later in this chapter. Any review of this type of material must be analyzed under the guise that any mechanical errors in the story affect the audience's ability to read the story.

Above and beyond reviewing for mechanical breaks in the article, the journalist must review if the story is being told using clear, concise, and precise language that the audience can easily understand. Understanding this concept does not mean talking down to the audience nor placating the audience. Instead, the point of analysis comes from the viewpoint that the audience and journalists must be able to communicate in a common language.

In this case, language goes beyond the textual into the realm of the visual and the aural. The presentation of mediated content must not dive into the realm of the artistic for aesthetic's sake, much like the textual content should not fall into the poetic realm for the sole purpose of making the story fanciful. The journalistic approach to language in the story should follow the paraphrased wisdom of Eric Rothenbuhler. He once told me that written works are like wheelbarrows that carry the knowledge to the audience. The pathway you take with that knowledge should be as straightforward as possible.

138

The model that all journalists follow for straightforwardly writing comes from the *Associated Press Stylebook*. This essential guide that all journalists must follow is used and followed to avoid common mistakes (issues with dates, proper names, captions, etc.). This guide must be used rather than making the journalist simplify their language. All journalists follow this guide because it helps them maintain a universal language in the story through the established practices of normative language behaviors. Associated Press shows a journalist in the field the expected guidelines to follow when writing any story and a template for presenting the information as clearly as possible by creating a common lexicon.

In terms of a mechanical rubric, there are a few elements to highlight. First is a simple proofreading of the article for typos. Word processing software most writers use for their stories can underline spelling and grammatical errors with some precision. Pay attention to those highlighted words and phrases as they can save you from embarrassment.

A review of AP style is also part of this level of analysis. For novice journalists, an evaluation of the density of paragraphs is reasonable. If every paragraph is written like an academic work, it's going to be boring. Looking over the work for passive voice will help maintain the narrative. For college and high school students, comma use tends to be a good point of analysis. Try to limit commas in journalistic work as commas tend to slow down the reading of textual elements and add a more poetic language to the story. Finally, a complete listening or viewing of a graphic or mediated assets will expose fundamental mechanical flaws.

Failure to fix these mistakes before they appear on the platform means that the author loses their credibility as a general writer and media practitioner. Also, the editors should be at fault for failing to mentor the producer of the story, failing to filter for quality, and failing to protect the platform. Finally, the platform suffers as the audience that looks at the story that fails at the mechanical level will be less likely to treat the platform as a professional news organization. The urgency to publish a story first should not circumvent good editing practices.

RHETORICAL

The **rhetorical** criteria of journalistic work come from the rhetorical traditions of communication. In the rhetorical tradition, all ideas presented represent a position or an argument. Any position or argument within a given story must be explained enough for the audience to understand the clear implications of the story (Lunsford & Ruszkiewicz, 2014). Clearly defining the story must include presenting all of the relevant information related to the story in a manner that highlights the information that the audience must know about the story to make an informed decision (Campbell, Huxman, & Burkholder, 2015).

Rhetorical situations related to journalism borrow from the older means of studying rhetoric, which comprises of five interrelated conditions. Messaging is the most crucial part of the rhetorical situation as it is the **message** that connects the communicator with the audience. **Communicators** deliver that message with a **purpose** (the reasoning that the communication is crafting that message) in mind within a given **setting** (time, place, culture, and society in which the message is delivered). The **audience** must decide if the communicator is competent in their presentation of the message and will interpret it based on the effectiveness of the communicator and the message itself.

In multimedia journalism, and journalistic content in general, there are multiple mediums to use to deliver the narrative of the story beyond the pure expression of information and facts. The elements explained in this section of the essay are taking the rhetorical elements of speech and applying them to evaluating journalistic works.

An **inartistic** evaluation of journalistic work will look at any journalistic work element that is "builds from evidence and observation to a final conclusion" (Lunsford & Ruszkiewicz, 2014). The first of these elements would be **forensic**, which is the factual description of a subject without the logos, pathos, or ethos of the subject matter (Bitzer, 1992). A journalistic work must be a compelling narrative, but it must include a truthful presentation of the fact related to the subject. The rubric's analysis point is if the journalist included enough facts to explain the underlying hook of the story.

Deliberative is the second of the inartistic elements. Traditionally, deliberative is a means to either the narrative direction of a subject or the future of Elements

(Lyon, 2013). The review of the story should look for a natural progression or schedule related to the subject without the logos, pathos, or ethos related to that subject. Also, the progression should lead to some action occurring in the future related to the subject.

Epideictic is considered the last of the inartistic elements for study. Culture, time, and occasion are the three themes discussed in the epideictic. In rhetoric, the epideictic speech is typically a celebratory one. However, journalistic content should avoid celebration for celebration's sake. Rather, a good journalist must acknowledge the time, culture, and occasion related to an issue, event, or idea without the logos, pathos, or ethos related to the issue, event, or idea. Cultural and social influences of the central theme of the story must be included. This acknowledgment helps those not only in the community better understand the complete picture of the story. It also helps those in the community better understand how the community's actions affect the different actors within a given story.

Beyond the inartistic evaluation of the work is artistic assessment. The **artistic** in rhetorical studies are the arguments that the speaker must invent. They include rational appeal (logos), emotional appeal (pathos), and ethical appeal (ethos) (Eidenmuller, 2011). These "invented elements" of the rhetoric are not the same as creating a fictional representation of the world. It forces the communicator to explain how the Elements connect using a narrative supported by rationality, emotion, and credible communication practices.

Rational discussion in the rhetorical tradition means that the speaker attempts to persuade the audience with a series of logical conditions that they can follow and agree with the individual points. In the case of journalism, **logos** simply means that there must be a logical flow to the work. The reader must be able to follow the narrative. There must be a nice sense of flow to the work to connect the various facts presented in the writing. If the journalist fails to build the logical flow into the article, it becomes a series of bullet points rather than a journalistic work.

Pathos is the second artistic element for review. **Pathos** is how the communicator "attempts to persuade the audience by making them feel certain emotions" to connect with the audience and place the audience in the right emotional mindset (Williams, 2015). Journalistic pathos is represented by the emotions shown in the writing being proportional to the work's nature. One of the most common mistakes made by journalism students relates to pathos is the use of exclamation marks in journalistic work. It is sporadic to use an exclamation mark in an article. The better example of pathos in any journalistic work is how the journalist allows others to express emotion in the story via quotes and actions.

The final element of assessment in the rhetorical criteria of journalism is ethos. **Ethos** is made up of:

1. credible people referenced or quoted being connected to the subject at hand,

2. information being vetted by reliable sources, and

3. the journalist being "grounded" in the community related to the story.

The first two parts of the definition of ethos show up in many of the standards & practices founded in news organizations and the codes of ethics of professional associations (Tilton, 2016).

While the study of rhetoric is an older examination of communication practices, it is useful to apply those theories to this part of the review. Journalists owe a considered amount of their format for telling the news to these traditions. This consideration means that we owe it to our audiences to communicate what is happening within the story effectively. Understanding good rhetorical practices allows the journalist to be more effective in the telling of these compelling stories.

MEDIATION

Storytelling is more than just the textual content, especially as it relates to journalism. Journalists' ability to combine text, graphics, audio, video, and interactive elements allows for a complete telling of the story of the event, issue, point of interest, or topic to the community. Any good telling of a story needs the right media content to enhance the audience's understanding of a given subject.

A journalism student must recognize that Disruptive Journalism demands placing the right content within the structure of a story to enhance the person's understanding of a given story.

To piece the various pieces of content that may be connected to a given story, the reporter must recognize that all communication channels have strengths and weaknesses. A good multimedia journalist must realize which channel is most useful to tell the story. This section of the review will examine the non-textual channels of communication.

GRAPHICAL AND PHOTOGRAPHIC ASSESSMENT

Graphics must be evaluated based on their ability to present the relationship between Elements clearly. Journalistic graphics need to show complex data in a simplified form, which helps the audience process two streams of information simultaneously. Those two streams are:

1. textual information embedded in the graphic and

2. the visual information that comprises the work.

One of the areas to give journalist feedback is if the audience can easily understand the journalist's coding of the information within the graphic, specifically if the journalist is effective in connecting the visual with information in the graphic. The questions that come up often in this level of the examination are:

- Are the icons defined on the graphic?

- Are the colors' meanings explained clearly on the graphic?

- Are all of the critical visuals labeled in the graphic?

- What was the source of this information?

- How do the visual elements clarify the relationships between the Elements?

Reporters should come up with reasonable answers to these questions. One major issue with graphics is that visuals can clutter the story if they are overused or used ineffectively. Ineffective graphics misrepresent the nature of the story by not correctly labeling critical details of the visual or selectively manipulating the information on the graphic.

Assessing photographs means understanding what makes for a striking visual in journalistic work. The main criteria for examination when dealing with pictures are if the images capture "moments of action, shoot candid (un-posed) images at 'the precise moment' to reveal the drama of news stories" (Mortensen & Gade, 2018, p. 994). Still images in journalistic works must be expressive of the emotion of a community and its members that other mediums fail to capture. There must be an element of humanity that the audience recognizes as being authentic and presenting a piece of the story that the words can't. Finally, the caption must explain visuals within the photo and the photo's relationship to the overall story.

AUDIO ASSESSMENT

Based on the previous chapter on audio, journalists must examine audio content from four different perspectives based on the type of sound being presented. Raw audio content should make the audience feel like they are in the middle of the action. The audience will not feel like they are in the middle of the story if the audio is nothing more than a jumbled mess of incoherent sounds. There must be enough natural sound cues to give the listener a sense of place. Outside audio clips, for example, should sound like they are occurring in a natural setting. Birds chirping, wind blowing, people in the background are just some of the cues that would make sense to hear in a park.

Soundbytes from an interview should be judged if they add an emotional element that can not be transmitted by text and graphics alone. The reason this judgment point is valid is that audio helps set the tone of the story. Emotion is hard to capture in the text of the journalistic work, and graphics can, at best, expose a small part of a community's emotional experiences. An excellent audio quote does that type of emotional labor within the story.

Transparency in the third consideration when examining if the audio is practical within the article. Paul Bradshaw described the use of raw sound feeds as a useful way to be transparent. "In other words, next to an edited text interview, the journalist can post the interview in full (what is sometimes called 'wild footage') much more quickly than if they were to transcribe the whole thing" (Bradshaw, 2007, para. 6). Wild footage provides an audience with the entire interview without the journalist needing to take the time to produce a transcription.

The last consideration must be that the audio has a direct connection to the telling of the story. Audio can be tedious to an audience if the listeners have no reason to hear that content. The sounds that the audience hears must add to their understanding of the narrative or add context.

VIDEO ASSESSMENT

An analysis of video evolves from the previous section of this chapter as audio forms the foundations of any piece of video content. Also, this mode of assessment comes from chapter five of this book. Both of those sections point to one central truth about video content. Video content only works if there is enough motion to keep the attention of the viewer. Video without movement is just a series of photographs used poorly. Just use pictures in that case.

Another area to consider when deciding if to use video is if it explains Elements beyond the ability of normal communication modes. The audience is allowed to look at the speakers' non-verbal communication patterns, the environment of the story as selected by the videographer, the journalist, and the more subtle elements that may be present but left out through other communication channels. Those core components of a video should be in service of enhancing the story rather than being the flashy object that the journalist uses to grab the attention of the audience. Flashy objects (like a set of keys) are great for holding the gaze of a baby. Journalists should do more with this medium as it is the most contextually heavy of the primary forms of communication.

The last question the journalist should ask before deciding if a particular piece of video is appropriate for the story is if the camera is hiding key Elements. Remember that the camera has a limited range of vision, and the microphone has a limited pick-up. Journalists must always be concerned if a crucial part of the story is left out.

INTERACTIVE CONTENT ASSESSMENT

As this type of content is a composite of the previously listed forms of media, there are only two additional evaluation points to determine if the material works in the story. Ease of use should be the first evaluation point for this content. Interactive content is the right call if most of the audience can easily use the interactive elements within the work and understand what they mean. A good piece of interactive content should hide the technological complexity behind a user interface that allows the audience to learn it at their own pace.

As the content has been created, it is unfair to ask if the effort was worth it based on the importance of the story. A fair question to ask is, "Should this piece of content be on a stand-alone page?" Interactive content must not overshadow the importance of the narrative to gain engagement from the audience.

FINAL POINTS OF MEDIATED ASSESSMENT

Three overarching questions need to be addressed before determining the quality of the content.

- Does the mediation in the story connect with the topic being covered?

- Are the embedded links included in the story, and are they the "right links" for the story (e.g., the words attached to the embedded link are referenced within the link)?

- Is there audio, video, or both that helps enhance the audience's understanding of the story?

Once a journalist feels good about their story after reviewing all of the assessment points in this section of the Five Criteria of Journalistic Content, they can move on to the Contextual review of the story.

CONTEXTUAL

The contextual criteria for journalistic content are the first of the two "advanced" elements of journalistic writing. For this analysis, **context** is the ability to "speak" in the language of a given media platform. The language of a given media platform is:

- the style of storytelling used on a given platform,

- the formatting of a given story on a platform, and

- how a given story connects with the other stories presented on a given platform.

In the most basic sense context can also be defined as:

- the ability of a writer to "mimic" the style of the platform in a way that allows the audience to accept the work belonging on the platform,

- telling a story that fits the audience's version of reality, and

- awareness of the connection between the audience, the stories they are telling, and the platform's brand.

A good journalist can analyze a given media organization and describe the characteristics of the way that the organization tells a story.

The primary example of the analysis is describing the "NPR" storytelling style. NPR is normally described as:

- a male or female journalist speaking in a quasi-stylized soft monotone voice,

- with a normalized Midwestern accent to begin a story,

- a relatively long introduction to set up the story for the audience, and

- an interjection of natural sounds to reinforce the Elements.

The story's construction is a long-form version of audio journalism with a detailed narrative, long soundbytes from important actors within the story, and heavy use of natural sound to enhance the storytelling and narrative approach.

These criteria focus on if the journalist has a basic understanding of the platform itself. If the person writing or producing the story can not define the platform's essential characteristics, the writer or producer often will not be able to match the style of the other stories found in the given section of a platform. The reviewer should get the journalist to reread their article and try to mimic other stories' critical characteristics in the given section.

VOICE

The final of the five criteria is the concept of the voice. **Voice** is the ability of a journalist to be recognized regardless of the context of their work. This definition means that the audience should know the journalist solely by how she or he weaves a story together. This criterion is the toughest to teach, as it depends on the journalist's natural skill and how those journalists define themselves in the industry.

Unlike the contextual criteria, a journalist can not mimic the style of another journalist to develop their voice. The development of voice comes from working in a particular medium for a significant period and receiving thoughtful feedback that helps that journalist feel comfortable in the storytelling style within a given platform.

Exercises in a journalist's voice should have the student of the medium study famous modern journalists and identify what makes them distinctive within a given platform. For example, what makes David Carr's writing different and exciting in the framework of the style of the *New York Times* Media section? What makes Ira Glass a successful storyteller in the realm of *This American Life*? An analysis of professionals tends to be the first step in the process of developing a voice.

The second phase is for the journalist to identify:

1. their perceptions of the world,

2. the communities they serve, and

3. the relationship between themselves, the audience, and their journalistic peers.

Journalists who can articulate these three points clearly will have an easier time developing their voice than those who can not identify these critical concepts of the voice.

Any rubric in this criterion should examine how the journalist matches the context of a given platform while maintaining their perception of the events within the limitations of language and expression.

BREAKDOWN SESSION

The final element of consideration is the ability of journalists to evaluate other people's work to provide a guide for their work or strong feedback for a colleague. We conduct an initial breakdown session with the students in our writing and editing classes. The **breakdown session** is designed to be carried out in a group setting. We go over the Five Criteria of Journalistic Content, the characteristics of journalistic work defined in the first chapter of this book, and the lede, hook, & nut as they relate to the presented story.

The function of this exercise is to provide a base level of knowledge to the students regarding the right practices for producing journalistic works. Students must be engaged in this process. A group session seems to encourage communication and feedback between the members of the class. During the early part of the semester, the breakdowns are traditionally instructor-led (e.g., the instructor asks all of the questions of analysis). The following classes of the semester all have student-led breakdown sessions. This switch from instructor-led to student-led breakdown sessions allows for a more thorough assessment of the students' ability to evaluate their peers' journalistic content.

CONCLUSION

As defined in this chapter, journalistic work's characteristics and criteria are grounded in the standards and practices of past journalists in the field. Therefore, the criteria presented in this chapter evaluates work that matches the ideal representation of journalism praxis. There are fair criticisms that the points raised in this work match the historical perspective of journalism as opposed to its current state. Missing from this discussion is the influence of economic and editorial factors. Specifically, the definitions of journalism should be more adapting to the ebb and flow of journalistic practices that make up the changes found in most newsrooms. It is this last point that helps set the stage for the final part of the Journalism Breakdown. The people best able to speak on those changes are the editors and the executives that make up the newsroom and review the work of journalists in their organization.

POINTS TO PONDER

- Pick a journalistic platform you go to more than three times a week. What are the contextual characteristics of that platform?

- How does knowing your journalistic voice help you when producing journalistic work?

- How would you describe your journalistic voice to other journalists?

- How would you describe your journalistic voice to your audience?

- Pick a work published by a professional journalist on a journalistic platform. Perform a breakdown section on the piece based on the five criteria of journalistic content, the characteristics of journalistic work and the lede, hook, & nut as they relate to the presented story.

WORKS CITED

Bitzer, L. F. (1992). The Rhetorical Situation. *Philosophy & Rhetoric, 25*, 1-14.

Bradshaw, P. (2007). *Five Reasons for Audio Journalism: Actuality, debate, emotion, background, podcast.* Retrieved September 8, 2016 from https://web.archive.org/web/20150420222136/http://onlinejournalismblog.com/2007/02/28/five-reasons-for-audio-journalism-actuality-debate-emotion-background-podcast/

Campbell, K. K., Huxman, S. S., & Burkholder, T. R. (2015). *The Rhetorical Act: Thinking, speaking, and writing critically.* Cengage Learning

Deuze, M. (2005). What is Journalism? *Journalism: Theory, Practice & Criticism, 6*(4), 442-464. doi:10.1177/1464884905056815

Eidenmuller, M. (2011). *Scholarly Definitions of Rhetoric.* Retrieved July 31, 2016 from https:// web.archive.org/web/20160408093909/http://americanrhetoric.com/rhetoricdefinitions.htm

International Communication Association. (2020). *About the Journalism Studies Division.* International Communication Association. Retrieved July 20, 2016 https://web.archive.org/web/20170712031920/https://www.icahdq.org/members/group_content_view.asp?group=186103&id=631060.

Ireton, C., & Posetti, J. (2018). *Journalism, 'Fake News' & Disinformation: Handbook for journalism education and training.* United Nations Educational, Science, and Cultural Organization.

Kabutakapua, B. (2012, April 25). *Journalism Requires a Definition.* Retrieved May 10, 2020, from https://web.archive.org/web/20150424091248/http://mic.com/articles/6933/journalism-requires-a-definition

Kercsmar, S. & Kaufmann, R. (2012). *Composition and Communication Workbook.* Cengage

Kovach, B., & Rosenstiel, T. (2014). *The Elements of Journalism: What newspeople should know and the public should expect.* Three Rivers Press.

Lunsford, A. A., & Ruszkiewicz, J. J. (2014). *Everything's an Argument for the University of Kentucky (6th ed.)*. Bedford/St. Martins.

Lyon, A. (2013). *Deliberative Acts: Democracy, rhetoric, and rights (Vol. 7)*. Penn State Press.

Moran, C. (2019, April 2). *You may Hate Metrics. But they're making journalism better*. Retrieved May 10, 2020, from https://web.archive.org/web/20191222103703/https://www.cjr.org/innovations/you-may-hate-metrics-guardian-audience-twitter-images.php

Ng, W. (2012). Can we Teach Digital Natives Digital Literacy?. *Computers & Education, 59*(3), 1065-1078.

Poynter. *About Poynter*. Retrieved July 4, 2016 from https://web.archive.org/web/20200508210652/https://www.poynter.org/about/.

Press, J. (2015). A Campus-Wide J-School: News literacy as an avenue for journalism schools to connect with new students and a new generation. *Toward 2020: New Directions in Journalism Education,* 111–120.

Tilton, S. (2016). "Steve Jobs is Dead": iReport and the ethos of citizen journalism. In A. Davisson & P. Booth (Eds.), *Controversies in Digital Ethics,* (pp. 308-319). Bloomsbury.

Williams, G.H. (2015). *Ethos, Pathos, & Logos: The 3 rhetorical appeals*. Retrieved August 9, 2016 from https://web.archive.org/web/20160119213215/http://georgehwilliams.pbworks.com/w/page/14266873/Ethos-Pathos-Logos-The-3-Rhetorical-Appeals?

CHAPTER 10: EXECUTIVE AND EDITORIAL REVIEW

The final and most crucial part of the Journalism Breakdown is when a journalist gets constructive feedback for others. I felt it necessary to include this section into the Journalism Breakdown. It seemed to be an excellent way to engage with fellow journalists to improve the overall quality of work. It was not uncommon for alumni of my program to come back to me to ask for feedback on their work. This situation wasn't true for every student. But, it happened enough that I wanted to get a better understanding of why this was happening. I found out that the students liked the feedback sessions they received either during the Workshops I taught earlier in my career or in the Practicum session I currently teach. Based on this input, I feel the need to address the methods we use for our executive and editorial reviews. There are three points to note before going further with this discussion.

The first point is that this step in the process is as much the responsibility of the editorial staff of the news organization as it is the journalist's responsibility. It is vital to mention this fact because many of my former students acknowledged that this level of feedback is traditionally not offered to incoming journalists in the era of Disruptive Journalism. The story is completed, put into the workflow, and off to write the next story. Newer journalism workflows require a more engaged feedback system, either among peers or the traditional editorial review. Otherwise, the content becomes a flat representation of the events within the story.

The second point to note is that this process is what Andres Ericsson and Robert Pool (2017), scholars in the field of expertise, describe as deliberate practice. This idea of **deliberate practice** requires good, thoughtful feedback (which is why the ethical feedback model is vital to this process) given by trained professionals in the field based on work that challenges the journalists and exposes their weaknesses so they can work on them. It is fair to argue that the college experience should be the place to find that deliberate practice. However, the amount of time it takes to find a level of proficiency is around 10,000 hours (Gladwell, 2009), and expertise can take around 25,000 hours to achieve (Ericsson & Pool, 2017). This timeline is longer than most students will have in the practice of journalist work in college, which is around 4,500 hours during a typical college career of those that thrive in college and 1,200 hours during a college career of those that struggle in college (Beattie et al., 2019). This fact means that the editorial staff of most news organizations will need to spend some time helping journalists in the art of deliberate practice if they wish to maintain the quality of their platforms.

The final point to note is that there is a difference between an executive and editorial review. As a professor, I ONLY did executive reviews and not editorial review. An **executive review** focuses on the first three parts of the Five Criteria of Journalistic Content. An **editorial review** can focus on all five. This distinction is vital. I was not comfortable defining what the student media organization should produce, which is central to a critical contextual review of the work. I was also unwilling to influence the student's underlying view of the world, nor their way of presenting it as that is central to a critical voice review of their work.

This chapter acts as both the conclusion of the Journalism Breakdown process and a simple system to encourage conversations about the editorial process. The main subject of this chapter will be describing the core of both types of reviews and how journalists might apply this model in the digital newsroom environment in the era of Disruptive Journalism.

EXECUTIVE REVIEWS

Executive reviews are useful after most stories that most novice journalists write. The best format for this style of review is an informal sit-down between the journalist and a member of the editorial staff or a fellow journalist. I will often encourage journalists to form a peer review group that allows them to collaborate without editorial oversight. Short of that, I will perform an executive review with students during our weekly Practicum meetings.

It is fair to argue that the executive review's most prominent influence came from a 2017 Broadcast Education Association annual conference panel entitled "Examining the Journalism Entrance Exam: Innovative Methods to Better Prepare Students for News Reporting and Writing Jobs." In that session, the panelists allowed me to transform something that was mainly an unstructured assessment into a more formal discussion about the craft of journalism.

This level of review is vital because it should be used as a training component for journalists to address the most common misconception of the editorial workflow, which is that it is the responsibility of the editors to catch all of the mistakes journalists make in writing their stories. This discussion should help address the ten most common Associated Press style mistakes that journalists still make, according to Rick Brunson in his part of that 2017 presentation. It is fair to argue that these ten mistakes would be caught in a mechanical review of the journalistic content.

ISSUES WITH INTRODUCTIONS

The most common issue that I find in the executive review sessions deals with essential and nonessential clauses. The most significant area that most students work on is introductory clauses, phrases, and words. **Introductory clauses** are a group of words that contain a subject and a verb and are used to begin a sentence. They need further support within the sentence to make sense to an audience. A comma separates these clauses from the rest of the sentence. An example of an introductory clause would be:

> **Before the end of the second quarter**, Townsville's quarterback Rod Rodson threw three interceptions and was pulled from the game.

Introductory phrases are similar to clauses except that they lack a subject, verb, or both. **Introductory words** are a single word that begins a sentence and has a comma following them.

Introductory clauses appear in most forms of writing due to a factor that my colleague CarrieLynn D. Reinhard refers to as the inability to write forward. We understand the information that needs to be placed in the sentence and write it immediately. The problem with this writing style is that it introduces an uneven tone that makes the sentence harder to read. This choppiness goes against the short, clear, and concise language we strive for in journalistic works. It also increases the likelihood that the sentence will be a passive voice representation of the information embedded in those words.

Passive voice is a phrase that English and language arts teachers have thrown around since time immemorial[7]. I tend to like Kimberly Joki (2014) from Grammarly's definition of this term.

> Passive voice is when the noun being acted upon is made the subject of the sentence. Active voice is when the noun doing the action is the subject. (para. 2)

I find myself teaching the wisdom of Rebecca Johnson (2012) to see if the sentence is in the passive voice.

> I finally learned how to teach my guys to ID the passive voice. If you can insert "by zombies" after the verb, you have passive voice.

All of this discussion about passive voice offers a solution for dealing with the introductory clause issue. It helps to place the introductory clause in a different spot of the article. Let's go back to the original example and move the introductory clause to a logical place in the middle of the sentence.

> Townsville's quarterback Rod Rodson before the end of the second quarter threw three interceptions. He ended the half on the bench.

This sentence is clearer and more concise as it also was split into two sentences.

ISSUES WITH PRONOUNS

Brunson noted two specific issues that students have with pronouns. The first is the idea of the indefinite pronoun. **Indefinite pronouns** are words that substitute for nouns that do not specifically reference a person, object, or amount. The classic examples are the bodies (e.g., somebody, nobody, everybody, and anybody), the wheres (e.g., nowhere, somewhere, everywhere, and anywhere), and the others (either other itself or another). An example of

---

[7] A long, long, time ago that is beyond the reach of memory

indefinite pronouns comes from the classic Charles Osgood's work, *The Responsibility Poem.*

> Anybody could have told you that Everybody knew that this was something Somebody would surely have to do.

The previous sentence works well as a piece of literary prose but fails at the clarity that we would expect for journalistic work.

The second concern is related to pronoun confusion. This confusion occurs when the writer uses a pronoun where two or more of the subjects are of the same gender, or the wrong pronoun for the occasion is used. It is the second point of confusion that causes most of my time in the executive review. The two sets of pronouns that are confused most often would be who / whom and me / I. Who and whom are often confused in question form.

- If the answer to the question can be he, she, we, or they, the form is who.

- If the answer to the question can be him, her, us, or them, the form is whom.

The "me and I" issue occurs most often when they are pair with another object. The quick check to ensure the use of the right one by removing the pairing. For example:

- "The waitress handed Mark and me change from the bill" is correct because "The waitress handed me change from the bill" is correct, and "The waitress handed I change from the bill" is incorrect.

- "Mac and I are walking down the hill" is correct because "I am walking down the hill" is correct, and "Me am walking down the hill" is incorrect.

Pronoun issues can be resolved most often by adjusting the placement of words in the sentence and doing the necessary checks listed in this section.

ISSUES WITH MODIFIERS

The next two issues deal with modifiers. **Modifiers** alter a word or phrase in a sentence to clarify its condition, limit its meaning, change its definition, or qualify a component. Modifiers highlight in the form of an explanation or as a point of emphasis. The two types of modifiers that are problematic in journalistic writing are dangling modifiers and compound modifiers.

Dangling modifiers happen when it is not clear what word the modifier is altering. "Tired, the bed was the place to be" is an example of a dangling modifier as it sounds like the bed was tired. Restructuring the sentence would help. "I was tired and went to bed." **Compound modifiers** happen when the modifier uses two or more words. The *Associated Press Stylebook* generally recommends using a hyphen to make the meaning clearer. It is in the best interest of the journalist and editor to look at *Webster's New World College Dictionary* if there is a question about the proper form of the modifier.

The simple suggestion is to re-read a sentence containing a modifier to make sure that the meaning is clear.

OTHER MECHANICAL ISSUES

The last five points range the gamut of mechanical issues an editor might face regularly. The first of these is the "it's vs. its" and "effect vs. affect" misuse. Both of the misuses come from a misunderstanding of the meaning of the words.

- It's represents the contraction of it is and should be used in place of that combination. "It is my birthday" can be "it's my birthday."

- Its represents a possessive. "I will take the phone back to its owner" is the correct use of its in this sentence.

- Effect as a noun that means "something that inevitably follows an antecedent (such as a cause or agent)."[8]

---

[8] The definitions of these terms come from the *Websters' New World College Dictionary*.

- Affect is a verb that means "to produce an effect upon: such as to produce a material influence upon or alteration in or to act upon so as to effect a response."

- Effect as a verb "goes beyond mere influence; it refers to the actual achievement of a final result."

The recommendation is to refer to *Webster's New World College Dictionary* or this section of the chapter for further reference when these words come up in an article.

Another mechanical issue to focus on during an executive review session is the parallel construction within sentences. **Parallel construction** is crafting a list in a sentence using the same **parts of speech** (noun, verb, adjective, adverb, pronouns, prepositions, interjections, and conjunctions) and all of the ideas in the list coordinate with one another. "Journalistic writing must be short, clear, and concise" is an example of proper parallel construction. The most natural solution to bad parallel construction is to focus on the pattern. "I want to thank her for being an excellent author, skilled at editing, and knowledgeable enough to speak at length on a variety of topics" can be fixed by saying "I want to thank Ms. Bell for being an excellent author, editor, and public speaker."

Two mechanical issues from the list are discussed in some detail in the *Associated Press Stylebook*. They are collective nouns and subject-verb agreement. **Collective nouns** are those nouns that denote a group of objects or people. The *Associated Press Stylebook* typically provides clarity in the section on sports, the definition of collective nouns, and the "Ask the Experts" area of the Associated Press website. The **subject-verb agreement** simply refers to the idea that the subject and the verb must both be singular or plural in the sentence for it to make sense. The "Ask the Experts" area of the Associated Press website gives some guidance in this matter. I tend to refer students to the Purdue Writing Lab, our Writing Center at Ohio Northern University, or the Grammarly website. I find that using a service like Grammarly helps with issues that I miss during my reviews of student articles. Grammarly also helps with the last of the ten issues on Brunson's list.

Spelling and vocabulary is an extensive issue that impacts many of my students during their first year in the program. This issue tends to go beyond the time allotted for a typical executive review. I set three ground rules before meeting me for our first executive review. The first is completing at least ten of the Associated Press Style Quizzes on the Associated Press website. I will tell my students that it is an open book quiz. My rationale for doing that is that the purpose of the quiz is to make my students comfortable searching through the *Associated Press Stylebook*. Secondly, I will encourage them to read over their article one more time on the computer and look for the colored lines under their words. Sometimes, Microsoft Word and Google Doc know what it is talking about when highlighting the area on the screen. Finally, I encourage my students to either visit the Writing Center to go over the article with a professional or invest in a service like Grammarly. Both of these services help point out mistakes and give guidance to improve their writing..

RHETORICAL ISSUES

Unlike the mechanical issues listed earlier (which came from the 2017 panel), the next two sections are more from the last six years of teaching. It would be fair to note that Hagit Limor noted in the 2017 panel the rhetorical issues I found in my students' writing. "Writing is like music. It has a tempo, a style, and a pace." The primary issue is the lack of flow between the critical truths in the article. It is hard to overemphasize the number of articles that read like a PowerPoint slide of the events in the story instead of a journalistic narrative with flow. One of the questions I use to highlight this issue is asking the journalist, "Where should the reader be in the first part of your story?" I want the student to think about the audience's mindset. That question is followed up by:

- where is the reader at the end of the story, and

- how did they get to the end of the story?

Both framing questions should help the journalist understand the narrative direction of the story and examine the transitional elements that they used to connect the truths within the story. It is hard for the audience to follow the narrative if there is no flow within the story.

The biggest emotional issue that I address in these sessions if the willingness to include examination points in different areas of the story. It is rare (if at all) that

161

I will use an examination point in a journalistic work as it is the same as me SCREAMING THE WORDS OUT LOUD!!!! Emotion is a by-product of good quotes and better mediated in the story. It should not be brought in through the use of punctuation.

Student journalists do not use examination points in the stories.

Period.

The last major rhetorical issues in this part of this review, and it deals in the realm of credibility. There are two standard mistakes that journalists will make in this area of the review. The first being not used trustworthy sources in the embedded links of the story. It is effortless to use a search engine and get the information that lines up with a piece of evidence that supports a claim within a story. It is much harder to ensure that the information in the link passes the CRAAP Test mentioned earlier in the book. Part of the review is to go over all of the links for their credibility.

The second mistake is not having enough quotes from newsworthy sources within the story. Quotes are the transitional elements that drive the story further and ground it in the community's reality. Having the right people talking about the Elements can make all the difference in reporting a story.

MEDIATION ISSUES

Mediation is still an issue I have with my students when they first get into journalism. They might be comfortable with the textual part of multimedia journalism. However, they fail to see the connection between the words on the screen and the rest of the mediated works needed to make a compelling multimedia journalism piece. There are two areas that we address early on in the Practicum sessions.

Pictures with captions tend to be a point of review that comes up often. A student might be able to describe the visuals in the images briefly. I will see about six to eight words in the form of a sentence fragment in the caption's spot while describing a candid photo of friends posing while they are attending the event in question. The practice of photojournalism will be discussed in the later chapters. We can go over the art of crafting a quality caption now.

A caption must first tell the audience who might know nothing about the visuals in the image enough information for them to decide if the photos are newsworthy or not by itself. The second part is explaining how the picture fits into the narrative that the journalist is crafting. This explanation means understanding how the visual either helps define the Elements or provides another layer of information to the audience. Finally, whoever took the image should get credit for their work. The format that the Northern Review uses is after the caption a photo credit appears with the information in the following order:

> ([Organization's Name] [photo/graphic/illustration]/[Name of photographer/artist or file if we don't the name of the photographer/artist])

For example, a picture I take for the Northern Review has a photo credit of (Northern Review photo/Shane Tilton). We also distinguish between a photo, graphic, and illustration. **Photos** are unaltered images taken at the scene of a story by a photojournalist. An artist rendering of the Elements that honestly explains their relationship within the story is a **graphic**. **Illustrations** are the visuals that reflect a creative interpretation of Elements. This denotation is vital as it helps clarify what the audience sees. An image must be labeled as an illustration if it is photorealistic but not a photo.

It is also vital that the audience be literate enough to understand the differences between those three types of visuals. Photos must be actual events as they were unfolding during the time of the story. If there is a photograph taken after the events in the story, it is in the best interest of the journalist and editorial staff to note it as a graphic, illustration or **photo recreation** to ensure the honesty of the story.

The second of the mediation issues is when a journalist uses a written quote instead of an audio soundbyte. The mediation criteria from the Five Criteria of Journalistic Content explains that audio adds an element of emotion traditionally left out of the text of a story. The human voice is an emotional conduit that adds a layer to help the audience understand more of the actors' motivations within the story.

I find that having an audio soundbyte in the middle of the story does two useful functions. It acts as a secondary hook in the story that the audience wants to listen to if the journalist has given enough reason to listen to those words. It also provides a place within the story to pivot to a new direction by giving the journalist a bridging transition. **Bridging transitions** are points in a story that allows the journalist to change the focus to another narrative related to the previous narrative of the story.

EXECUTIVE REVIEW VS. COPY EDITING

This style of executive review borrows a considerable amount of its practices from copy editors. Still, it should not be a substitute for a good copy editing session. **Copy editing** is beyond simple spell checking. The method of copy editing refers to going over any written piece to help improve its readability by removing critical grammatical issues. Copy editing does some of the elements of face checking and proofreading to ensure that the work's quality meets the standards of publication.

Executive reviews are in line with the practices of journalism as it relates to multimedia work. The article needs to balance the story's fundamental writing with the mediated elements that enhance the work. Copy editing takes care of the former, while an excellent executive review focuses on both.

The last step in the Journalism Breakdown is the one before publication. The journalist must get the work approved by an editor to send it up the workflow. This part of the process means understanding what the editors are looking for in a completed piece of journalism.

EDITORIAL REVIEW

One of the areas that takes the most time as an educator is developing students to be editors. Journalism is one-third having good reporters crafting stories, one-third having rich stories to tell, and one-third having the right editorial staff to publish those stories. Reporting is a more manageable skill to train a student to have when compared to preparing a student to be an editor. I find that the classes I took in social psychology during grad school helped me the most in developing students to become competent editors.

The way we approach the editorial review at Ohio Northern is a practice and holistic approach to the evaluation and assessment of journalistic work. The idea of editorial review as a practice means that the editor learns something from the editorial review every time they perform one. Holistic development means improving more than the basic writing skills of the journalist.

This style of the editorial review came from the work of Carl Sessions Stepp, a professor of journalism at the Philip Merrill College of Journalism at the University of Maryland. My editing course would use his (2013) *Editing for Today's Newsroom* as a foundational text. This section is not meant to replace that masterwork, but rather highlight the three central takeaways from that text.

First, an editor must master the technical, conceptual, and people skills to maintain a high-functioning newsroom. *The Journalism Breakdown* should be a guide to the technical skills needed in journalism. Conceptually, the editor must have the right vision of what their platform means to their audience and what they are getting from the content published on that platform. The remaining of the three is people skills. The editorial review is the way that the editor practices their people skills regularly.

The second highlight recognizes that the editor must balance their roles as a businessperson, planner, manager, decision-maker, coach, and journalist in the modern newsroom. It is impossible to do all of those tasks at all times. The editor must develop a sense of priorities when managing the various responsibilities of the position. There also must be a different set of ethical standards for the editor due to the multiple roles they perform. They have a higher level of responsibility to the platform and the newsroom staff, which leads to the last of the highlights from Stepp's book.

Editors must finally remember that they are the guardian of the legal and ethical responsibilities of the platform. This acknowledgment means that the editor is responsible for something beyond themselves: the platform itself and journalism as a practice of social and community good. Failing to live up to those standards damages the editor's reputation, the platform's credibility, and journalism as a whole.

As a position, the editor should be held in high regard when one understands the rights and responsibilities associated with that position.

Stepp's three highlights of the editor should set up the beginning of the editorial review. The editor and reporter should schedule at least ten minutes to talk about the story. The first one-on-one can be as long as an hour. It is essential to establish realistic expectations of how long these meetings can be as necessary to take up the time allotted in order to be productive.

The first question that I want my editors to ask the reporter during this review is, "What did you find to be the most difficult part in completing this story?" It provides a great place to start the conversation. The editor can refer back to their experiences to provide guidance to the reporter and help develop the skills needed to deal with those issues productively.

Follow-up questions require a careful reading of the article with an examination of all media and embedded links within the work. Those follow-up questions must be framed using the ethical feedback model with the Five Criteria of Journalistic Content as the rationales for examples selected in the review. Understanding the five criteria makes the editor a better reviewer in this part of the process.

There are three significant thresholds beyond the previously listed questions that the story must pass to meet publication standards.

First, the journalistic quality of the work is judged. Editors must go over the breakdown elements to ensure the quality of the story is satisfactory for publication on the platform. Individually, editors and other support staff will check to make sure that the story fits the platform's mission and the purpose. Every platform will have a journalistic checklist with requirements that define editorial quality. The individual list and standards should be in line with the characteristics of journalists discussed early in this article. Otherwise, the platform should question if it is meeting the needs of its audience.

Second, the legality of the story must be examined by the editors. The editorial staff has a responsibility to protect the platform from potential lawsuits and legal issues (like subpoenas). The editors of a platform may need to consult experts to understand elements of a given story that may be in the grey areas of the laws and other extralegal concerns related to publishing a story. Most grey areas and extralegal problems come from undercover newsgathering techniques (like hidden camera work) or obtaining private records that impact the public's knowledge of a story.

Finally, the editorial staff should check the ethical issues associated with the publication of a given story. All ethical reviews are based on the profession's code of ethics (e.g., the Society for Professional Journalists Code of Ethics), the organization, and the individual journalist. As a rule of thumb, a journalist must develop a code of ethics to ensure that they do not put themselves in situations they are not comfortable performing.

CONCLUSION

Both the executive and editorial reviews serve a place in the era of Disruptive Journalism as it ensures the accuracy of a given piece of journalistic content by maintaining the field's traditions. These reviews allow experts to explain what it takes to produce quality news on their platform. These experts' feedback must be in service of doing more than getting a single story ready for publication. Rather, the process in use to improve the work of a single journalist. That level of improvement will enhance the quality of journalism on a given platform and, perhaps, enhance journalism as a whole.

This review of the work should help journalists reflect on the process that they use to produce a story. By being reflective, a journalist can determine what worked and what didn't after finishing up the piece that they wrote. One of the points that help journalists improve is reading over the story when their work is published. This step helps as it places their work in the context of the platform. Acknowledging how their work fits into the platform's structure will make it more likely that the journalist will continue to publish on that platform in the future.

POINTS TO PONDER

- Think about a skill that you consider yourself good at performing. How long did it take to get good at that craft? What support did you need to improve that ability?

- Talk to an editor of a local news organization. Find out what it took for that person to feel comfortable in that role.

- Think about how often you look back at work that you wrote last month, last year, or even five years ago. What wisdom do you gain from critically examining your past writing?

- Pretend to do an editorial review on a professional journalist over a piece they wrote on a platform that you read often. How would you perform that editorial review?

- Perform an executive review with a classmate or friend on a piece of writing they did. How did you incorporate the ethical feedback model in that review?

WORKS CITED

Beattie, G., Laliberté, J. P., Michaud-Leclerc, C., & Oreopoulos, P. (2019). What Sets College Thrivers and Divers Apart? A contrast in study habits, attitudes, and mental health. *Economics Letters, 178*, 50-53. doi:10.1016/j.econlet.2018.12.026

Ericsson, A., & Pool, R. (2017). *Peak: Secrets from the new science of expertise*. Eamon Dolan.

Gladwell, M. (2009). *Outliers: The story of success*. Penguin Books.

Johnson, R. (2012, October 18). *I Finally Learned How to Teach my Guys to Id the Passive Voice. If you can insert "by zombies" after the verb, you have passive voice.* Retrieved June 1, 2020 from https://twitter.com/johnsonr/status/259012668298506240.

Joki, K. (2014, October 12). *A Scary-easy Way to Help you Find Passive Voice!* Retrieved June 1, 2020 from. https://www.grammarly.com/blog/a-scary-easy-way-to-help-you-find-passive-voice/.

Stepp, C. S. (2013). *Editing for Today's Newsroom*. Taylor and Francis.

PART 1: CONCLUSION

October 15, 2019.

That was the date that I was most proud of being a journalism professor. We had seven students attend the fourth Democratic Presidential Debate at Otterbein University. The 90 minute trip from Ada to Columbus in the afternoon gave my students a chance to run over their gameplans for covering the debate. They were talking about the Fundamental Research they completed on their selected candidate. Also, they discuss the themes they expected to emerge before, during, and after the debate. These discussions were grounded in the multiple training sessions they completed the six weeks before the event.

All of that was possible, thanks to the Journalism Breakdown. This editorial process gave my students the foundation to go to a national news event and cover it with the mindset to think what their audience needed to know about what was happening that night.

The other point to note about that experience was that our university sent seven journalists representing three campus news organizations. The only other two universities that sent student journalists were the host campus (Otterbein) and the state's flagship campus. Otterbein and the other school each sent two. This factoid made me appreciate all of the hard work my students put in to prepare for this event.

They were engaging with professionals from NPR, CNN, NBC, Fox News, the Columbus Dispatch, and a wide variety of state, regional, national, and international news organizations. Everyone was amazingly gracious with their time. My students had a chance to talk to one or two reporters before the start of the debate. Everyone, to a person, treated my students with respect and kindness. Their interactions with my students ensured that the future of journalism would be taken care of by this new generation.

My students looked over their progressions one final time before the start of the debate about thirty minutes before the candidates took the stage. They reviewed their notes and added information based on what they gathered from the other reporters. We then discussed the plan of attack for covering the debate. Everybody (including myself) had an assignment to cover the key themes from the talking points of our candidates. I drew Biden and the other candidates that the students didn't get assigned.

Once the debate started, we were off. One person was typing on the Google Doc we created for this moment. The others were either taking pictures of the press area, writing down notes of their candidate's actions, or asking me questions. This experience felt like the old days when I worked for NBC covering local elections in Ohio. It was a collaborative process that demanded everyone be in sync with what others in the newsroom were doing. That level of sync-up depended on everybody knowing the workflow of the organization. Understanding the Journalism Breakdown helped my students better understand the flow of news events and how to cover them. Before the event, the preparation meant that they were ready to go the first moment they were in the building, and when the real action happened.

Thirty minutes after the end of the debate was the time that the spin room opened up. This opening up was the moment when the candidates and their representatives would come out and address the press. Every student got up before the closing remarks and scouted a position to do interviews, take pictures, and get a lay of the land. It was essential to remind them that journalism is not a stationary activity. They needed to be ready to move where the action was coming to instead of merely following the action.

They were on the floor for a good two hours, outlasting many of their colleagues from other organizations. Not every candidate made an appearance in the spin room, but many did. The ones in the room answered the questions posed by my students and gave them reasonable responses to those questions. Students took those answers and worked their way back to our base of operations (a couple of tables in the back of the room). They typed a paragraph on two in the communal document from the safety of their seat and ran back into the thick of it. It was the fourth or fifth student running back to the table that made me realize that the best role I could perform was getting out of their way and coaching them from our tables. They knew what they were doing.

The CNN crew gave the fifteen-minute warning that they were going to close the room around one in the morning. My students were hanging around the central CNN platform when Jake Tapper stopped by to talk to them. They spent the last minutes of the night asking this professional a few questions about the craft of journalism. He posed with them for a couple of pictures at the end, and we left utterly exhausted.

Students spent the next week finishing their features on the debate for the campus television channel, radio station, and newspaper. It was a team effort that showed the power of multimedia journalism. The newspaper stories used audio and video content to enhance the narratives of the night. Both the television and the radio crews took the information from the newspaper crew created to provide more context on the event.

Fast forward to May. Alex, my station manager and one of the journalists who went to Otterbein, knocked on my door. "Shane, I wanted to say thanks for everything. I felt like a real journalist at Otterbein." I handed him the award they won from the Society for Collegiate Journalists for the debate coverage. I tell him, "Well... you are a journalist. That's why you feel like one."

The moral of this story is that you don't have to follow the Journalism Breakdown in its entirety. You will find the part that works for you. Use this text as a guide to becoming a better journalist.

That is the way to happiness.

The next part of the book will act as a series of sessions to help improve some of the skills required to become an award-winning journalist.

PART 2: PRACTICUM MODULES

Practicums and Workshops are one of my favorite courses to teach. It's the opportunity to work with a student who is developing a project that they are passionate about or helping the student improve their media and journalism skills. It also means getting to the root of what they care about and what they see themselves doing after graduation. This set of courses allows me to be more proactive in the student's program of study during the semester. Every Workshop and Practicum is different as the student's view of the world evolves the longer they attend college. It is from that point of view that I want to discuss this next section of the book. There is a direct connection between the Journalism Breakdown and the following ten chapters relating to the development of the journalistic mind. It comes back to providing quality feedback that allows the students to maintain a level of deliberative practice as a journalist.

Quality feedback occurs when both the expert and student are engaged with the process, focusing on a clear plan to ensure the successful completion of the project. Engagement is directly related to both parties sharing the same outcomes for the meeting. The act of commitment also depends on understanding the plan of our time together. This part of the book lays out those plans to help current college students and ways to improve journalistic skills for others.

Practicums involve two distinct but vital parts. Students are required to share several stories with me as part of an executive review. As I stated in the tenth chapter, I do not want to influence the publication of the campus newspaper. In that spirit, I explain the first requirement for an executive review, which is the story that MUST have already been published. This type of discussion in the Practicum session aims to improve the quality of the student's work using the ethical feedback model to help facilitate the process. Another requirement is that I will only do one executive review per week per student. I encourage the student to schedule these types of meetings no sooner than one week apart. I want them to reflect on the elements discussed in the review and not to rush their work. They must also write down a reflective analysis of their article before the meeting based on the Five Criteria of Journalistic Content. I want them to have some understanding of what it takes to make a quality piece of journalism. The **reflective analysis** uses those criteria as the central questions in the assignment. They are required to submit a 1,000-word reflective analysis of their work over the semester during finals week.

Beyond the executive review, the other part of the Practicum is the modules. I have developed ten modules during the last decade to inject skills training in the sessions. The students will go over six modules depending on their past work, their role in campus media, and where they are as a journalist. Typically, modules have three sections. The first is an explanation of why we are going over the given module. This discussion helps frame the module to their development as a journalist. Part two is the bootcamp of the core requirements of the module. I use the term **bootcamp** as an educational practice representing a hands-on exercise, a step-by-step tutorial, or expanded reading of:

1.) a technical skill,

2.) a piece of software, or

3.) an industry practice that is central to their advancement as a journalist.

The final part of the module is an assessment related to the elements referred to in the bootcamp. I usually prepare two levels of evaluation. The basic tier is those that are taking the module for the first time. Some of the students will repeat modules as they are required to complete three to six Practicums to graduate the program. Those students that repeat the module will get the advanced tier of evaluation.

The first module that all students complete is the review of the Journalism Breakdown. We go over the rationale for this being the first module during our introductory one-on-one session. I feel that the student must be grounded in this system to be successful in our program. We go over the requirements for the Practicum in the syllabus. Students sign a contract before the end of our first meeting, stating that they will complete all parts of the Practicum assigned before their deadlines.

They are given a summary of the Journalism Breakdown either in graphic form or in written form. They are expected to have either the ten bullet points of the Journalism Breakdown memorized before our next meeting if this is their first time taking Practicum or reflect on how they used the system in their past work if they have taken this course with me in the past. This action is the bootcamp part of this module.

The basic evaluation of this module is relatively simple. We sit down next week. The student is asked if they reviewed the Journalism Breakdown before meeting with me. If they are familiar with the system, the next step is that they have to go over all ten levels of the Journalism Breakdown and what those steps mean for a typical journalist. I will generally divide Fundamental Research and Freewriting as separate steps in the Breakdown and combine the editorial and executive reviews as one step for simplicity. They will pass the module if they can explain those ten steps and their meaning to the point that I feel they are proficient in understanding the system.

Advanced evaluation of this module required the student to explain how they applied the Journalism Breakdown to one of their past stories. They must be able to describe how the different steps in the process were relevant to the creation of their content in some detail. This level of evaluation allows me a chance to examine their method of newsgathering. It also provides an opportunity to tweak the Practicum to be more helpful towards their development as a journalist.

The rest of the modules can be divided into two categories. Content creation makes up the first set of modules, including photojournalism, audio production, video production, social media and feature writing. The other set of modules includes skills needed to help improve the overall abilities of a multimedia journalist. Those modules are journalistic ethics, math for journalists, infographics, writing feature articles, and crafting executive summaries. We use the first two weeks to determine which five from the list of ten would be the best use of their time during the semester.

A typical semester would alternate between executive reviews of an article that hasn't been reviewed by me before and completing a module. This schedule plans out for 13 weeks if they are completing this course for one credit hour. The eighth week of the semester is traditionally a midterm review to see what they have learned over the past seven weeks. The 15th week is a dead week where they can submit their reflective analysis for this semester's Practicum or turn it in during finals week. The rest of the chapters in this part of the book explain the modules in more detail.

CHAPTER 11:
PHOTOJOURNALISM

Photojournalists serve an essential role in society. The ability of photojournalists to tell stories that explain the reality of the situation at locations that are unfamiliar to the general public is part of that service. Those pictures taken by trained photojournalists lead to more conversations about the issues of the day and creates a more informed public by knowing about those events.

Photojournalists create narratives with images. Those narratives are driven by images' ability to create a sense of pathos. One of the means that photojournalists can create pathos in the image is by focusing on the subject's face (especially the eyes). Facial expressions can tell as much of the story as the words that propel the narrative. One only needs to look at the classic covers from *National Geographic* or *Time* to see this aesthetic practice.

Photojournalism can also capture the spirit of a location that can often be overlooked due to motion and sound. The stillness of the medium allows the audience to witness a snapshot of reality within a given community. This media allows the audience to slow down and observe the community and its members in a natural way. Photojournalists become the powerful recorders of a community's history as long as those journalists follow the best standards and practices of ethical journalism.

This recording of a community's history means that the photojournalists essentially zooms in to highlight a single moment. That moment can be expanded in the structure of the story so the audience can clearly understand the significance of those actors and actions shown in the image. Photojournalists can preserve the crucial moments of a community that would otherwise be lost in time.

PHOTOJOURNALISM IN THE ERA OF SMARTPHONES

The change for standard SLR 35mm analog cameras to their digital counterparts has meant that photojournalists have become more accustomed to the smaller kit for photojournalism. Chase Jarvis (2010), an award-winning photographer, is known for his famous saying, "The best camera is the one that's with you." The larger argument that Jarvis makes is that the photographer should be able to identify a good photo based on the photographer's understanding of how a photograph speaks to the experience shown in the image. My addition to that adage is, "The best camera is the one that's with you as long as you understand how it works."

This bootcamp will focus on both DSLR and phone cameras as both will be the standard tools that a multimedia photojournalist will use daily. **DSLRs** are digital cameras that typically use a single interchangeable set of lens that transmits the visual information from the lens and captures it digitally via a **single lens reflex (SLR)** mechanism. That mechanism allows the camera to function similarly to the traditional 35mm film camera. Photographers can control many functions from the body of the camera, with some elements being controlled on the lens. An excellent up-to-date DSLR will traditionally outperform a smartphone for most news stories. Smartphones tend to be good enough for most stories as they act as a Swiss Army Knife for newsgathering. Like a Swiss Army Knife, the smartphone represents the most basic quality needed to produce a piece of multimedia journalism (Hobbis, 2020).

PREPARING TO USE A SMARTPHONE

In this section of the chapter, it is fair to note that the gap between a smartphone camera and the DSLR is slowly becoming smaller. Smartphone cameras may entirely replace the use of DSLR soon. As of the writing of this book, some of the significant issues of the smartphone cameras need to be addressed before using them in the field. The most significant wisdom I can give is to set the smartphone to airplane mode when you plan on using the smartphone as a camera. Using airplane mode removes some of the technical failures that can occur in the field. The main technical failure that most journalists will experience using a smartphone as their primary camera is if you get a phone call while taking the picture, the phone will not take the picture. That picture could be a once-in-a-lifetime image.

One must essentially strip most of the functionality of the phone in order for it to act as a high-quality camera. This process also requires turning off the "high-efficiency photo" mode of the smartphone. This mode might be labeled as the "HEIF/HEVC Format" on some models of phones. The issue we ran into when the phone was in this mode was that the images taken in that mode were unusable in print and other edited forms of media.

The final bit of wisdom I give that is exclusive to smartphones is not going beyond a 2x zoom on the camera. Most smartphones use a dual-zoom build. Everything before the 2x zoom uses the lenses to zoom in to the image. Control of the phone's physical lenses to perform a zoom is using the **optical zoom** function of the phone. This type of zoom is a real representation of whatever is being captured by the camera. Pushing the zoom past the 2x mark forces most phones to use the computer to approximate the phone's visual frame. This type of computer-aided zoom is called the **digital zoom** function of the phone. Using the digital zoom introduces more imperfections to the photo. The rule of thumb is (if it can be done safely) to move closer to the action and using the optical zoom to get closer to the action of the scene.

PREPARING TO USE A DSLR

The hardest element for novice DSLR users to remember is that it requires a keen understanding of how the camera's body and the interchangeable lenses work to be a successful photojournalist. This point means knowing the camera as a whole and its core components. This knowledge goes beyond making sure all parts of the camera (especially the battery) are in good shape. Photographers must be comfortable with their camera to ensure a quality image at the end of the day.

Beginning photographers will typically need to understand each of the parts of the camera to find that level of comfort. This understanding means remembering to put caps back on the body to keep the inside of the body clear from dust and dirt. I also require students to protect the screens of the camera.

Most of the cameras we use have a back screen that can flip. The screen must be flipped close when it is put back into the bag. Another piece of wisdom I want my students to know is how long it takes to charge a battery after it has been drained fully. This knowledge allows the students to recognize when to charge a battery before going out to a shoot and understanding they should probably be charging the backup battery if possible while they are in the field.

The next step is getting a feeling for the functions on the body of the camera. We will often take a day in class and make the students use the dial functions on the camera to understand how the camera changes the information coming into the camera from the lens. Having this level of awareness of what each body setting does requires reading the manual or tutorials and practicing on those settings for at least eight to ten hours.

This process of playing with all settings takes a full class period for us as I can give feedback on proper camera use. After this training session, I will reassure the students that using the automatic setting on the body of the camera for the first several sessions in the field is okay. The body's automatic setting tends to provide the evenest quality of work. They can concentrate on the flow of action in the field. It takes a few assignments in the field and several hours practicing with the camera away from the field to feel more comfortable adjusting the camera on the fly.

The last part of the camera to have proficiency in before using the camera in a field assignment is understanding how to work the lenses. A reasonable place to start with this education is to examine the nine different types of lenses that most photojournalists will use during their careers.

Standard lenses are the most common lenses used with DSLR kits. They tend to be set between 40-60 mm focal length, as it is the perspective that is most like how humans see the world (Modrak & Anthes, 2011). **Focal length** is essentially the distance between the lens and the charged coupled device in a DSLR. Longer focal lengths allow for higher magnifications, while smaller focal lengths allow for a wider angle of view in photography (Erkelens, 2018). For example, the lens I use most often when I shoot is an 18-55 mm lens. The denotation of 18-55 mm is the focal length range of the lens. This lens also gets into the wide lens range as the range of those lenses tends to be at the 24-35 mm range.

Wide lenses have an excellent ability to place more of the scene into the image by distorting the perspective (Třebický et al., 2016). An ultra-wide lens tends to have a smaller than 20 mm focal length, as that is the perspective that creates a more climactic view of the world. Photojournalists should limit the use of wide and ultra-wide lenses whenever possible. It dramatically shifts the visual information within the image. This shift fundamentally alters the visual narrative of the photo.

The other end of the focal length spectrum is commonly used in photojournalism. Telephoto lenses tend to have around 100 to 150 mm focal length. That focal length allows photojournalists to capture sporting events without risk their safety. The ability to capture faraway objects allows the audience to understand better what is happening during a match. Super telephoto lenses have more than a 200 mm focal length. Action shots are taken with these lenses. Those types of shots require the photojournalist to be stationary, as those lenses are relatively massive compared to other lenses. They require either a tripod or monopod to be held still enough to take an image (Collins, 2018). The final of the variable focal length lenses is portrait lenses. Portrait lenses have a 60-100 mm focal length range as those lenses help photographers frame the image clearly within the photo. Like wide and ultra-wide lenses, photojournalists should limit their use of these lenses as it influences the audience's perception of the actors within the image.

The last three lenses tend to have a fixed focal length. All lenses that are fixed focal length tend to be referred to as prime lenses. Prime lenses trade-off the flexibility of the zoom by providing a high-quality image within the given focal length of the lens. A prime lens used for photographing small subjects at close distances is called macro lenses. It is typically set around 35 to 60 mm (Thompson, 2018). Fisheyes are the prime lenses that have their focal lengths set between 4 to 40 mm. It creates a circular effect as the horizontal lines are distorted to provide a flatten and an extremely wide-angle view of the world (Tu, 2015).

Both smartphone cameras and DSLRs are merely tools that require the photojournalist to understand how to take newsworthy images with it.

PREPARING THE PHOTOJOURNALIST

A photojournalist should take as much time to be mentally prepared to cover the story as they take to prepare their camera for fieldwork. This next section represents how my students get ready to cover a story as a photojournalist.

The first point of wisdom is that the photojournalist must know that their equipment is in good working order and ready to go. This checkpoint means making sure that the camera battery is fully charged before arriving at the scene of the story. I still recommend having backup batteries or USB batteries charged and ready to go as well. Having extra memory cards for DSLR is useful. A smart multimedia journalist will take a few practice photos with their camera before leaving for the scene.

Knowing the **tripod stance** is the second point of wisdom that I want students to know before they cover the story. We practice this stance in class and as part of the Practicum. The stance requires the student to hold the camera with both hands. Smartphone cameras require the photojournalist to grasp the corners of the phone with their thumbs on the bottom of the phone and their middle fingers on the top corners. Their elbows must be extended slightly wider than the width of their bodies. They will take the photo with their pointer finger and make sure the other fingers are out of the way.

The DSLR tripod stance is a little different. The full left hand holds the bottom of the camera. In contrast, the right hand should rest comfortably on the side of the camera with the right pointer finger on the shutter button. Both elbows are again slightly wider than the width of the body.

Elbow position is the most vital element of this stance. It first provides stability when the photojournalist takes the shot. The camera will be also more likely to be level if both elbows are the same distance apart. Finally, getting into the tripod position forces the photojournalist to be aware of the bodies. This placement is unnatural. We do not traditionally move around with our elbows that far out. It grounds us to be focused on capturing newsworthy images.

The last three points of wisdom do not apply until they arrive at the scene of the story. Photojournalists must scan the surrounding area before getting out of their vehicle to cover the story. This third point of wisdom is more than having the photojournalist think about their safety. That is part of the rationale for this wisdom. It is never a bad idea to find the escape routes from the scene early just in case issues happen. The more significant concept is finding the best places to take photos. A good photographer should understand the flow of the crowd, the negative spaces in the area, and all of the elements that will help or hinder the photojournalist from doing their job. This level of scanning helps the journalist work within space's limitations instead of being limited working within the space.

Understanding the nature of the story is the fourth point of wisdom worth going over. It will inform the photographer of the essential aspects to cover. This knowledge will allow the photojournalist to prepare to take the pictures necessary to explain the story to the audience. Great photojournalists know where and when to spend their time, attention, and effort while on the scene. Otherwise, they will waste their time take pictures of non-newsworthy content, not focusing on the right subject at the scene, and will waste their efforts by producing photos that do not tell a story.

The final point of wisdom I want my students to remember is that photojournalism is not a stationary action. This reminder allows the students to get comfortable moving throughout the scene to find the best views of the story and take pictures that encapsulate the spirit of the narrative.

UNDERSTANDING THE FUNDAMENTAL SHOTS USED IN PHOTOJOURNALISM

The next five shots listed in the chapter will make up most of the images that a multimedia journalist will take during their careers. These categories of photojournalistic images are a summary of Duy Linh Tu's (2015) book *Feature and Narrative Storytelling for Multimedia Journalists*. This text is one of the books I recommend to read as the lessons from that book help develop the photojournalist's mindset. I also recommend Terence Wright's (2016) *The Photography Handbook*. It provides much more detail regarding the history, theory, and practice of quality photography. Both books are incredibly useful for photojournalists to help them develop their work and become masters of the craft.

Mastering these five shots listed below will allow multimedia journalists to be more sophisticated in their storytelling practices and more effective in focusing on critical aspects of the story. Understanding the weakness mentioned in the other visuals help the photojournalist narrow what images they should use when telling the visual story of the events happening in their given communities.

LANDSCAPE

An example of a landscape. This photo shows the James Lehr Kennedy building before the start of the Fall 2019 semester at Ohio Northern University (Northern Review photo/Kelly Kern).

This first category of photographs is one of the easiest ones to begin with, in the career of a photojournalist. **Landscapes**, for photojournalistic works, are photographs that focus more on the features of a given piece of land and less on the humans that live in the land. These types of images tend to show the relationship between the natural world and the human-made society. These images represent how a community exists within the boundaries of the architecture that defines the community and the ecological system that naturally supports it (Zhao et al., 2017). The story within those images is driven by the lack of human actors in the picture. Those visual elements recognizable to community members drive the narrative in a landscape (e.g., skyscapes of Chicago, New York City, London, or Tokyo are iconic markers of those cities). These images tend to work best for environmental, life and culture, and opinion and editorials pieces. Multimedia journalists can also find places to use these types of images in other types of stories if the narrative supports the audience viewing those images.

ACTION SHOTS

An example of an action shot. This photo shows Paige Hartings moves in for a spike over two Muskingum defenders (Northern Review photo/McKenzie Wilson).

As a counterbalance to the relative stillness of the landscape, the second category of images is all about movement. **Action shots** are images that help show off motion missed in the blink of an eye. The power of this type of image comes from the ability to contrast the stillness of the final image with the projected direction in which the elements in the image are going.

Action shots, by their nature, visually explain what is happening during the story. Time slows down in the image allowing the audience to reflect on the development of the narrative by capturing what actors are doing. The best action shots go beyond the whats of the story to answer the hows and whys. Actors within the image make up the whos within the story. Hows get addressed in the image by giving the audience a clear view of the actor's critical movements to accomplish a given goal. The reactions of the actors in the images will often explain the emotional why of the story. Excellent action shots address the story's Essential Questions far better than any textual write-up of the events.

STAGED SHOTS

An example of a staged shot. This photo shows Dr. Susan Meyer giving the 2020 Sebok Lecture in the Freed Center for the Performance Arts at Ohio Northern University (Northern Review photo/Kelly Kern).

Most of the time that the general public thinks about photojournalism is when they see rows of photojournalists at a press conference, covering political leaders, or some other regularly scheduled event. These events often produce staged shots. **Staged shots** are any image that comes from an event that includes artificial lighting and props on a set. All of these parts are typically controlled by another organization outside the control of media companies that sent photojournalists. These pre-arranged stories script all movements, speeches, and other actions to the second.

Photojournalists should recognize that their attendance at the event feeds into the "stagecraft" of the event. The media covering a given event makes the event more significant regardless of the substance of the event. All public speeches, scheduled live events, or other pre-arranged stories that have a media presence depend on all of the parties at the event being aware of the agenda of the event to be effective in the coverage and to hit crucial media deadlines (e.g., having a story ready for the local six o'clock newscast).

The best staged shots a photojournalist can take show two relationships. The first relationship explains the typical rhetorical situation with the connection between the speaker, audience, and the occasion on display in the image. This relationship shows the newsworthiness of the event with the image alone. A classic example that shows this relationship is showing the crowd cheering with the politician on the stage in front of a sign highlighting a key talking point of the speech like "Steel Still Drives American Growth."

The second relationship is a little more meta, as it will show the relationship between media coverage and the rhetorical situation. An explanation of this relationship typically takes a caption that hits the three significant criteria listed earlier in the book. The photo credit allows the audience to judge who is interpreting the actions happening at the public event—describing the elements of the image with precision hits on the elements of the rhetorical situation. The ultimate criteria for explaining how the image connects to the story gets to that meta-level of the event. The photographer can not simply write that they took the image because they were there. Captions allow the audience to judge if the event is genuinely newsworthy or just a public spectacle.

CANDIDS

An example of a candid photo. This photo shows Ellie Schroeder performing a song with her guitar for the Battle of the Bears. (Northern Review photo/Amanda Trogus).

The last two types of photojournalistic work addressed in this chapter come from focusing on community members within the image to tell the story. One to three actors within a given image create a **candid** photo. The primary focus of such an image is how the people are acting naturally within their environment. Candid photos are most effective when the individuals' interactions and behaviors are clearly explained within the context of the image and the caption. These types of images often get to the whys of the stories. They reveal a small part of the community's psychology in how the community members see themselves within the broader social and cultural elements that influence their daily lives.

Candids are best when they explore how people use objects usually found in the community. The objects themselves may have some significance to the community but hold some worth to specific community members. A classic example can be ringing the victory bell after the home football team wins a game. The facial expressions plus the objects in the images tell some of the story. Photographers explain what those objects mean to the community.

Finally, the photojournalist is responsible for how the actors in the images impact the audience's reading of the events in the image. This understanding means that the photojournalist must capture the reality of the situation in the image.

Candids work well within a multimedia journalism story if the audience can identify who is being shown in the image. A good caption will take care of the identification of those people. The other part that is more vital is that the image must explain what the significance is of the time, place, or objects in the image to those community members. That significance is best framed by explaining to the audience why the time, place, or object should be significant to them. Photojournalism strikes a connection with the audience when the viewers find commonality with the subjects and objects being shown.

SLICE-OF-LIFE

An example of a slice-of-life photo. This photo show students gathering before the COVID-19 announcement at Ohio Northern University. (Northern Review photo/Doug DeNoi).

Images that contain more than three people and show some aspects of communal life are slice-of-life photos. The focus of these types of images is on the interactions between the people seen in the images. **Slice-of-life** images focus more on the rituals and performances of the group. Any actions in the image must have a clear explanation of what they mean within the broader community context. Unlike candids, slice-of-life images tend to focus on the actions people take towards each other.

An excellent slice-of-life photo is one that identifies the cultural significance of the image. Much like the candid, the caption does most of the heavy lifting when it comes to explaining the significance of the image to the community at large. Unlike the candid, the photojournalist needs to be aware of the collective whole being shown, as opposed to a singular focus.

The final point to note about both the slice-of-life and candid images is about having expertise in the community. This form of expertise should come from either a community member that can honestly explain what is happening in the image during the time it was taken (a.k.a. a community **gatekeeper**) or the photojournalist themselves having the lived experience of being a member of the given community. An expert on the sociological or psychological elements of community and community members is the third-best option when the first two are not available.

OTHER IMAGES

The last style of photography to note is an image where one or more people are posing in front of a neutral background with a sense of limited movement by those people. These **mug shots** were used in the printed newspaper due to limited space on the page and limited use of color on the medium. Mug shots must be avoided whenever possible in multimedia journalism articles as they are boring and virtually add no new information to the story. This type of picture is an artifact of Legacy Journalism and should be removed from our ability to tell stories.

Most other artificial images should be used sparingly and only if they are labeled as a graphic (photorealistic) or illustration (not photorealistic). The only exception to this rule is infographics, as they tend to make the complex relationships in the story simple. Audiences can interpret the information in these types of graphics due to previous exposure in the media.

CONCLUSION

The photojournalism bootcamp, like the following modules in this book, depends on two key elements to ensure success. The first element is the repeated practice to fine-tune the technical skills of the photojournalist. Having an open mind for feedback and improvement is the second element. The bootcamps in the modules can be done in the field for the seasoned journalist, but better serves the student journalists if these bootcamps are part of the classroom experience..

BOOTCAMP PRACTICE

The bootcamp practice is to take five examples of the five named shots above (not the mug shot) for a total of 25 images. Students would generally share one of each of those types of images and create a caption shared with the rest of the class. This bootcamp uses the ethical feedback model as each student that is not presenting their work must verbally share their ethical feedback with the student presenting. Those not using this chapter should work with another journalist and practice the five listed shots to improve their photography quality.

Photojournalism is a reasonable second module to work on (after going over the Journalism Breakdown) as it allows for a richer understanding of multimedia storytelling in journalistic works. Improving the quality of photographs that a journalist takes helps improve the narrative being presented to the audience.

ASSESSING THE MODULE

Basic: What are the criteria that make for a successful work of photojournalism?

Intermediate: What techniques do you use to ensure a good photograph for a multimedia journalism story? Take one of each of the named shots in the chapter and incorporate them into a story.

Advanced: Provide a personal critique in the form of a reflective analysis of a series of photos in one story that you created.

WORKS CITED

Collins, R. F. (2018). *Photocommunication Across Media: Beginning photography for professionals in mass media*. Routledge.

Erkelens, C. (2018). Multiple Photographs of a Perspective Scene Reveal the Principles of Picture Perception. *Vision, 2*(3). https://doi.org/10.3390/vision2030026

Hobbis, G. (2020). A Digital Swiss Army Knife. In *Digitizing Family: An ethnography of Melanesian smartphones* (pp. 73-93). Springer Nature. doi:10.1007/978-3-030-34929-5_4

Jarvis, C. (2010). *The Best Camera is the One That's with You: iPhone photography*. New Riders.

Modrak, R., & Anthes, B. (2011). *Reframing Photography: Theory and practice*. Routledge.

Thompson, R. (2018). *Close-up and Macro Photography: Its art and fieldcraft techniques*. Routledge.

Třebický, V., Fialová, J., Kleisner, K., & Havlíček, J. (2016). Focal Length Affects Depicted Shape and Perception of Facial Images. *PLOS One, 11*(2). https://doi.org/10.1371/journal.pone.0149313

Tu, D. L. (2015). *Feature and Narrative Storytelling for Multimedia Journalists*. Focal Press.

Wright, T. (2016). *The Photography Handbook*. Routledge.

Zhao, J., Wang, R., Luo, P., Xing, L., & Sun, T. (2017). Visual Ecology: Exploring the relationships between ecological quality and aesthetic preference. *Landscape and Ecological Engineering, 13*(1), 107-118.

CHAPTER 12: AUDIO PRODUCTION

Audio content within a story has the capability of adding a sense of ethos (by providing natural sound from the location of the story), pathos (by allowing the listener to hear the emotion in the interviewees' voices), and logos (by adding to the logical progression of the narrative). This chapter will focus on creating content that fits in naturally within the context of a larger multimedia journalism story or as a stand-alone podcast. The exercises within this chapter will help journalists develop some basic techniques to improve the recording quality. Work in this area is vital as those audio assets can be used in the compelling telling of a given story.

It is fair to argue that multimedia journalism content will mostly be recorded on a smartphone. This idea was one of the central points from Chapter 11 as a smartphone will likely be the recording device that will be closest to you throughout the day. Therefore, it will be essential to understand how to record successfully from that device. The first level of knowledge required to produce a successful audio recording is a baseline understanding of how audio recording works. This basic primer should give you a foundation for planning and recording great audio content for a multimedia journalism story.

There are two types of sounds that journalists should focus on when creating journalistic content. **Soundbytes** are audio clips that contain a human voice providing a little bit of pathos. These audio clips allow the listener to connect with the Elements and reinforce the story's written components. Great soundbytes gives the audience more context to the story and breaks up the reporter's narrative to provide a more balanced view of the story.

The other types of sounds that journalists will record for their stories are natural sounds. **Natural sounds** will usually be the environmental sounds that allow the journalist to connect the listener with the story's location. The two most common places that reporters will use natural sounds are background sounds for parts of the story or a transitional effect for longer stories. NPR has many examples of practical uses of natural sounds in a piece of audio journalism on its website.

A reasonable place to begin this understanding of audio production is with a simple primer of audio and some technical components. This primer should only be seen as a simplification of producing sound in the real world and capturing it for later broadcast. There will be many, many elements left out to get to the core of what journalists need to remember about the best practices of recording sound.

AUDIO PRIMER

We need to begin this module about audio production by defining some terms. **Audio** is the study of all acoustic (e.g., an unamplified human voice), mechanical (e.g., a music box), and electronic (e.g., a synthesizer) devices that create waves that can be picked up by human ears. **Sound** is the result of human ears picking up the audio impressions created by the waves produced by the previously listed devices. When sound from audio devices is captured, edited, and transmitted, we say that it is **audio production** (Kern, 2012).

The next element that is vital to understand is how sound gets from those audio devices. We are surrounded by invisible particles every day. Those particles transmit heat, light, and sound through their vibrations. The amount of times that a particle vibrates is measured in **Hertzs**. A particle vibrating once per second would have a frequency of one Hertz (or 1 Hz). **Frequency** represents the property of a given particle or spectrum of particles in space. A wave is the motion created by the vibration of particles as particles tend to reflect the motion of other particles nearby. The human ears have these mechanisms (the eardrum, bones in the ear, fluid in the cochlea of the ear, and thousands of tiny hair cells) that can pick up the particles' vibrations and translate those vibrations into sound (Rodero, Diaz-Rodriguez, and Larrea, 2018).

This understanding of sound's natural production is vital as a journalist needs to acknowledge how the characteristics of the space they are recording will impact the quality of the recording. This knowledge of **acoustics** allows the journalist to prepare to record sound in a way that promotes the highest clarity or **fidelity** of the recording. There are some general principles for recording audio journalism pieces regardless of the technology being used to record to guarantee better recordings (Bartlett & Bartlett, 2016).

GENERAL PRINCIPLES OF AUDIO RECORDING FOR JOURNALISM

There tend to be some basic rules that students need to be aware of in this module to ensure an excellent audio recording. All of these tips help journalists collect their thoughts and prepare for a recording session in earnest.

The first tip is for the journalist to get a sense of the recording location before they start their recording session. There are three types of recording locations that a multimedia journalist must be aware of to prepare to record. The optimal space would be inside a recording studio or a space meant for audio projects (like a band/choir room in a high school, a music practice space, or some other sound isolation room). Using a recording studio means being aware of the equipment in the room if using such devices. It is in the journalist's best interest to make friends with the audio engineer or the person responsible for maintaining the space. They will provide training far better than this short chapter can with the space remaining. Take the time to learn as much as possible. If the space is not a traditional recording studio, walk around the room and talk out loud. Listen for the way sounds change while moving around the room. Once locating a few spaces that sound good, take a minute to sit down and start recording. Playing back that practice recording will give a better sense of what the recording might sound like when recording in that area. I will often record one to two minutes of pure background sounds (called **atmos**) before an actual recording session. I can use the atmos as part of the editing process to cover up some non-essential audio from the recording.

The second types of recording space are indoor spaces that are not traditionally used for audio recording. The wisdom of walking around and practice recording still holds here. Beyond that basic walkthrough, a journalist needs to be aware of all electronic devices in the room. They can produce intermittent sounds of being turned on and off, give off electrical interference, or even just a background hum. A test recording will discover most of these issues before the actual recording. Also, be aware of HVAC vents and fans in the ceiling, walls, and floor of the room as they can kick on and drown out all sound in the room. A visual scan of the area should help spot those problems.

Finally, there is recording outside. Scanning the area is vital as there tend to be five issues with recording away from the comfort of a building. Being near a road means thinking about how traffic will impact the recording. The conventional wisdom is finding a quiet time when there is less traffic and record during that period. Otherwise, the best advice is to face away from the road and attempt to dampen those sounds.

WC Fields, a famous comedian from the 20th century, had this famous quote, "Never work with children and animals" (Maasz, 2004, pg. 87). This expression has been exaggerated in the media for several years. However, it is worth noting that those two groups make up the second and third issues on this list, as both groups can add a sense of randomness to the process. Kids tend to be easier to work with if they are involved with the process of recording. They are often curious about how everything works. They will not be afraid to interrupt to poke around and ask questions (Siegel & Bryson, 2019). Animals, whether they are domesticated or wild, can cause their own form of chaos. The only solution is that a journalist might need to move to get a good recording.

Crowds of people are the fourth issue to be aware of when recording. Some crowd noises are vital for the audience to feel they are at the scene of the recording. Too much crowd noise can drown out the journalists and other participants on the recording. Journalists need to watch the waves of the recording, volume meter, or other indicators of sound input to make sure that there is not too much noise for the recording.

We need to address the most prominent problem recording outside, and that is the weather. It is known that water and electronics do not play well together. Checking out a weather report should prevent that issue from happening. Beyond that, the environment sounds can overwhelm a recording. One of the most prominent environmental sounds we deal with in Ada is the wind. It is a requirement to get some sort of windscreen for the microphone to cut out that issue.

Placing the microphone in a reasonable place that will allow for a good pick-up of the session is the next element that needs to be worked out once the location has been selected. This placement means sitting the recording device or microphone down several different ways to make sure it picks up all of the necessary audio from the session. One must know their equipment well enough to know:

- what their microphone can pick up,

- how long the battery will last during a recording session, and

- other limitations of the device that can prevent a quality sound recording.

This knowledge is vital in ensuring the recording will be suitable for a multimedia journalism article.

A final consideration that journalists must acknowledge before starting a recording session is a more fundamental difference between the microphone and its human analog, the ear. We need to deal with the psychology of sound to understand the best techniques for audio production. **Psychoacoustics** is that examination of the psychology of sound (Howard & Angus, 2017). The broader theory of psychoacoustics states that a person hears a sound. Soundwaves are picked up by the ear and travel to the brain for interpretation of the noise. A person's brain sends appropriate signals throughout the nervous system to cause the body to react.

Understanding psychoacoustic from the journalistic standpoint means that knowing the difference between what the ears pick up and what is heard. A microphone is essentially the same as what the ears pick up. The vibrations that make up sound waves would enter the ear canal in the same way they would cause the ribbon to vibrate in a ribbon microphone or a membrane to vibrate in a condenser microphone (Connelly, 2017). The microphone will pick up all sounds, whether they are wanted or not, as recording systems do not transitionally have a filter designed to know the difference between what is wanted versus unwanted. The mind allows for the recognition and rejection of sounds that are not useful to a person. Unwanted sounds become part of the background noises of daily life that people do not focus on or consider important. Audio recordings do not.

The last part of psychoacoustic to consider when thinking about a recording session is that hearing is part of people's sense-making systems that indicates how information should be processed. Human beings use sight, smell, touch, taste, and other senses to understand the world and make decisions about it (Schwartz & Krantz, 2019). As all devices do not have these human senses, the recording process removes most environmental information to maintain a select few streams of information into the recording. It is important to note everything else crucial to the project that can not be captured mechanically or electronically.

Wrapping up the General Principles of Audio Recording for Journalism requires one additional element before recording with others. It is a requirement to have any other person being recorded:

- to say and spell their names,

- tell you what organization they represent with their title in that organization (with any spellings that might be tricky), and

- give you verbal permission to record and use the recording for publication or broadcasting.

This step is vital for several reasons. First, it allows the journalist to have their waiver recorded. This waiver acts as informed content that they understand the purpose of this recording. This style of introduction also ensures an actual record of the person being recorded. Finally, it acts as a final test to make sure that all of the equipment is working before the start of the session.

With this point of understanding, we should discuss the three means that most journalists will use to record audio.

RECORDING FROM A SMARTPHONE

One of those old jokes about smartphones is that they do everything well except make a phone call. The issue that journalists run into using a device like a smartphone for journalistic work is forgetting rule number one, "Technology fails" (Tilton, 2020). One way to reduce the number of failure points is to optimize the recording process at the point of capturing sound. Optimizing the phone for recording first means knowing where the microphone is on the phone. Most of the time, there will be a small hole near the charging port of the phone. More likely than not, that will be the microphone for the phone. Knowing the placement of the microphone will allow the journalist to position the phone for the best pick-up. The best pick-up position is typically a balanced position.

A **balanced position** depends on who or what is being recorded. Placement should be about one to three feet away if only one person or object will need to be picked up by the microphone. This placement allows for the best pick-up while allowing some room sounds to enter the recording without overwhelming the focus of the recording.

Beyond testing the phone to check the quality of the recording, the only other wisdom that I find that works with a smartphone is reducing its functionally. It is best to make the device perform as nothing more than a digital audio recorder. Turning on the airplane mode on the phone is the best way to accomplish that feat. The recording will shut off if a phone call comes into the phone. Other notifications can make sounds that the phone will pick up. It is best to limit those issues. Finally, it is also best to close as many apps that are not currently being used on the phone as one can. Apps can cause the phone to vibrate or make strange noises. It is best to limit those by shutting down as many apps as can be feasibly done.

RECORDING FROM A DIGITAL AUDIO RECORDER

Digital audio recorders are any device exclusively designed to capture sound and translate those sounds into digital files. This process of translating analog sound to a digital format happens through the process of sampling the sounds. **Sampling** refers to a computer using a microphone to capture the relative location of a wave in space, coding its location many times per second, and saving it as a file (Toulson, 2020). It is crucial to understand this process because the digital recording is not a perfect replication of the analog sound wave, but rather a "good enough" copy of the sound (Capps, 2009).

The first point to go over is the recording format. I will tend to record in a WAV format at a 24-bit/192kHz resolution. **WAV** is the Waveform Audio File Format developed by Microsoft to contain the information captured by the digital microphone and wrap up that information in a format that most computers can read (Whibley et al., 2016). The WAV format is a lossless file format. **Lossless formats** do not lose information by being saved or transferred to other computers. File formats like mp3, AAC, m4a, and ogg are **lossy**, which refers to how the format compresses the data in the file to make the files use the least amount of memory. The more a file is compressed, the more the file will sound or look less like the objects that are supposed to be represented.

24-bit depth means that each sample of the wave that the computer takes is turned into a binary code that uses 24 bits (an one or a zero). That level of nuance to the recording means that the computer is sensitive enough to place the wave in one of 16 million locations within the digital construction of the waveform. A 16-bit depth (a.k.a. the resolution of most CDs ^) can place the wave in one of 65 thousand locations. A 12-bit depth can place the wave in one of four thousand locations. The trade-off to that level of precision is that the file size will take up more memory in the 24-bit resolution than 16 or 12-bit resolution.

192kHz sample rate refers to the computer taking 192,000 samples per second of the sounds being produced. The more samples of the wave the computer takes, the more the digital file will be closer to the shape of the actual wave recorded. It will never be a perfect representation of the wave as the computer will guess the way the wave should look (Savery et al., 2019). As you might be able to guess by now, the higher the sample rate means that the recording file will take up more memory.

I do not worry about making these files use much memory thanks to the increases in storage cards and the actual size of the files. According to Colin Crawley (2018), a one-minute recording stored on a 24-bit/192kHz WAV file should take around 10 MB. This quick piece of math means I can record around 6,000 minutes on a 64 GB memory card. That means I have 100 hours of recording space on my device for sounds that will be as close to original quality as I can get with current technology.

The next item to understand about digital audio recorders is the type of microphone pick-up. **Microphone pick-up** is simply what areas near the device will the soundwaves be easily captured (Ward, 2016). Most digital audio recorders I have used had an omnidirectional pick-up. **Omnidirectional microphones** pick up sounds from all directions equally. I found this type of record pretty versatile as it does not require the subject being recorded to stay in one spot. The major disadvantage is that they pick up more unwanted noise than other types of microphone pick-ups.

Another type of microphone pick-up used by journalists is cardioid. **Cardioid microphones** will tend to have that heart-shaped pick-up using one microphone. This pick-up reduces (but does not entirely get rid of) unwanted sounds. The Zoom H4n recorder has two microphones on top, which creates a heart-shaped recording pick-up. I still carry it in my kit when I know there will be a press conference or a chance for an interview. I find it useful as that recorder gives me the most control in terms of the recording's quality and format.

A Zoom H4n Recorder is a digital audio recorder with a cardioid pickup that uses two Lobar (or Unidirectional) microphone to control the pickup. Each of those microphones can be turned off to provide a single Lobar pickup (file photo).

Hypercardioid and **supercardioid** microphones are the pick-ups of **shotgun microphone**, the type of microphone used in films, television productions, and on top of DLSRs. The example of a shotgun microphone is the one that I attach to the top of my DSLR. I use a Rode Video Mic as it provides a better pick-up than the microphone on the camera.

A Rode Videomic is one that is traditionally used on top of DLSRs to enhance the sound pickup during video recording. It has a hypercardioid pickup which tends to focus the capturing of sound to the direction that the microphone is pointing (in this case this microphone's pickup is the area in front of the R of Rode) (file photo).

The last two microphone pick-ups are the most controlled of the ones listed. A **bidirectional** microphone allows for the most pick-up towards the front of the microphone with some pick-up behind the microphone. These types of microphones are great for podcasts. I have a Blue Yeti in my recording space for recording one-on-one interviews. I will position the microphone between the two of us when the interview starts.

The **Lobar Polar pick-up** is the closest pick-up to a unidirectional pick-up (Tierno, 2020). There is a minimum amount of pick-up behind the microphone with most of the pick-up in front. I will tend to use a Shure SM55 microphone as my unidirectional microphone as it has a limited cardioid pattern. The other microphone that I have used in the past that has an actual Lobar pick-up is a Shure SM7B. The difference between the two is the SM7B is around $400, while the SM55 is $249 and looks a lot cooler.

The Shure 55SM (left) and Shure SM7B both have unidirectional pickups. The 55SM is a super cardioid pickup while the SM7B uses a Lobar Polar pickup (file photos).

The last bit of wisdom about the digital audio recorder is to do several test recordings before taking it out into the field for an assignment. The most common regret is not checking to see if the device is recording. Most digital audio recorders (like the Zoom H4n) have a standby mode, which pauses the recorder. It is most likely that you will need to hit the record button twice to make the recorder start recording. Please read over the instructions carefully and try the device out multiple times before you will need it.

RECORDING AN INTERNET CONVERSATION

The last of the recording techniques worth noting in this section is recording an Internet conversation via Skype or other programs. **Skype** tends to be the most natural program to use for an Internet interview for a couple of reasons. The most significant reason is that there is built-in recording functionality in Skype, which makes it perfect as a journalism interviewing tool. It also informs the other parties that you are recording the conversation. Hitting the recording button should happen before you ask all parties for their consent to be recorded. The journalist must make sure that the interviewees' oral consent is recorded for future reference.

There are two vital reminders before fully recording the conversation. Unless it is vital to have a video for the conversation, avoid turning on webcams. The recording changes from an **mp3** (audio) format to a **mpeg4** (video) format when Skype detects a video feed in the conversation. That change makes it much more challenging to edit the conversation.

I also suggest having all participants in the conversation record their end of the conversation. This practice ensures typically at least one of the people has a recording of the conversation. It also improves the quality of the interview if the journalist can edit the various recordings into one file. The ability of others to record the conversation and the journalist edit those recordings can be done quickly with Audacity.

EDITING

My first audio editing experience was in 1997 with 1/4" analog tape, editor's tape, razor blade, cutting board, and red wax pencil for a class. I am happy to say that I have not edited audio projects since the late 20th century. The nature of digital non-linear editing has made this process much more manageable. **Non-linear editing** refers to the ability of the editor to edit a project anywhere along the track. This editing style is in contrast to linear editing, which requires the editor to start at the beginning of the track and edit the work in chronological order.

I do most of my audio editing in Audacity. **Audacity**, according to their website, is a "Free, open-source, cross-platform audio software...[that is] an easy-to-use, multi-track audio editor and recorder for Windows, macOS, GNU/Linux and other operating systems." I mentioned earlier in this book that I wanted to avoid naming specific tools as I felt that it was essential to know the techniques of the craft of journalism. This area is one exception that I am willing to make. It is easy to recommend using this program because journalists should avoid overproducing their audio work as it impacts the ability of the audience to trust the content (Ireton & Posetti, 2018). Audacity is a piece of streamlined audio editing software that borrows a lot of its functionally from other applications.

It is fair to compare Audacity to software like Microsoft Word and Google Docs as it has some of the same key commands as those pieces of software. Users can highlight sections of audio they are unhappy with and hit the delete button or control/command-x to remove them from the recording. The copy function also works in Audacity. The instructions are simple and allow users to start editing right away. Part of my classes used to have a step-by-step tutorial for Adobe Audition. I found it easier to do the bootcamp practice listed below to help them feel comfortable with audio editing.

The other nice feature of Audacity is that a journalist can convert those raw WAV files they recorded in the field into mp3 files. That means that most people can access their work on their phones and other devices as most phones can easily play mp3 files.

BOOTCAMP PRACTICE

Students will select a partner to work with for this bootcamp. It is okay to have a group of three if there is an odd number in the class or Practicum. Each student will be creating a one-minute audio package for either radio or a journalism website. Students will interview their partner about a subject of their choice for no less than five minutes. Any subject that would be suitable for broadcast is acceptable for this assignment. A reasonable interview protocol is required for this bootcamp.

Students must take notes during the interview. Once the interview is done, the students need to look over their notes and find a way to incorporate two natural sounds into their package. They will use editing software to complete this bootcamp. Those packages will be presented for review within the classroom using the ethical feedback model described earlier.

ASSESSING THE MODULE

Basic: What are the criteria that make for a successful work of audio journalism?

Intermediate: What techniques do you use to ensure proper audio for a multimedia journalism story?

Advanced: Provide a personal critique in the form of a reflective analysis of a piece of audio journalism that you have created.

WORKS CITED

Bartlett, B., & Bartlett, J. (2016). *Practical Recording Techniques: The step-by-step approach to professional audio recording.* CRC Press.

Capps, R. (2009). The Good Enough Revolution: When cheap and simple is just fine. *Wired, 17*(9), 110.

Connelly, D. W. (2017). *Digital Radio Production.* Waveland Press.

Crawley, C. (2018, May 14). *Audio Duration Calculator.* Retrieved June 4, 2020 from https://www.colincrawley.com/audio-duration-calculator/.

Howard, D. M., & Angus, J. (2017). *Acoustics and Psychoacoustics.* Taylor & Francis.

Ireton, C., & Posetti, J. (2018). *Journalism, Fake News & Disinformation: Handbook for journalism education and training.* UNESCO Publishing.

Kern, J. (2012). *Sound Reporting: The NPR guide to audio journalism and production.* University of Chicago Press.

Maasz, R. (2004). *A Cast of Shadows.* Scarecrow Press.

Rodero, E., Diaz-Rodriguez, C., & Larrea, O. (2018). A Training Model for Improving Journalists' Voice. *Journal of Voice, 32*(3), 386.e11-386.e19.

Savery, R., Genchel, B., Smith, J., Caulkins, A., Jones, M., & Savery, A. (2019). *Learning from History: Recreating and repurposing Sister Harriet Padberg's computer composed canon and free fugue.* arXiv preprint arXiv:1907.04470.

Schwartz, B. L., & Krantz, J. H. (2019). *Sensation & Perception.* SAGE.

Siegel, D. J., & Bryson, T. P. (2019). *The Yes Brain: How to cultivate courage, curiosity, and resilience in your child.* Bantam.

Tierno, M. (2020). *Location and Postproduction Sound for Low-Budget Filmmakers.* Routledge.

Tilton, S. (2020). *Tilton's Laws of Academic Universe.* Createspace.

Toulson, R. (2020). *Changing Technologies of Music Distribution.* Bloomsbury.

Ward, C. (2016, January 11). *6 Microphone Pickup Patterns Every Filmmaker Should Know.* Retrieved June 4, 2020 from. https://www.premiumbeat.com/blog/6-microphone-pickup-patterns-every-filmmaker-should-know/.

Whibley, S., Day, M., May, P., & Pennock, M. (2016). *WAV Format Preservation Assessment.* Retrieved June 4, 2020 from http://wiki.dpconline.org/images/4/46/WAVAssessmentv1.0.pdf.

CHAPTER 13: VIDEO PRODUCTION

Video is often one of the first elements people will think about when they hear the term multimedia journalist, as it reflects the changes to journalism in the past fifteen years. The term "pivot to video" is both a reflection of social media companies forcing news organizations to move away from traditional journalism story-telling techniques in favor of more short-form content (Moore, 2017) and the fundamental shift in newsrooms because of those demands by social media companies (Madrigal & Meyer. 2018). While video journalism is not replacing all forms of journalism, it is essential to recognize the power of video for journalistic works.

A good video can better enhance a person's understanding of a given story. It can provide clarity of Elements and allow the audience to see and hear some of the actors. A great video, by extension, can connect the narrative to the broader community. Those videos allow the community to represent itself by showing the audience the people, locations, and interactions that make it up. This distinction is only essential if the video amplifies the overall narrative by not merely repeating other Elements.

Part of the underlying purpose of this chapter is to help think about the broader implications of shooting, editing, and adding video to a journalistic work. Producing video takes a significant amount of time to create. It will be crucial to know if your time is best spent working on that type of content. This chapter will address which parts of the video production process require the most time and how you such spend that time wisely. This underlying purpose means that the reader will be working through an essential checklist to create good video journalistic content.

The more critical objective of this chapter is working through all of the necessary shots and practices of videography. While shots were discussed earlier in this book, this chapter will apply those shots to everyday situations that the journalist will face. The exercises within this chapter are designed to have the reader practice with a phone, DSLR, and traditional field video camera setup. After reading this chapter, readers will understand the differences between these three types of cameras and how the differences impact the reporter's ability to tell a story using video.

A reasonable place to start this discussion about video production is time and resource management in the standard three phases of video production. These three phases are common to all forms of video production (not just journalism) to make the content creation process smoother. It is also important to note that this chapter summarizes this process as journalism tends to be less rigorous than other forms of video production (Blankenship, 2016).

PRE-PRODUCTION, PRODUCTION, AND POST-PRODUCTION

One of the most common mistakes multimedia journalists make regarding video is the idea that mistakes made in the filming of a project can be fixed in post-production. The three stages of video production need an explanation to understand why that line of thinking is a mistake.

Pre-production for most videos (even journalistic works) is the planning stage of the project. It is when the script is written along with the planning of the shots. The **pre-production** section of any project requires the content creators to work out any issues they might have so that the rest of the video can go smoothly. This stage is more than having a clear concept that everybody can follow. It requires an understanding of how to implement that concept in the real world. The more work that happens during the pre-production phase to ensure the project's success means that less time is spent during the production and post-production phases of the project. A responsible multimedia journalist should spend a little time working out all of the story's angles before going out into the field, even if that story is a breaking news story.

The **production** phase of the project is the time when the crew goes out and shoots the video. It is nearly impossible to improve the quality of any video in the post-production phase of a project. It is better to shoot more footage in this part of the process than you think you will need. The rule of thumb is that there is a six-to-one ratio with regards to production. Every minute a person spends planning the video in pre-production will save the person six minutes in the production phase. A person will also need to have at least six minutes of footage for every minute that the project is supposed to be at the end of the post-production phase of the project. During this part of the project, it is constructive to keep a detailed log of the filming to have good notes for editing the video.

Post-production is when the shooting concludes, and editing begins. It requires an exquisite sense of knowing how to organize, cut, and put the various shots together to create a clear narrative throughout the video. It is also fair to note that this phase takes the most amount of time compared to the rest of the aspects of creating a video. It is also during the post-production phase that leads to the shaping of the video's final narrative.

The journalism version of those three phases is more condensed due to deadlines and other external forces (such as competing news sites pushing the news out at a rapid rate). Workflows will dictate when a video needs to be completed. These factors mean that journalists must be proficient and efficient in producing quality videos for their organization. Being skilled and competent in this medium means knowing how to self-evaluate to focus on the aesthetic quality of the video.

EVALUATING VIDEOS AS A PIECE OF AESTHETIC WORK

There tend to be six areas that I will give feedback to a student regarding their videos. These six criteria form the rubric that I use when I have discussions with those students. It is important to note that we look for growth if the student completes this module for their Practicum course. We will generally have this module in every Practicum course a student signs up for during their academic career. The rationale for this decision is to promote improvement in the quality of a student's video before they graduate.

The first criterion we focus on is that the student must demonstrate the ability to edit a visual work with a solid comprehension of the given medium's mechanics. This criterion allows me to concentrate on the student's ability to do well in the project's post-production phase. One of the reasons I tend to focus on this area is that editing is the most time-intensive part of the project. Editing is also the area that I have the most input to offer, as I was a line editor for nearly a decade.

An excellent multimedia journalism video is edited with only high-quality shots remaining in the package. **High-quality shots** contain:

- no blurred images,

- add to the story's overall narrative, and

- reflect the right narrative statement based on the functions of those shots discussed earlier in this book.

Each shot is incorporated seamlessly into the final project, which allows the video to move smoothly through the various scenes. A variety of transitions help communicate the main idea and smooth the flow from one scene to the next. The final element worth examining is the use of limited digital effects within the video to emphasize critical parts of the story.

Beyond clarity of visual editing, an excellent work of video journalism must consider the audio in the package. The student must be able to demonstrate the ability to edit audio with a solid comprehension of the technical elements. I focus on this criterion as it is easy to overlook the sound as much of the journalist's focus is on the screen, looking at the shot's quality. The main element I am listening for is the audio being clearly understood in the package while effectively assisting with communicating the main idea of the story. This clarity also means that the background audio in the package must work in balance with the rest of the video's elements.

A common complaint about video content is that it can be that it is too dark to see the elements on the screen. Therefore, the third criterion we examine is the ability of the student to demonstrate the ability to use lighting with a solid comprehension of a shot's aesthetics. Journalists must consider having enough illumination when shooting their video and using additional light to eliminate shadows and glares. A proficiency in lighting means that the journalist has sufficient brightness for the viewer to see the action on the screen easily.

The fourth criterion is grounded in the production of the video. Specifically, it examines if the student demonstrates the ability to use proper camera techniques with a solid comprehension of applying the different media elements correctly within the story. I want the student to be concerned with making sure that all shots are clearly focused and well framed. To shoot the video well, the

212

camera operator must use an excellent technique to keep the camera steady with a few pans and zooms. The use of proper camera techniques also means understanding the focus of the story. A well-practiced videographer will use closeups to show the audience who or what to focus on in the story.

It is helpful, like mimicking the writing style of a platform that a student would like to work, to craft content in the manner suited for a given organization. This knowledge means that the student must demonstrate the ability to use moving images with a solid comprehension of how those movements fit within the given context of a media platform. Journalists must be purposeful in using motion in the video to help create emphasis within the storyline. The video must also look planned out to highlight all of the critical Elements. Finally, stand-ups or "talking head" shots must be used when addressing essential facts to the audience.

Lastly, I want to make sure that the student demonstrates the ability to use timing effectively that represents a sense of style within the context of the story. This criterion means that the video clips must exhibit the classic **three-beat timing**, which means that the journalist shows three natural actions per clip or three related clips per event (Frechette, 2012). This technique allows the journalist to be thoughtful in their display of actions within the story.

All six of these criteria depend on the journalist understanding what it takes to construct a video package for journalism platforms.

CONSTRUCTING A VIDEO PACKAGE

Video packages are the self-contained pieces of visual content that allow the journalist to explain the story's concepts. Packages are useful from a journalistic standpoint. They can be plugged into websites, newscasts, and other editorial content as a means of addressing more critical stories. All video packages begin with a script that covers the Elements visually. Writing scripts happens after all of the videos are captured for the story. It is the videos that determine the direction of the package. Well-crafted progressions also usually help move the narrative flow of the story while connecting to the story's central truths.

Ledes are essential in video packages as they make up the first ten to fifteen seconds of the story. The lede's purpose is to address the Essential Questions in such a way that it makes the audience want to know more about the story. A compelling lede in a video package is a descriptive lede. The level of the lede's description needed depends on the journalist's ability to pick an angle of the story that allows for the Elements to be explored to the point of clarity. The only way a lede can reach this level of precision is through extensive fundamental research about the Elements.

Fundamental research for a video package requires the journalist to do a good deal of background reading on the person, issue, or event they are writing about. A solid story is built on this research level, especially if that research leads to the development of a good protagonist for the story. In multimedia journalism, protagonists must be presented beyond an oversimplification of the narratives surrounding the actors in the story. They must fully explain the actor's connection to the rest of the Elements (Meyers, 2019). The protagonist explained well allows the audience to be more engaged with the story as they can see the story through the eyes of that person (Hartsock, 2019).

Explaining the protagonist to the audience take quotes that hit the three artistic rhetorical points. There must be some quotes that emotionally appeal to the heart. Some hit the logical sweet spot in the audience's mind, and others impress the audience with how they are grounded in the community's ethos. Picking a variety of quotes that meet those rhetorical requirements will allow the video package to impress the audience.

The final point to note in the construction of video packages is how to end them with a bang. The package's conclusion depends on whether the package would be classified as a hard news story or a soft news story. **Hard news stories** are often those narratives that most directly relate to dramatic changes to the audience's view of the world with regards to political leaders, major social issues, or disruptions to the status quo (Otto, Glogger, and Boukes, 2017). The best ending for a hard news story is one that uses the facts present in the story to reach a logical conclusion about the state of the story. The contrasting **soft news stories** will deal with figures in the public eye that the audience will find more entertaining than informative (Glogger, 2019). These stories end best when the conclusion sticks within the mind of the audience. This style of ending requires a strong emotional completion of the narrative or a call to the audience's ethical sensibilities. Both of these endings should force the audience to think about the story long after its conclusion.

These standard practices of video packages work best when used within the context of a specific type of video package. This next section will review those types discussed earlier in this book.

REVIEW OF MULTIMEDIA JOURNALISM VIDEO PACKAGES

The fifth chapter provided a summary of the five types of videos used by journalists in multimedia journalism works (Tu, 2015). Journalists need to recognize how to use each of these types to amplify critical parts of a given story. Raw videos should be used within a story to present an unedited account of the events. These types of videos might require additional content to explain the video's context but should be untouched by the journalist. Compelling raw videos in a story must also be verified as an honest representation of the events described in the article.

Explainers will help the audience better understand a topic, issue, point of interest, or event only if there are experts in the video that can simplify the complex Elements. The complexity of the subject can be clarified by incorporating graphics that show all of the relevant facts. Journalists must be transparent in the crafting of explainers by citing all of the sources they used in the creation of the video. This final step adds to the credibility of the journalist by allowing the audience to check their work.

Broadcast clips lose their effectiveness if the textual story is nothing more than a transcription of the video. This knowledge means that the journalist must add more context to the story that was left out of the original broadcast. Journalists need to watch the video and ask Essential Questions based solely on the content of the video. The answer to those questions should frame the progression of the other mediated elements for this story.

Creating a feature video for a story requires spending enough time with the person or location or doing enough research about the moment to get to the distinctive elements for the video. That time spent with the person / location or doing the research means finding the visuals or archived videos that clarify the subject to the audience. Feature videos become dull if they only show interviews without other supporting visual elements.

Documentary videos are the most complex ones to use for multimedia journalism. These types of videos are stand-alone stories. They will take the most time. It is not usual for these projects to take months or even years to finish. The only wisdom I can offer is to make sure you have a precise pre-production, production, and post-production plan for this type of work. I would encourage completing the Executive Summary bootcamp in chapter 20 before tackling a project of this scope and magnitude.

Journalists working in video (either in the form of a package or just supporting content for a larger story) should be able to tell the story by selecting the right shots effectively.

REVIEW OF THE BASIC VIDEO SHOTS

Videographers tend to have five different types of shots to explain what is happening in the story's narrative. **Extreme wide shots** (EWS) or **extra long shots** (XLS) occur when the camera is so far from the subject that they are not visible. This type of shot establishes the scene of a video. It is a useful shot as it helps the audience better understand where the action is taking place. The audience can feel that they are on location by seeing all of the surroundings. Typically, no one person is highlighted in this shot.

Wide shots (WS) have the subject take up the full screen to place the actor within the scene. The purpose of these shots is to place the subject in the context of the rest of the scene. Subjects in this shot should have some "breathing room" away for the sides of the frame as it is easy to remove part of the subject. This issue happens when a journalist is not careful about how they are shooting their subjects. Another element to keep in mind is that subjects will look awkward if their feet are precisely on the bottom of the screen or the top of their head is touching the top of the screen.

The most common style of shooting that journalists will use is the medium shot. **Medium shots** (MS) show some part of the subject in more detail while allowing the audience to feel that they are looking at the whole subject. This shot is considered the most neutral and the best for delivering information. It is used when the actor's quotes are not too emotional or require the audience to concentrate on a particular area of the scene. Medium shots are also neutral because they are frequently used by journalists when they appear on the screen. That framing of the journalist in the medium shot allows them to use hand gestures to highlight critical facts and move around the screen to point out Elements.

A counterpoint to a MS in an interview would be the closeup. Closeup **shots** (CU) usually refer to a tight shot of a person's face. CUs are any shot that a videographer chooses to focus on a particular feature or part of the subject by making that feature or section take up most of the frame. These shots are best at highlighting the actor's emotions as they exaggerate the critical visual for emotions, which are facial expressions.

The last of the primary modes of shooting a video is the **extreme closeup** (XCU). XCUs allow the journalist to add tension to the story by getting closer to a subject than a person would generally be. These shots are useful for highlighting reactions in the subject if the journalist has a sense of the actor's response to a question or action.

These five shots make up some of the visual languages that multimedia journalism use in video. One final note before shooting a video is that a journalist should understand some of the basic rules for video before putting together any video for a multimedia journalism story.

AUDIO TECHNIQUES FOR VIDEO PRODUCTIONS

Chapter 12 explained how to produce audio for a journalistic project and the fundamental theory that drives the study of acoustics. It is essential to refer back to the section as those aspects get overlooked when working on a video package. The old practice was to hook up a set of headphones to the camera to listen to the incoming audio for problems. The issue is that most equipment now is more streamlined with limited input to hook up such devices as a headphone with a 1/8" or 1/4" plug. This understanding of the limitations of the now means a journalist needs to be more prepared for failure.

The best bit of wisdom I have when it comes to the audio is having another device recording the sound while filming on the phone. This act doubles the chances that you will get something useful while in the field. It gives another audio track that can be edited into the final mix of the video package. Even a small digital audio recorder is better than nothing.

I also find that having an adapter that hooks up in the power / data slot of the phone can output the audio without interfering with the audio recording. Those devices are traditionally called **pass-throughs**, as the sound will pass through from the phone to the journalist.

Typically, DSLRs have a headphone jack that journalists can plug a set of headphones to give them a sense of how the audio sounds. It is important to keep listening through the headphones as ears tend to hear different sounds than the microphone picks up.

There are three types of microphones that a journalist should be familiar with to capture news on video. **Shotgun microphones** were the ones discussed in the previous chapter. Those types of microphones allow journalists to record from a distance with some clarity. The nice aspect of this microphone style is that it provides a balanced sound that picks up everything it is pointed at, making it one of the best all-around microphones when you need a one-piece solution (the microscope attached to the camera) recording a package.

Handheld microphones are traditionally what most people think of when they hear the word microphone. These microphones are generally light-weight and easy to control. A journalist just needs to point the mic at the person speaking or placing on a stand when recording more than one person. Handhelds can be set up some distance away from the camera as they use an XLR cord and jacks. XLR cords are normally shielded so the signal can travel a considerable distance (about 50 feet without amplification) between the microphone and the camera or any other piece of audio equipment.

Lapel mics are the last of the three conventional microphones used by multimedia journalists. These small microphones will attach to a piece of clothing via a lapel clip. They usually need to be reasonably close to a jack (around 12 feet at the most) unamplified. They tend to be ones that journalists like to use for studio interviews. However, they work wonderfully for all interviews. They will minimize the amount of background noise picked up on the recording.

It is helpful to do a test recording to ensure that anything is working correctly. Playing back that test footage helps check the levels and other aspects of the recording before actually filming anything important.

SOME FINAL CONSIDERATIONS FOR MULTIMEDIA JOURNALISM VIDEOS

This section should help journalists use video more effectively in multimedia stories. These concepts are borrowed for basic film practices but will assist in the crafting of more compelling videos. The most important thing to remember when applying these concepts is that they should not diminish the truths or facts from the story. These six ideas are part of the editorial process of getting the information out to the audience to help them better understand what is happening in their local community.

The first basic consideration when putting together the final video is that it is better to show the story's critical actions rather than letting people just talk about them. The nature of any video is dynamic. It demands narratives to be supported by a visual reinforcement of what is happening in the story. Getting experts to talk about the unfoldings within the story is a second-best solution if it is impossible to show the actions related to the story. This consideration also means having a detailed log of all of the shots taken for a given project, so the best shots are easier to find at the end of the project.

The camera having a limited range of vision is the second consideration of video. This understanding is similar to the discussion points about the microphone from the previous chapter. A camera does not work the same as the human eye. It can be extended or augmented based on the additional component on the camera. The camera's sole job is to control the highlighted and focused area within the entire scene. Cameras spotlight the crucial visual elements that the audience needs to see.

Shot selection matters is another consideration as each shot adds a different contextual piece of information to the overall presentation of the story. Selecting the correct shot for the right moment of the story amplifies the audience's understanding of the narrative. The order of the shot also plays into the selection. Two aesthetic effects are useful to understand when discussing shot selection.

Kuleshov effect is the juxtaposing of different visual elements within a single piece of flow to create a different interpretation of the various aspects of the story. The classic example of this effect is showing a person and then showing a plate with one cookie. The person appears on screen again, followed by a full plate of cookies. The last sequence of shots begins with the same person and editing with a plate filled with cookie crumbs. The assumption the audience is left with is that the person ate the cookies. This narrative device allows the videographer to control the video's narrative by carefully considering the order that the audience is shown specific visual elements (Calbi et al., 2017). Journalists need to be aware of this effect as their shots and editing may unethically affect the audience's perception of the Elements.

Chiaroscuro is the use of light and shadows on the screen to reinforce tension in the scene. The reason that this concept is essential to note that a good work of multimedia journalism depends on the video narrative having enough light to make the elements of the scene visible to the audience. Adding levels of darkness in most videos will help create a dramatic moment. This technique should be avoided as it may unethically affect the audience's emotional responses to the Elements (Kay, 2019).

Understanding the camera angle is the fourth consideration of video as it also impacts how the audience reads the visuals on the screen. Journalistic videos should be shot as much as possible using a neutral angle. The **eye-level angle shot** is the one in which the camera is placed at the subject's height. They will not look up or down if they are looking at the lens. They are perfect for journalistic works as they add not dramatic context to the shot. Low and high angle shots have some issues that tend to make them inappropriate for journalism. **High angle shots** have the camera looking down on a subject from above. This position makes the people on the screen look weak, submissive, or frightened. This type of shot is in contrast to the **low angle shot**, which shoots the person from below them to look up at the person. Low angles make the people on the screen appear to be dominant, aggressive, or ominous (Moura,

2014). Changing the angle from an eye-level perspective will impact how the audience views the people on the screen.

The fifth consideration of video is that great sound is vital. Audio is often overlooked as a necessary part of video work. The best wisdom for this consideration is reviewing this book's audio production section and being comfortable with all aspects.

Finally, a solid work of multimedia journalism video will have a takeaway and strong visual at its end. It is fair to bring this up as the last of the six considerations as it will reinforce the rationale for using this technique. The **serial-position effect** refers to a psychological concept in which people are more likely to remember the first idea they are exposed to when presented information (**primacy effect**) and the last fact that they see in a story (**recency effect**) when compared to all of the other pieces of information in a given story (Kelly & Risko, 2019). Having a compelling visual at the end of the video means that the audience is more likely to remember the takeaway.

The last concept we will need to discuss is how to use the cameras when shooting video. Two of the types of cameras were presented in a previous chapter as a smartphone and DSLR are the ones more likely to be used to shoot multimedia journalism content. The last type of camera is more commonly found in Legacy Journalism newsrooms.

USING A FIELD CAMERA

A **field camera** can use either a digital medium or tape to record the information coming in from the lens. These cameras tend to be larger than the DSLRs and have a singular focus of recording just video. Using a field camera means understanding the functionally of the specific camera in front of you. A DSLR that can shoot video is still primarily used for taking still images. The functionally of that camera serves that purpose. Field cameras are meant for video. The lens controls, depth of field, and other functions are supposed to make it easier for the videographer to record the video's quality that matches the needs of a given project. The suggestion for dealing with this camera is simple.

Read the manual and play around with the camera before taking it out for a real story. The bootcamp should help you practice with the camera.

VIDEO EDITING

Editing represents the post-production process of video journalism. It also can be the most complex part when producing a video. This section will be a simplified way to edit as opposed to a tutorial. The first step is to download all videos onto a series of backups (both computer and cloud drive) as soon as possible. Technology has a way to fail at the worst time. The rule for backups is 3:2:1. A digital asset is not backed up until it is in **three different locations** on **two different mediums or devices**, with **one of those copies being in the cloud**. Once the files are backed up, the next step is to review the log for the best shots. One of those best shots should begin the video, and another one should end it.

The third step happens before the computer is turned on to start editing. It is finalizing the script. The script is a combination of the truths from the progression, the videos that have been captured, and the video overs (VO) needed to explain the video the audience is watching. We use the **three-column system** when crafting a script. The top of the script typically includes the name of the project, a one to four-word description of the project (i.e., **the slug**), the people responsible for completing the video (e.g., the videographer, editor, journalist), and the deadline for the project. Below that information is a three-column spreadsheet. The left column is the running clock of the project, starting at 0:00. The middle column tends to note all of the audio that the audience will hear in the video. These pieces of audio include VOs, natural sounds, soundbytes, and other sound effects. The rightmost column is where the editor (or responsible party for the script) will write down all of the video content that are supposed to be in the project. The audio and video assets in the center and right columns need to line up to the correct time indicated on the left column. Voice overs might need to be recorded in another space as editing areas can be noisy. Use a smartphone or digital audio recorder to record the voice over.

Once the script is done, the next step is adding the asset to the timeline of the video editing software. If you have an Apple Computer, iMovie is a reasonable piece of video editing software to use if you have limited experience with editing. Adobe Premiere is another that works well as Adobe offers good tutorials for the software, and the cost is reasonable as a monthly subscription at the time this book was written.

The final step in the process is compiling the video into one file. Most news organizations use an mpeg4 format for a final project. However, it is based on whatever format your organization or software requires you to use.

BOOTCAMP PRACTICE

This bootcamp requires shooting both inside and outside. Shoot each of the five shots (EWS, WS, MS, CU, and XCU) discussed earlier in this chapter at an eye-level angle both at an indoor location and outdoor location. Shoot at least one minute of each of the shots at both locations for a minimum of ten shots. Edit those shots into a minute-long story. Write the script out first before putting the video together. Either use a class session or peer group to perform an ethical feedback review on the work.

ASSESSMENT OF THE MODULE

Basic: What are the criteria that make for a successful work of video journalism?

Intermediate: What techniques do you use to ensure proper video for a multimedia journalism story?

Advanced: Provide a personal critique in the form of a reflective analysis of a piece of video journalism that you have created.

WORKS CITED

Blankenship, J. C. (2016). Losing Their "Mojo"? Mobile journalism and the deprofessionalization of television news work. *Journalism Practice, 10*(8), 1055-1071.

Calbi, M., Heimann, K., Barratt, D., Siri, F., Umiltà, M. A., & Gallese, V. (2017). How Context Influences Our Perception of Emotional Faces: A behavioral study on the Kuleshov Effect. *Frontiers in Psychology, 8,* 1-10. https://doi.org/10.3389/fpsyg.2017.01684

Frechette, C. (2012, August 13). How Journalists can Improve Video Stories with Shot Sequences. Retrieved June 9, 2020 from https://www.poynter.org/newsletters/2012/how-journalists-can-improve-video-stories-with-shot-sequences/.

Glogger, I. (2019). Soft Spot for Soft News? Influences of journalistic role conceptions on hard and soft news coverage. *Journalism Studies, 20*(16), 2293–2311. https://doi.org/10.1080/1461670x.2019.1588149

Hartsock, J. C. (2019). Exploring the Referentiality of Narrative Literary Journalism. *The Routledge Companion to American Literary Journalism,* 325–344. https://doi.org/10.4324/9781315526010-23

Kay, J. (2019). *Chiaroscuro.* Oberon Books.

Kelly, M. O., & Risko, E. F. (2019). Offloading Memory: Serial position effects. *Psychonomic Bulletin & Review, 26*(4), 1347–1353. https://doi.org/10.3758/s13423-019-01615-8

Madrigal, A. C., & Meyer, R. (2018, October 25). *How Facebook's Chaotic Push Into Video Cost Hundreds of Journalists Their Jobs.* Retrieved June 9, 2020 from https://www.theatlantic.com/technology/archive/2018/10/facebook-driven-video-push-may-have-cost-483-journalists-their-jobs/573403/.

Meyers, O. (2019). The Critical Potential of Commemorative Journalism. *Journalism, 146488491986571*. https://doi.org/10.1177/1464884919865717

Moore, H. N. (2017, September 26). The Secret Cost of Pivoting to Video. Retrieved June 9, 2020 from https://www.cjr.org/business_of_news/pivot-to-video.php.

Moura, G. (2014, June 3). Camera Angles: The art of manipulation. Retrieved June 9, 2020 from http://www.elementsofcinema.com/cinematography/camera-angles-and-composition/.

Otto, L., Glogger, I., & Boukes, M. (2016). The Softening of Journalistic Political Communication: A comprehensive framework model of sensationalism, soft news, infotainment, and tabloidization. *Communication Theory, 27*(2), 136–155. https://doi.org/10.1111/comt.12102.

CHAPTER 14: SOCIAL MEDIA

The second chapter focused on how to approach progressions on social media platforms. By their nature, those progressions are supposed to provide a means to describe the Elements within the platform's limitations. Like the other medium for distributing the news, social media has its strengths and weaknesses that can interfere with the audience gaining access to the information vital for engaging with their local communities. Understanding how to use the advantages of the various platforms without being caught up by their disadvantages makes one a more effective multimedia journalist.

DEFINING SOCIAL MEDIA

Christian Fuchs (2017) asked the right question about this topic when he wrote, "What is Social about Social Media?" Fuchs mentions that **social media** is any platform online that allows people to discuss what is on their mind, collaborate with a community of users, and develop relationships with others online through the various communication tools available on that platform. That definition is a good start but needs a little more refining to work within the context of journalism.

The second chapter of this book breaks down social media platforms in six-different types. Looking at social media platforms as community-driven, microblogging, media-driven, ephemeral, professional network, or another form of social media is a useful way to think about how journalists engage with those various user groups. That method of categories allows journalists to craft stories on those platforms in a manner that will enable the users to gain some benefit for those stories. That chapter also pointed to the prime example of each of those platforms by highlighting how to write progressions for Facebook, Twitter, Instagram, YouTube, Snapchat, and LinkedIn. Keen multimedia journalists will note there are more than those six services being used online. New social media sites are being introduced rapidly as communication technologies make these services more accessible to the general public. The obvious question from this knowledge is, "What social media site should I have an account on?"

The answer to that question is not so straightforward. The six listed services above seem to be where most journalists spend their time and energy either in the act of newsgathering or creating content for those platforms. Adding a new service to be a part of will take away your time and energy from doing journalism on your primary platform or the social media platforms already supported by our organization. One should add a platform to be a part of if there is:

- a critical mass of users,

- a diversity of experiences and opinions shared by those users,

- the ability to interact with a wide range of people through thoughtful engagement on the site, and

- there is some underlying value in engaging with those users.

Critical mass of users on a social network has two parts:

1. there must be enough people on the platform to make the website subjectively feels like it is an active community, and

2. those people who use the platform get to the point that they feel confident to use the platform regularly (Al-Taie & Kadry, 2017).

Both parts should impact the decision to join a social media platform as a journalist. It makes virtually no sense to take the time and effort to craft stories for a small audience where the content will have limited views, feedback, or shares.

Diversity of experiences and opinions shared by those users means that the platform is more than an echo chamber of the same ideologies (Ladini et al., 2018). The **echo chamber** means that like-minded individuals are repeating the same political, cultural, and social positions about subjects in the public sphere that essentially become the polarized outliers in public discourse and debate (Balsamo et al., 2019). Echo chambers have limited use as a crystallized representation of a position held by one sub-group with a community or the general public. Presenting journalists' work in those spaces becomes problematic as stories will fail to line up with those deep-seated positions and cause conflict. Content is propaganda and not journalism if all articles support those positions expressed in the echo chamber.

Journalists should find in a platform that has a diversity of experiences and opinions that multiple positions are expressed about subjects of community importance. Expressions of those positions aren't necessarily going to be civil but should feel like there is some form of debate happening. The critical takeaway from seeing those exchanges is that there is a free marketplace of ideas occurring within the platform. The final result of a genuinely **free marketplace of ideas** is that the truthful presentations of reality will find some form of success on the platform. At the same time, false representations will be buried underneath the noise on the site (Schroeder, 2020).

The third idea of a social media platform having interactivity through thoughtful engagement is a byproduct of two forces. **Interactivity** happens when suitable communication technologies allow members of a community to connect through smooth and secure interactions to exchange information. The **thoughtful engagement** occurs between community members when those users take the time to process that information to turn it into knowledge about their community and come to a rational conclusion expressed via the social network. As with the diversity of experiences and opinions, this process will not happen all the time within the system. But, it happens enough that it feels like community dialogues are happening on the site (Tully et al., 2018).

This series of definitions now makes its way to the most important of the four. **Underlying value** can refer to:

- a revenue source for the organization (Goyanes et al., 2020),

- access to people, stories, and communities that are newsworthy (Parks, 2020),

- controlling a particular market (Boyles, 2020),

- promoting democratic practices and culture (Anderson, 2018),

- advancing pro-social behaviors and ideals (Craig, 2020),

- maintaining a sense of local community (Poepsel, 2018),

- access to users that can craft compelling narratives that might gain an audience for the organization (Dunham, 2019),

- or a combination of the above-listed definitions.

These value arguments boil down to a reason to stay on the social network platform once setting up the account. A journalist can not devote the time to a given social media website if they do not see a benefit or the value in the site. This understanding of the value or benefit might come for using the site as a regular user. Only by playing with the functionality of the website can one see the potential value as a journalistic platform.

Addressing the four listed rationales for joining a social media platform is not a binary selection process. Journalists and organizations might find that the overwhelming value of joining a social media service outweighs a lack of a critical mass or one of the other rationales. The definition of those rationales listed above should be redefined and assessed based on the organization's needs or the individual journalist's requirements for getting the news out.

Once the decision has been made to join a given social media network, the next step should be creating content EVEN BEFORE ACTUALLY JOINING THE SERVICE. There are three different categories of content that journalists and organizations can produce for those websites.

SOCIAL MEDIA PROMOTION

Promoting the content produced on a given organization's primary platform tends to be the first step that most news organizations take when creating an account on a new social media service. Doing this level of promotion well means understanding what drives interactions and engagement on the given platform.

Community-driven sites (like Facebook) require a discussion point within the posting. Most organizations seem to think that a discussion point is the same as asking questions that the users can answer in the comments. Most of the time, this approach doesn't work because there's no reason for the users to respond to the question. Those questions are crafted in a way that fails to consider what questions the audience would have about the story. Writing a question without thinking about the audience is the same as asking "Any questions?" at the end of any speech. Silence will follow both of those situations.

Creating discussion points means knowing what the audience is concerned about or about the topic, issue, point of interest, or event. This post should be a beginning point for a civil discussion. Content from the primary platform should be driving this discussion with the audience engaged with the subject at hand. This level of engagement requires good moderation to ensure that the conversation does not go off the rails. It is useful to have some ground rules written down on the main page of the account, so everybody knows what content is out of bounds (Borges & Gambarato, 2019).

Promoting content on microblogging sites (like Twitter) means framing the post as an extended headline for the article. There are four parts to any post on a microblogging site: the message, hashtag, URL, and media asset. The message acts as an extended headline. A journalist has anywhere from 80 to 170 characters to use to provide clarity for a given story and encourage the audience to learn more about it by going to the primary platform referenced in the URL of the post. The right hashtag in the post will connect the audience with the story. Finally, a compelling piece of media related to the story will get the audience to stop for a moment, pay attention to the post, and possibly click on the link to go to the story. Effective content on a microblogging site means understanding the reactions to a given post.

Media-driven social media sites (like Instagram and YouTube) depend on high-quality images, audio, or video to keep the users engaged with the platform. Content that follows the practice described in the fifth chapter of this book will find an audience on this type of service. The media leads the narrative (as suggested by the name of this type of social media network) and audience engagement. Crafting journalistic work on the platform comes down to knowing what about the content posted speaks to the audience. Visual narratives on services like Instagram often address the humanity of the people captured within the image (Tilton & Fleck, 2019), a more profound political message supported by a group of users on the site (Lalancette & Raynauld, 2019), aspects of culture that the casual person might miss (Becker, 2017), or a deeper understanding of the personal lives of others (Carpenter et al., 2016). Promoting content from a primary platform onto a visual media-driven social media website means finding those narratives that the audience connects with and are willing to share with their friends online.

Those sites that depend on audio media to drive users to their platform (like SoundCloud) are traditionally looking for something shorter than a podcast. Professionally produced short (around two to four minutes) pieces of audio that tells the story of a local community in a way that the audience was not expecting. This content should make them feel that they learned something by listening is the goal that journalists and news organizations strive for when producing content on those types of platforms.

Ephemeral social media websites (like Snapchat) depend on a consistent stream of live news to fill their service as old stories virtually disappear off their platform after some time. There is not a sense of a publicly accessible news archive due to the nature of how the site functions. Promoting a news organization or journalist of this type of platform means producing short segments of news that summarize what is happening in the world in a manner that grabs the audience's attention quickly to the point that the audience is excited to receive the content you are producing. It also means being literate about how users communicate on the site. Snapchat is a different level of visual rhetoric that is not found on other websites. Playing around on this type of social media platform is vital to sound authentic when producing content.

LinkedIn, like other professional social media networks, depend on the journalists to write in a manner that sounds professional. There is less of a creative narrative in the journalism articles found on those platforms. The central truth from the articles published on the primary platform connects with some insight about a market, consumers, or a given industry. It seems those that find success on these types of platforms produce in a style that appears to combine journalistic inquiry, marketing knowledge, sociological theory, psychological motivations, and a level of awareness about effective business practices. Networking on these platforms is transactional in nature, therefore content produced for this site should also be seen as transactional. If the journalist or organization gives enough insights that the audience considers valuable, they will gain more of an audience on those platforms.

Newer social media platforms might be developed that do not fit into the five listed categories above. In that case, the critical wisdom is related to the advice already expressed in the chapter. Journalists that find use in a social media site not discussed above will first need to play around on the site to see how others interact within the social network. Interactions on social media websites are traditional communication based, which makes sense as social media platforms at their core are communication technologies. The next step is finding out what type of information and knowledge is most often shared. Asking friends who use the site is a reasonable starting point in understanding the kinds of information users find interesting, useful, and valuable. The last bit of intelligence one should get before starting to produce journalism for a newer social media platform is to get a sense of how individual users interact with groups and companies on the site. It is fair to argue that users can be uneasy that corporations are entering these public spaces to influence public opinions about their brands (Byard, 2019). The research listed in this paragraph will give journalists and news organizations a better sense of the lay of the land when entering a new social media network.

DISSEMINATING THE NEWS VIA SOCIAL MEDIA

The next step a journalist or media organization will take once they have the promotion component of the social media platform down is to create exclusive programming for the platform. This level of engagement requires the organization to understand its purpose to meet the needs of the audience. It is beneficial to develop an executive summary as a proof of concept for this product. Crafting an executive summary is covered in chapter 20 of this book. Once a journalist has reporting the news on a social media platform down, the final step is reporting on a breaking news story or live event on social media.

REPORTING BREAKING NEWS AND LIVE STORIES VIA SOCIAL MEDIA

One of the defining moments for any journalist is the first time that they cover a breaking news event or report on a story live on location. Social media sites tend to be where most new journalists will get that experience. This next section is designed to help those who have not had this experience to be better prepared before reporting live.

DEFINITIONS OF PRACTICE

Live news describes a wide-stroke of news stories currently happening while the journalist is reporting about the subject. **Breaking news** should only reference newly received information about an event that is presently occurring or developing. The focus of this presentation of the report is how this breaking news event will generally impact the audience currently. **Continuing coverage** adds to a breaking news story by adding more details about the story that are happening away from the main action of the breaking news story. Once the news media have broken the breaking news story, additional information will be reported by journalists in the form of a **developing story**. The main focus of a developing story is how the story has changed since the last time it was reported. This reporting should add to the audience's understanding of the story. A **news flash** is any single piece of news that interrupts the current flow of programming with **alerts** being the most serious of these news flashes. They broadcast warnings related to dangers, threats, and problems to the given community (Georgakopoulou, 2013).

COVERING LIVE NEWS ON SOCIAL MEDIA

The best way to cover events live is usually to set up a liveblog/livestream on your primary platform by auto-feeding the page with social media postings. This coverage level is tricky, especially for those who have never covered a breaking news story before. One of the keys to doing this type of coverage well is to have a conversation with the audience about the subject of the live news event.

Covering live events works best when the journalist focuses on the audience members with a high-interest level about the subject rather than for the average audience member, as they can learn about the topic by reading other sources. This focus on the high-interest audience member means providing more detail and analysis in the postings. Engaging with the public also works well in this environment if the journalists can focus on the feed of questions coming in at the same time as unfolding live events. Otherwise, focus on the details of the story.

It helps to do as much research as you can with the limited time you have to make sense of what about this particular event is newsworthy or worth the audience's attention. Performing the Fundamental Research step suggested in the first chapter of this book is not a bad way to answer those questions.

Most live events will have a video feed (either directly set-up by the journalist or rebroadcasted from another source). It is essential early on in the process to determine how you are using the video. For example, press conferences should not have interjections by the journalist. Raw footage requires the journalist to explain what is happening.

Regardless if there is a live video feed or not, the journalist is required to set the tone of the live coverage early. This setting of the tone means that the journalist should explain their vantage point for the coverage (on the sideline, in the press box, watching on TV, curating tweets from your desk or home). It is also useful to give some context for the live event (explain why this subject is newsworthy, provide links for reference, and explain why it is essential they are there covering the event).

Hashtags tend to work well to inform the audience you are covering a live event (as long as the audience understands what the hashtag refers to) and organizing posts around one subject. The use of the hashtag allows audience members to respond to the posts live and provide feedback on the coverage of the story. Using a hashtag effectively means typically having the support of another journalist so they can moderate the feed for questions for the journalist or track down additional information related to the story.

The coverage of the breaking news does not require a full transcription of the actions. People can watch those aspects of the event after the fact. A journalist should use the news judgment to determine what description, explanations, and analysis are required to make sense of what is happening. This feed is often the "public notebook" of the post-event coverage of a given breaking news story.

It is useful to keep the audience informed of what the lack of action means. Sometimes it is as simple as explaining that the journalist needs to take a break to get some water. Other times, it is telling the audience that the people are sitting around because never new has happened. A lack of action is the best time for journalists to leave their vantage point to do some additional newsgathering. The journalist is not required to remain at one location while covering a live event or breaking news (unless told so by authorities). They should feel free to move around to find out what is happening.

There is a need to provide some fact-checking on the fly. Most of the time, this will happen if someone mentions a report, video, or statistic in the context of the event. It is useful to search for that material and determine if it is a reliable source of information (using the CRAAP test mentioned in the first chapter of this book). A link to the source can be posted if the content passes the CRAAP test. A journalist is also responsible for not allowing inaccurate information to go unchallenged. It is up to the reporter to report the truth and explain why a fact being repeated is false or correcting the claim in a piece of misinformation.

Wrapping up a live event means providing a recap for the audience about what happened during the live coverage, what the takeaways are, and where the audience can go to find more information about the events that just happened. Those wrap-ups act as a moment of clarity after the chaos of the live. Use that time to make sense of what happened and provide some closing thoughts.

CONCLUSION

One of the defining elements of the era of Disruptive Journalism is the introduction of social media as a means of delivering news to the audience. Social media is still a communication channel that depends on journalists to gather the news and transform the information about subjects affecting a community into knowledge that allows the audience to make good decisions about their daily lives and have a better understanding of the state of the world.

Social media is a mode of engagement between the journalist, the audience they are serving, and the community from which the journalist's story is coming from. It is critical for the journalist to use news judgment to filter all of the information coming from these various sources to produce a truth representation of the reality that the community is experiencing.

BOOTCAMP PRACTICE

Find a story online and cover that story using two different social media platforms. How are those social media presentations of that story supported by and enhancing the coverage found on the primary platform?

ASSESSMENT OF THE MODULE

Basic: Look at a journalistic organization that has content on three separate platforms. Compare and contrast those three individual platforms, followed by comparing and contrasting their social media content with the content they produce on their primary platform.

Intermediate: Produce journalistic content postings for a social media platform at least once a day for two weeks. Perform an executive review over the social media content.

Advanced: Find a live event and cover the story using the techniques described in this chapter on a social media platform. Take careful notes about the event and write up a story once the live event has ended. Perform an executive review over the social media coverage of the event and the post-event story.

WORKS CITED

Al-Taie, M. Z. (2017). Information Diffusion in Social Networks. In S. Kadry (Ed.), *Python for Graph and Network Analysis* (pp. 165-184). Springer Link.

Anderson, C. W. (2018). Journalism as Procedure, Journalism as Values. *Journalism, 20*(1), 8-12. https://doi.org/10.1177/1464884918806732

Balsamo, D., Gelardi, V., Han, C., Rama, D., Samantray, A., Zucca, C., & Starnini, M. (2019, June 27). *Inside the Echo Chamber: Disentangling network dynamics from polarization.* https://arxiv.org/abs/1906.09076.

Becker, D. (2017). Instagram as a Potential Platform for Alternative Visual Culture in South Africa. In M. Bunce, S. Franks, & C. Paterson (Eds.), *Africa's media image in the 21st century: from the "Heart of darkness" to "Africa rising"* (pp. 120-130). Routledge.

Borges, P. M., & Gambarato, R. R. (2019). The Role of Beliefs and Behavior on Facebook: A semiotic approach to algorithms, fake news, and transmedia journalism. *International Journal of Communication, 13,* 603-618.

Boyles, J. L. (2020). First-movers and Industry Shakeups: How public newspapers define value. *Newspaper Research Journal, 41*(2), 231-245. https://doi.org/10.1177/0739532920919824

Byard, N. (2019, October 9). *Silence, BRAND.* Retrieved July 8, 2020 http://www.thefactorytimes.com/factory-times/2019/10/8/silence-brand.

Carpenter, S., Kanver, D., & Timmons, R. (2016). It's About Me: A study of journalists' self-presentation of their visual and verbal selves. *Journalism Practice, 11*(10), 1246-1266. https://doi.org/10.1080/17512786.2016.1245587

Dunham, R. S. (2019). Keys to Effective Journalism in the Multimedia Era. *Multimedia Reporting,* 23-39. https://doi.org/10.1007/978-981-13-6163-0_2

Fuchs, C. (2017). *Social Media: A critical introduction.* Sage.

Georgakopoulou, A. (2013). Storytelling on the go: Breaking news as a travelling narrative genre. In M. Hatavara, Hyden Lars-Christer, & Hyvarinen Matti (Eds.), *Travelling Concepts of Narrative* (pp. 201-226). John Benjamins Publishing Company.

Goyanes, M., Rodriguez-Castro, M., & Campos-Freire, F. (2020). Value and Intelligence of Business Models in Journalism. In J. Vaizquez-Herrero, S. Direito-Rebollal, A. Silva-Rodriguez, & X. Lopez-Garcia (Eds.), *Journalistic Metamorphosis* (pp. 171-184). Springer Link.

Ladini, R., Mancosu, M., & Vezzoni, C. (2018, August 11). *Electoral Participation, Disagreement, and Diversity in Social Networks: A matter of intimacy?* Retrieved July 7, 2020 from https://journals.sagepub.com/doi/full/10.1177/0093650218792794.

Lalancette, M., & Raynauld, V. (2017). The Power of Political Image: Justin Trudeau, Instagram, and celebrity politics. *American Behavioral Scientist, 63*(7), 888-924. https://doi.org/10.1177/0002764217744838

Parks, P. (2019). The Ultimate News Value: Journalism textbooks, the U.S. Presidency, and the normalization of Donald Trump. *Journalism Studies, 21*(4), 512-529. https://doi.org/10.1080/1461670x.2019.1686413

Poepsel, M. (2019). Community and Small-Town Journalism. *The International Encyclopedia of Journalism Studies*, 1-7. https://doi.org/10.1002/9781118841570.iejs0120

Schroeder, J. (2020, June 15). Free-Expression Rationales, Truth, and the Marketplace of Ideas. Retrieved July 7, 2020 from https://ssrn.com/abstract=3606549.

Tilton, S. (2019, February 23). Accelerating the Photojournalist: An analysis of how media brands use Instagram for brand promotion. Retrieved July 7, 2020 from http://www.academia.edu/download/62846325/20190305f_Accelerating_Photojournalist_CCA_2018.pdf.

Tully, M., Vraga, E. K., & Smithson, A.-B. (2018). News Media Literacy, Perceptions of Bias, and Interpretation of News. *Journalism, 21*(2), 209-226. https://doi.org/10.1177/1464884918805262

CHAPTER 15: FEATURE WRITING

Feature writing is a style of writing that presents an in-depth view of a singular event, location, or (most often) person with the right amount of detail that allows the audience to understand that event, location, or person better. This chapter will focus on how to turn this traditional "soft-news, human interest essay" into a more comprehensive narrative that connects the subject of the feature to the broad community. The exercises within the chapter will focus on feature writing progressions and effectively incorporate media assets into this type of story.

Features often distinguish themselves from other forms of journalistic work. The feature article is a long-form piece of writing that allows the story to develop slowly throughout the narrative. Most other forms of journalistic work are short-form writing, focusing on the story being on the crafting of a solid lede, hook, and nut in writing. Sources are also different in this style of writing, as most journalistic work depends on at least two quotes from two sources to complete the story. Features will use quotes from four or more people to allow the audience a better understanding of the feature's primary focus. A great feature will humanize the story's subject to the point that the audience has more clarity regarding the motives of the subject's actions and their rationales for their decisions. Other works will only address the critical details of the story from the vantage point of a "dispassionate" member of the community to tell the narrative surrounding the whos and the whats of the story.

Multimedia journalists who want to excel in this form of writing must first put the audience in the mindset of the key actors within the story. Without this crucial connection, the audience will quickly lose interest in the narrative and will no longer care about the story. Connecting the audience to the subject allows the journalist to add the second important characteristic of a robust feature article. The narrative must place the actors within the story within the context of the community's culture and the broader issues facing society. This process allows the reader to go beyond the psychological components of the story to the more sociological aspects of the narrative. These sociological aspects allow the reader to understand the connection between community and audience concerning the actors in the story. A great feature article finally must leave one or two minor questions unanswered. These questions are different from the ones addressed in progression and the interviews. Instead, those minor unanswered questions allow the reader to mentally go over the narrative to find their own answers to those questions.

The rest of this chapter will go over the seven types of feature articles that most multimedia journalists will tend to write throughout their careers. To effectively write those types of articles, it is crucial to understand how to structure those stories. Those discussions will go over the strengths and weaknesses of each of the four structures used to craft feature articles. This basic rundown of one of the quintessential modes of journalistic writing is framed more as a tutorial for those not familiar in writing in this style as opposed to a series of hard and fast edicts coming down from the master of all things journalism. Feature articles are the primary means that journalists find their voice in the industry. It will take some time to perfect that voice. Consider this chapter as a set of training wheels for practicing that development using the feature article format as the practice medium.

SEVEN TYPES OF FEATURE ARTICLES

It is fair to argue that these seven archetypes of feature articles expand on the standards and practices of journalism discussed earlier in this book (Fritz, 2013). They tend to provide different angles for understanding the various relationships between Elements while grounding that understanding in an easy-to-follow narrative. Journalists must be familiar with these seven types as all can be used depending on the supporting facts, quotes, and other information that will determine how the audience will view the feature's subjects.

The most common type of feature article that a journalist will write is the human-interest feature. **Human-interest features** use the hero's journey model described earlier in this book to explain the tragedy or struggles people face. Those tragedies or struggles follow one of the six **classic narrative conflicts of literature** (Brown, 2019). A person versus themselves allows the reader to examine an internal, moral argument or see the effects of mental illness on an individual. A person's desires are often amplified in the narrative when the conflict is with someone else. Man versus nature explores how the untamed world can cause a person to struggle against the elements. Technology is the fourth type of conflict, as society's tools can trap a person to perform actions or go against their beliefs. The fifth of these conflicts is when a person is going against the status quo or social institutions because those elements threaten that person's survival, ethical standards, and emotional wellbeing. The last of the six conflicts are rarely covered in journalist work as it deals with the conflict between a person and the supernatural. When written well, this type of feature allows the audience to somewhat internalize the struggle the individual faces in the story.

Informational feature articles typically have a narrative driven by research, statistics, and other references. This style of a feature should not be considered an encyclopedia article as the facts of the subject are still interwoven with quotes and a solid narrative. The audience should be given detailed information about the Elements so that they feel smarter for reading the work.

News features create a personal connection to the newsworthy event. The primary purpose of this feature is for the journalist to put a human-interest angle on the central facts of the story. A news feature is different from a long-form news story as a news feature must explain the newsworthiness of the story and humanize all of the central Elements. Journalists must drawl on the community angle in this style of story to highlight the story's components that the average audience member would miss in other sources of information about the Elements.

Personality features tend to be best suited for journalists who find creative writing one of their strengths. These features depend on the right person or group of people that the audience will find interesting. The focus of the article does not need to be famous in the traditional sense. There should be some reason or reasons that the community and audience should recognize the subject(s) of the article. The most successful features of this nature tend to present the article's subject(s) in a similar style to the characters readers would see in well-crafted fictional works. Readers depend on a level of detail that focuses on the most minute aspect of the people being highlighted and explain why those aspects matter.

An excellent **how-to feature** article is written somewhere between an explainer video and an informative article that focuses on expert commentary. The how-to feature must avoid being merely a step-by-step series of directions as there is little insight gained from that form of writing. The how-to steps in this type of feature are in service of explaining why knowing these steps are beneficial to the audience.

Past events feature articles are more than a simple history lesson as the work should be a documentary-style dive that places human voices and faces to dusty tomes of the legacy of a community. The best past events feature articles that must present an honest retelling of the Elements that avoids whitewashing the dark truths of the event in question. Repeating half-truths in service of dodging conflict does not help the legacy of the community. It merely delays the truth from being revealed until a later time. Journalists must reflect the community for better or worse.

"The Best" feature article is a montage of successful actions performed by the article's subjects. These articles depend heavily on good mediated content to support the claims within the story. The journalist must avoid the article sounding like a series of brags or tall tales about the subject. Quotes will tend to drive a majority of this style of feature as the information will be best framed by others more familiar with the subject of the article. Narrative transitions must be long enough to allow the audience a moment to reflect on the information given as quotes. Journalists must also be careful not to turn the story into a hagiography as the sainting of subjects that do not deserve that type of treatment (Borins & Herst, 2019).

FOUR TYPES OF FEATURE ARTICLE STRUCTURES

The most straightforward way to structure a feature article is to use a **traditional feature structure**. It starts with a well-crafted descriptive lede. This lede must address more than the how and the why questions the audience would have about the story. Once those questions have been addressed in the lede, the journalist shifts their attention to providing the audience a reasonable takeaway about what they should discover while reading the article. What tends to follow this modified nut graf is an alternating series of quotes and narrative transitions. The interviewees drive most of the narrative movement in a traditional feature article structure with the transitional elements shaping the story's direction. The strength of this structure is that if the quotes are compelling on their own and the transitional elements contain "detailed description and vivid writing" (Acton, 2018, pg. 2) that the feature will be relatively strong and compelling enough for the audience to want to read the work. The weakness is that this structure can also lead to formulaic writing, which makes the article dull. A back-and-forth whiplash happens when balancing between quotes and transitions. This jarring style makes it difficult for the audience to develop the credibility of the subject or the interviewees in the article. This format tends to soften the overall focus if the narrative does not fit the context of the quotes.

Quotes need to be longer when addressing the mindset of an individual. A single sentence is often not sufficient enough to explain the psychological state of the person being referenced. Journalists must also ground the key actors in the story within the context of the community's culture and the more significant issues facing society by writing long blocks of narrative in the transitional elements of the story. This balanced act is delicate for the best writers and is often spoiled by those writing the first feature. Human-interest and information-driven features are best suited for this structure. There are three additional structures to consider using based on the type of feature article being crafted.

DOLLAR SIGN STRUCTURE

One structure that helps address a topic that can be expanded from a local story to one of national relevance or how the general state of the world impacts a more specific and narrowly defined issue. The **dollar sign structure** provides clarity on connecting the two focuses of the story together into one coherent narrative (Blundell, 1988). The term dollar sign refers to the structure's visual representation, as there is a straightforward narrative that drives the overall story. The straight line represents that narrative through the middle of the dollar. The leftmost curve of the dollar sign is the first progression, while the right-most curve is the next progression. The top of the dollar sign is the introduction to the story. A conclusion makes the bottom part of the dollar sign, with a pivot is in the middle of the dollar sign.

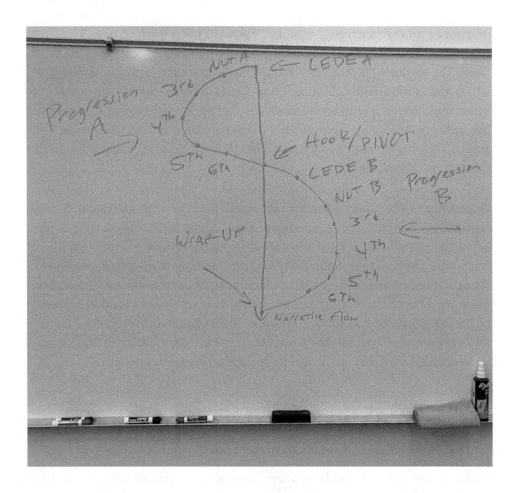

A whiteboard drawing of the dollar sign structure for feature articles.

A story that follows the dollar sign structure opens with an anecdotal, descriptive, or narrative lede (specific examples) that focus one of four different narratives:

1. a broad overview of a subject of general interest,

2. a narrowly constructed lead-in explaining the relevance of a specific subject to the audience,

3. highlights that make a national story newsworthy, or

4. provides details of a story of local interest that the casual reader may have missed in previous news coverage.

Regardless of which of the four types of ledes are chosen for this part of the story, the next step is to craft a nut graf that provides more explanation. Those details must extend the narrative so that the audience is better grounded for the rest of the story. Nut grafs in the first half of the dollar sign features are vital as those sections of writing lead into the first mini-progression of the story. The first mini-progression requires supporting information in the form of quotes, facts, and other developments to flesh out the more significant truths addressed in the first lede and the first nut of the story. Mini-progressions are often three to four truths in which the first truth is built off of both the first lede and the first nut. A mini-progression should end when the last truth in the mini-progression reveals something fundamentally different than what was addressed in the lede or the nut. It is up to every journalist to determine what fundamentally different means in this context. The most straightforward answer is that the ultimate truth of the mini-progression does not sound like a repeat of the lede or the nut. The narrative distance between the ultimate truth and the lede should feel like the journalist has told the short story. The effective use of quotes, as defined in the previous chapters of this book, flesh out the mini-progression.

Journalists should work on the second mini-progression next. The lede in this section should be counter to the first segment of the story. If the first mini-progression was a broad overview of a subject of general interest, the lede for the second mini-progression should be a narrowly constructed lead-in explaining the relevance of a specific subject to the audience. Highlighting the Elements that make a national story newsworthy should be followed by the journalist providing details of a local interest story that the casual reader may have missed in previous news coverage. The nut and the rest of the mini-progression follow the same pattern as the first mini-progression of the feature. A successfully crafted second mini-progression must flip the focus of the feature in a different narrative direction.

The next step in crafting a dollar sign feature is to develop the pivot of the story. A **pivot** has two essential functions within the context of the story. It must be the hook that also connects the two mini-progression to form one overall cohesive narrative. This style of the hook must be written more as a transition between the two progressions as less as a rationale to continue reading the story. The primary question that the pivot must address is, "How do these two mini-progressions connect?"

One of the toughest parts in writing a dollar sign feature is writing a conclusion that summarizes the two mini-progressions. At the same time, conclusions must provide one final takeaway for the audience that explains why understanding the connection between those two progressions is useful for the audience to know. Concluding this story style should not be longer than three paragraphs. Anything longer often becomes the beginning of a new progression. The purpose of the conclusion is to wrap-up the various components to one final statement and not lead the reader down additional narrative pathways.

An optional last step is to create an introduction of two or three paragraphs that bring in concepts early into the story that prepares the reader for the content within the two mini-progressions.

The two types of features that work well for this structure are the past events feature and the news features. Past events fit this structure nicely as the critical facts from the past form the first mini-progression while the current implication of those past events forms the second mini-progression. This format enhances news features as the story becomes more than a one-dimensional retelling of the facts in the story. Both the past events feature and the news feature fit this structure as these types of stories often get minimized in the process of traditional journalism. The narrative flattening that often happens while covering important stories means that critical details are left out of the article in service of a short, clear, and concise telling of the facts of the story. The dollar sign feature needs those facts to tell the story entirely.

THE CHRISTMAS TREE STRUCTURE

Christmas Tree structure also gets its name from the visual model created when crafting this structure. The "trunk" of the tree is formed from the standard five to seven truth progression. It is beneficial to make the narrative distance between these truths to be farther than a typical progression. The reason for the more massive narrative gap is that all of the truths coming from the trunk become the primary truths of five separate progressions.

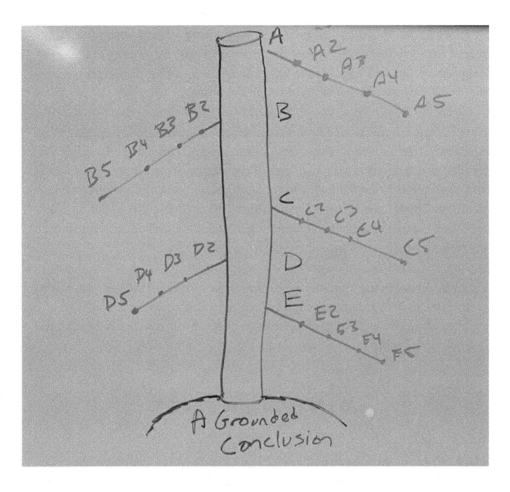

A whiteboard drawing of the Christmas Tree structure for
feature articles.

Assign each of the truths in the first progression a letter. The first truth is "A,"
second "B," and so on. The "A" truth is followed by four to six truths to form the
"A" progression. The most significant rule of the "A" progression is that this
progression can not repeat the same truths from the other lettered truths as the
"A" should act as a meta-lede for the article. It will connect all of the other truths
in this progression through some aspect of the narrative. The "B" truth will act
as the meta nut for the article with the "B" progression supporting why that
truth is the most critical piece of knowledge the audience should have about the
story. The rest of the lettered progression will follow the standard practice of the
Writing Progression with the additional rule that none of the Christmas Tree
truths can repeat. The journalist must expand the size of the metaphorical tree
by drilling down several angles of the story. The "E" progression is followed by a

solid conclusion that keeps all progressions centered around one theme. The last part of the story must tie together the initial progression with the branches of the progression. The "star" of the Christmas Tree is a solid paragraph or two that leads into the themes brought out in the story.

How-to features are the one best feature articles served by following the Christmas Tree structure as the step-by-step process is enhanced by using the lettered progressions. Those branches of the tree clarify the steps in the story and allow for additional information that might be left out of a traditional how-to article. Those branches of the story often give the journalist a chance to add mediated content to help the audience understand the individual steps in the process.

Other features can use this structure if there are discrete elements within the story that can be highlighted in the Christmas tree context. This ability to highlight core elements of the story means that the journalist goes beyond the basic facts and more into the contextual core that defines the story.

MINI-VIGNETTES

The toughest of the four structures to do well is the mini-vignettes. **Mini-vignettes** are mainly short (200-to-300 word) stories that can stand alone from the rest of the article while addressing some of the central themes that run throughout the feature.   Crafting this progression is a little different than the previous four examples listed in this book. The progression begins with the journalist defining three to five themes present in the facts of the story. Those themes do not themselves form any sense of flow, but they represent the concepts that are vital in the telling of this feature. All themes must be one or two simple declarative sentences that a layperson would understand without additional explanation or context. It helps if each of the themes is denoted by a different color of highlighter, pen, marker, or some other mode of color-coding the themes.

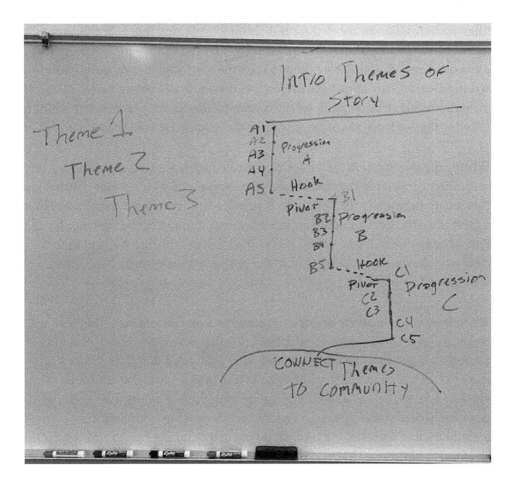

A whiteboard drawing of the mini-vignette structure for feature articles.

The next step is to craft three to five progressions with around five to six truths per progression that will form the foundations of the mini-vignettes within the story. Journalists then need to underline the truth of the progression that addresses one of the themes from the previous steps once each of the mini-vignette progressions is done. Each of the themes must be addressed at least three times, or it isn't a theme of the story. A new theme must be crafted if an older theme does not have at least three supporting truths in the various mini-vignette progressions.

Laying out the progressions in some manner comes next as the journalist must look for connective elements between the progressions to create transitions between the progressions generally in the form of writing a hook between the mini-vignettes. Hooks are vital for this feature, as writing this style of feature means crafting at least three mini-conclusions for the various mini-vignettes. A transition must do the heavy lifting to keep the story together. It seems that writing a well-constructed hook can handle the strain of holding two mini-vignettes together by focusing on the commonalities of the progressions while allowing the audience to continue reading the next section of the feature.

Writing the introduction for a mini-vignette feature tends to make the most sense after connecting the themes with the progression as it clarifies which themes are potentially the strongest. A strong narrative about a theme makes for a great introduction to a mini-vignette feature as it prepares the audience for the type of story that will be reading. It is crucial to write the introduction to make clear why the themes developed from the progression are worth the audience's time to read.

A conclusion for this style of feature represents a meta-"so what." Themes presented in this story need to be grounded in the day-to-day reality of the audience's experiences with the communities referenced in the feature and the reader's everyday interactions with others. It is in this spirit that the mini-vignette feature does a fantastic job highlighting the key points from both the personality-driven and "The Best" feature article types as both need the amplification of narratives that explain what makes up the stories that make up the focuses of these articles.

CONCLUSION

It is essential to understand what makes up a good feature article. Those articles tend to be the ones spotlighted in a portfolio for getting hired or for award consideration. Mastering this format allows for more opportunities to cover exciting subjects and topics using a keen vantage point of the world. The well-written feature also provides a bridge between the journalist and the community they serve if the feature is a truthful representation of that community. This chapter should provide the foundation for such a quality feature article.

BOOTCAMP PRACTICE

Pick a topic that would be the perfect subject to write a feature about for a given journalistic platform. Use each of the four structures mentioned in this chapter to craft the foundations for those articles. Which type of feature article is best suited for each of the structures you have crafted?

ASSESSMENT OF THE MODULE

Basic: Perform a reflective analysis of a feature article. Explain the type of feature article it is and why you believe the journalist used that type of feature article when crafting their narrative? Also, develop a progression that matches one that the journalist might have used to craft their story.

Intermediate: Use one of the progressions from the bootcamp to write a feature article.

Advanced: Provide a personal critique in the form of a reflective analysis of a feature article that you have created.

WORKS CITED

Acton, J. (2018). *Feature Articles*. Retrieved June 18, 2020, from https://www.uiltexas.org/files/academics/journalism/feature_2018b.pdf

Blundell, W. E. (1988). *The Art and Craft of Feature Writing: Based on the Wall Street Journal guide*. New American Library.

Borins, S., & Herst, B. (2019, September 12). *Beyond "Woodstein": Narratives of investigative journalism*. Retrieved June 18, 2020, from https://www.tandfonline.com/doi/abs/10.1080/17512786.2019.1664927.

Brown, D. (2019, August 16). *What Is Conflict in Literature? 6 different types of literary conflict and how to create conflict in writing*. Retrieved June 18, 2020, from https://www.masterclass.com/articles/what-is-conflict-in-literature-6-different-types-of-literary-conflict-and-how-to-create-conflict-in-writing

Fritz, M. (2013, January 31). *7 Types of Feature Articles*. Retrieved June 18, 2020, from https://prezi.com/uyoop0ttwaka/7-types-of-feature-articles/

CHAPTER 16: JOURNALISTIC ETHICS

The *New York Times* (NYT) introduces their overview of ethical journalism by stating the connection between their organization and society,

> The goal of The New York Times is to cover the news as impartially as possible — "without fear or favor," in the words of Adolph Ochs, our patriarch — and to treat readers, news sources, advertisers and others fairly and openly, and to be seen to be doing so. The reputation of The Times rests upon such perceptions, and so do the professional reputations of its staff members. Thus The Times and members of its news department and editorial page staff share an interest in avoiding conflicts of interest or an appearance of a conflict.

It is fair to argue that many news organizations share a similar worldview with the NYT regarding how they see their connection with others in society. Being concerned with one's reputation is a reasonable starting point in this discussion about journalistic ethics. A single journalist can damage the public's perception of journalism, even if that journalist is not an official member of a news organization (Tilton, 2016). Ethical journalism is more than merely protecting the institution of journalism from bad actors. It also acts as a reminder of the characteristics that define the social role of journalism.

This chapter will address the common themes among the professional organizations' code of ethics and the standards and practices found in most news organizations. This discussion will lead to the development of a personal code of ethics.

ETHICS AS A GENERAL PRACTICE

The idea of **ethics** begins with the study of the impact of a person's actions on the internal factors that make up the day-to-day life of the individual and the external factors that an individual might deal with regularly. For example, an internal factor would be how a reporter works with others in their newsroom. External factors would include how a reporter talks to someone from the general public about a story. Every action has some consequences. Journalists need to recognize what those consequences can potentially be as they may impact the ability to write stories, work with the community, or even maintain employment. Good ethical awareness helps a journalist do their job better.

One of the common mistakes in this topic is conflating ethics with morality. Both of these concepts deal with understanding the right way to interact with others. The idea of **morality** is grounded in beliefs that become the values that guide day-to-day actions. It is those values that lead people to understand the world through interactions with others using a given attitude for a given situation (Rae, 2018). Ethics are external to the individual, as those actions that a person takes determines ethical decisions (Christians et al., 2020). Morals must work within the context of the ethics of the situation.

THE THREE LEVELS OF ETHICAL CODES

Three levels of ethical guidelines drive the profession as journalism is an interdependent industry. **Professional codes of conduct** and ethics tend to be the umbrella standards that all journalists must follow regardless of the organization that they work for or any other factors. These statements come from a position of expressing the consensus of the journalists that belong to those organizations about how journalists should conduct themselves. Organizations like the Society of Professional Journalists (SPJ), the Radio Television Digital News Association (RTDNA), and the Poynter Institute use these documents to help shape journalism and allow everybody in the profession to know what is acceptable behavior for a journalist (Carey, 2000).

Understanding the acceptable behaviors of a journalist allows those entering the field to define the actions they will and will not perform in service of gathering the news. It is this level of critical reflection that should make journalists write down a personal code of ethics. A **personal code of ethics** is best when written out as it codifies the abstraction in a person's mind. This action requires sitting down and thinking about the characteristics that define a good, ethical multimedia journalist. Most of the personal code of ethics that students have

254

written explains how they will fairly present an honest narrative about the actions and actors that form the basis of their story. Their codes of ethics also address how they will be diligent in gathering facts, objective in the interpretation of those facts, and accountable to the audience. This personal level of analysis must consider how they will avoid conflicts of interest now and in the future.

It is useful to perform this crucial action early on in a journalist's career as it helps maintain their ethical center when they are selecting a story to write or even which organizations to work for. Developing a personal code of ethics should happen before a person begins crafting stories for a news organization. Journalists must review that code at least once a year to see if they are still following the tenets of their code or if revisions are needed.

Journalists who find them hired by a news organization will come across the last of the three types of ethical documents. These **organizational standards and practices** (S&Ps) focus on the values that define how the brand and platforms shall interact with others. It is fair to argue that out of the three types of documents, S&Ps tend to focus on how the organization will minimize harm, maintain the branding of the organization, and reduce the chances of facing a lawsuit (Bugeja, 2018). S&Ps can also provide insight into what the organization feels are the essential tenets of journalism and mediated communication.

COMMON CORNERSTONES OF ETHICAL JOURNALISTIC PRACTICES

Regardless of the type of ethical code, it is impossible to account for all of the issues one will face in the cold reality of being a journalist. The various professional codes, organizational practices, & personal codes of ethics are built on past experiences. They are revisable based on newer situations that can not be accounted for in those documents. These next several sections are a meta-analysis of all of the ethical codes from the three largest journalism organizations in the United States; SPJ (2014), the RTDNA (2015), and the Poynter Institute (2019). Seven themes emerged from a reading of these three documents.

REPRESENTING REALITY WITHIN THE CONTEXT OF THE MEDIUM

This book has addressed the concept of reality in the previous chapters. SPJ (2014) makes this one of its cornerstones with the statement as a journalist must "seek truth and report it." A journalist can only be an ethical reporter of the news if they are "honest, fair and courageous in gathering, reporting and interpreting information." The RTDNA (2015) frames this discussion by making the concept of truth one of their cornerstones.

> The facts should get in the way of a good story. Journalism requires more than merely reporting remarks, claims or comments. Journalism verifies, provides relevant context, tells the rest of the story and acknowledges the absence of important additional information.

Both of these quotes reflect the first part of journalism's definition as it reminds the journalist to explain a topic, issue, point of interest, or event of current interest using a truthful, compelling narrative about a community to a given audience. A journalist can do that requirement by gathering enough objective facts about the topic, issue, point of interest, or event to present the reality of the story that the community would think is a truthful telling of that story.

There might be times that a majority of community members would reject a story is being untruthful even though the reporter presented objective facts in the story. This conflict often boils down to the interpretation of the facts rather than the mere reporting of those facts. A reasonable reporter must question based on all of the evidence around them if the interpretation is wrong. One way to check your interpretation is by incorporating an interview question to clarify that interpretation. There are two actions to take if the answer you get from that question does not support your interpretation. The first potential action is to retune your interpretation of the situation's reality by creating a new Writing Progression. Otherwise, you will need to have a couple more conversations to triangulate the truth of the story.

JOURNALISTS MUST BE A FAIR REPRESENTATIVE OF THE COMMUNITY THEY ARE COVERING

Communities are not monoliths in terms of opinions, values, or even voices. Journalists reporting on the actions happening in a community must remember to allow for a diversity of expressions, thoughts, and comments. This level of reporting is enhanced by allowing those who traditionally left out of media coverage to add their voice. The RTDNA codes this value in their description of fairness with the statement, "Professional electronic journalists should present the news fairly and impartially, placing primary value on significance and relevance." The significance and relevance in the RTDNA statement should remind the journalist that presentations of members of the community should not be done for spectacle but rather as a means of showing what the community feels about the aspects of a given story.

Poynter makes this case much more explicit in their section on diversity issues. They write in *The Poynter Institute Codes of Ethics and Conduct*, "One of the most challenging issues faced by newspapers is dealing with matters of diversity, including the use of race as an identifier in stories and matters of racial stereotyping." This focus is vital as it helps minimize the unnecessary othering of community members (Gutsche & Hess, 2018).

SPJ also addresses this issue in their section of minimizing harm, "Journalists should show compassion for those who may be affected adversely by news coverage. Use special sensitivity when dealing with children and inexperienced sources or subjects." It is easy to get the same interviewee time and time again as they are the most accessible. Therefore, a journalist might have a general disposition when interviewing others. Journalists need to understand how to reframe questions to get the most information from a variety of interviewees. All of these points manage to help frame the more beneficial discussion regarding highlighting the community's critical aspects that the audience needs to know about to make sense of a given story.

The ability to get to the critical aspects of a story from the community's perspective is the primary reason that the audience and general public trust journalists to perform their jobs. The RTDNA makes this point clear in their writing about the public trust. "Professional electronic journalists should recognize that service in the public interest creates an obligation to reflect the diversity of the community and guard against oversimplification of issues or events." That oversimplification often comes in the form of stereotyping the community or narrative flattening. Journalists must ensure that the articles they are writing are an accurate representation of the community and its citizens. Otherwise, the journalist is merely feeding into the oversimplification of the news.

This underlying fight against the news's oversimplification is vital due to the last ethical point of this section. Poynter refers to the understanding of being a guest "in our readers' homes, and as such, we hold to high standards of decency, courtesy, responsibility and community" as how the profession of journalism maintains good public relations. The more significant point is that journalists should understand the role they play for the audience and society at large. Treating the audience and community with respect means understanding the humanity of the narrative and the people involved with it.

JOURNALISTS HAVE A SOCIETAL ROLE AS THE FOURTH ESTATE

The idea of journalists having a vital role in society comes from 18th century France and the United Kingdom. The French Revolution pushed writers and journalists to the forefront to observe the aristocracy, church, and military actions (Carlyle et al., 2019). While Edmund Burke adopted the concept of the estates to cover the three estates of Parliament in the forms of:

1. the Lords Spiritual (bishops who serve in the House of Lords),

2. the Lords Temporal (the other Lords in the House of Lords), and

3. the Commons (elected Members of Parliament (MPs)) (Newman et al., 2011)

in the United Kingdom version of this structure, the United States' version of the Estates borrows for the traditional structure of American governance with the Legislature, Judiciary, and Executive branches making up the first three estates. The press serves the **Fourth Estate** role as they oversee the actions of the first three and report those actions to the Fifth and Sixth Estates (business leaders and citizens). This idea of the press also has come to include citizen journalists performing this watchdog role (Benkler, 2007).

Being an effective watchdog of government actions means avoiding conflicts of interest. The Poynter Institute gives simple directions to avoid some of these conflicts. "Don't accept outrageously valuable gifts you can't pay for and avoid conflicts of interest." Valuable gifts are not specifically physical. Any action performed by influential individuals or organizations (whether those individuals or organizations are associated with the government, businesses, or other places of power) for the benefit of a journalist has a potential conflict of interest issue. Accepting anything of value for those one report makes it very difficult to act independently from those individuals. SPJ notes that issue in their Code of Ethics. "Journalists should be free of obligation to any interest other than the public's right to know." The audience's right to know the actions taken by public figures that have some impact on the daily lives of the people reading your story is the first priority of any journalist.

This connection to the audience is in line with another principle from SPJ about being accountable. "Journalists are accountable to their readers, listeners, viewers and each other." The interconnected nature of this industry forces journalists to recognize how they are part of a more extensive social system that requires journalists to understand the impact of their actions on the community, their audience, and the industry. This natural order means that the journalist must have integrity in their interactions with others in reporting on the news of the day. This type of integrity is a cornerstone of the RTDNA Code of Ethics. "Journalism's proud tradition of holding the powerful accountable provides no exception for powerful journalists or the powerful organizations that employ them."

The only value a journalist has is the ability to present the truth to their audience. Anything that interferes in that process hurts the journalist.

The last point to consider about the Fourth Estate argument is that the only way the Fourth Estate functions is to be independent of the other listed estates in this section. This point represents two areas highlighted in the professional codes of ethics. RTDNA focuses on the journalist's ability to be independent while Poynter frames this discussion as editorial independence. "Independence from influences that conflict with public interest remains an essential ideal of journalism. Transparency provides the public with the means to assess credibility and determine who deserves trust" This is the main takeaway that the RTDNA gives journalists in their code of ethics.

JOURNALISM AS "THE CORNERSTONE OF SOCIETY"

Beyond this watchdog role, journalism is a means for a community to have a permanent record of the present as a means of future citizens to understand who were the people in that community and what they did. The RTDNA labels this as part of the public trust as it calls on reporters to understand those actions and if those actions caused harm. "Transparency requires reflection, reconsideration and honest openness to the possibility that an action, however well intended, was wrong." This statement goes for the reporters and the people covered in the story that the journalist produces.

This concept of the cornerstone of society also means understanding what type of news the audience depends on and ensuring that they get the information they need to make decisions about their day.

ETHICS AS A TECHNOLOGICAL ISSUE

One of the challenges to ethical standards in journalism has been how quickly communication technologies have evolved as a means for journalists to gather the news, community members being able to report what is happening locally, and the audience members' ability to quickly consume the news efficiently. Poynter denotes this concern in their discussion about new technology. They argue that journalists must be able to "Apply our high standards for accuracy and attribution to anything you find using electronic services. Make certain a communication is genuine and information accurate before using it in a story" regardless of the speed of the world. Society has instant access to the news of the world on phones, tablets, and other smart devices.

Communication technology has fundamentally changed all social interactions throughout the world. The morning, afternoon, and evening editions of the newspapers became the hourly news reports on radio, leading to television newscasts and the 24-hour news cycle of cable news to finally instant news coverage via the Internet and smart devices. The speed of the news cycle seems to be getting faster and faster. The ethical consideration of this ethical area is that the news still needs to be presenting honestly. Avoid getting an incomplete story published for the honor of the first ones to break the story.

ENFORCING VIOLATIONS OF THE CODE

The last point to understand about journalism is what happens when a journalist fails to meet the profession's ethical standards. The most straightforward answer is that most nations do not issue a journalism license. No blacklist prevents journalists from working in the industry. This understanding means that it is up to the journalism community to focus on maintaining accountability and enforcement of ethical principles by calling out those that violate those principles. RTDNA highlights this in their section on accountability,

> Journalism accepts responsibility, articulates its reasons and opens its processes to public scrutiny... Responsible reporting means considering the consequences of both the newsgathering – even if the information is never made public – and of the material's potential dissemination.

The process of newsgathering is where most journalists can step in and help those that are not following good ethical practices by guiding them to improve the problematic actions. Journalism should be considered a community of practice that should be focused on improving the quality of journalism by training others on the ethical practices of newsgathering and reporting.

This need to improve journalism leads to the more significant point raised by the Poynter Institute in their section on enforcement, "No code can anticipate all problems, suggesting the need for consultation with supervisors whenever a potential problem arises." Any violation of journalism's ethical standards should invite discussion about how to resolve the problem and the actions needed for those resolutions. Those discussions should be open enough for feedback from enough sources that can provide a reasoned analysis of the problem and clarity of how to address the issue now and in the future. Otherwise, journalism will be more exposed to more criticisms by not addressing vital flaws in the industry's ethical standards.

CONCLUSION

Ethical journalism practices are crucial now, as the criticisms about journalism have reached a critical mass. "Fake news" has become the rallying cry of those threatened by the power of covering communities and putting a spotlight on the area in society that audiences should be aware of to make sense of what is happening in the world. Journalists must practice their craft beyond reproach. This chapter serves as a reminder to follow professional journalism standards and practices by crafting a code of ethics that matches the news organizations one might want to work for and the code of ethics established by the professional organizations.

BOOTCAMP PRACTICE

Write down a personal code of ethics for your writing based on the point raised in this chapter. It would be beneficial to reflect on any work completed in the past to help make this document more concrete. Otherwise, look over the professional code of ethics and S&Ps from organizations you might want to work for in the future.

ASSESSMENT OF THE MODULE

Basic: Complete a personal code of ethics before the end of the semester with a value statement.

Intermediate: Find the standards and practices statement of a media brand you like. How does this statement work with the personal code of ethics you have created?

Advanced: Show how you apply the code of ethics you have created to your journalism work. Provide three examples from past stories to show how you are following your code of ethics.

WORKS CITED

Benkler, Y. (2007). *The Wealth of Networks: How social production transforms markets and freedom*. Yale University Press.

Bugeja, M. J. (2019). *Living Media Ethics: Across platforms*. Routledge.

Carey, J. W. (2000). Some Personal Notes on US Journalism Education. *Journalism: Theory, Practice & Criticism, 1*(1), 12–23. https://doi.org/10.1177/146488490000100103

Carlyle, T., Sorensen, D. R., Kinser, B. E., & Engel, M. (2019). *The French Revolution: A history*. Oxford University Press.

Christians, C. G., Fackler, M., McKee, K. B., & Kreshel, P. J. (2020). *Media Ethics: Cases and moral reasoning*. Routledge.

Gutsche, R. E., & Hess, K. (2018). Contesting Communities: The problem of journalism and social order. *Journalism Studies, 19*(4), 473–482. https://doi.org/10.1080/1461670x.2017.1397933

Newman, N., Dutton, W. H., & Blank, G. (2011). *Social Media in the Changing Ecology of News Production and Consumption: The case in Britain*. Retrieved July 4,2020 from https://papers.ssrn.com/sol3/papers.cfm?abstract_id=1826647

Rae, S. B. (2018). *Moral Choices: An introduction to ethics* (4th ed.). Grand Zondervan.

Tilton, S. (2016). "Steve Jobs is Dead": iReport and the ethos of citizen journalism. In A. Davisson & P. Booth (Eds.), *Controversies in Digital Ethics*, (pp. 308-319). Bloomsbury.

CHAPTER 17: MATH FOR JOURNALISTS

One of the running jokes in our program is that math is a four-letter word. Students' faces contort into a look of panic when I mention that they need to take a math course to graduate. When the discussion of numbers comes up, a level of anxiety rises usually reserved for root canals, nails on a chalkboard, and seeing someone that has made your life miserable for years. We, as a field, need to understand mathematical concepts are more than just a requirement for a well-rounded student of the liberal arts to earn their degree.

Numbers are becoming more and more part of explaining what is happening in local communities. If journalism's definition is grounded in presenting truthful, compelling narratives about a community for an audience to understand and care about that community, then math is one of the core means to explain those relationships. Newsworthy stories are often dictated by changes to the community, something that exists outside the status quo, or a striking pattern of actions that impact community members' daily lives. All of those requirements for newsworthy stories can be discussed with the application of some mathematical concepts.

It's not just me in my position as a college professor that has expressed this need to be better at math. This chapter is directly influenced by Heather Dunn's lecture in 2017 during the Broadcast Education Association annual conference regarding how to help students find their footing in journalism, Robert Niles' excellent website about stats (http://www.robertniles.com/stats/), and the work of the Society of Professional Journalists in the form of their Journalist's Toolbox. It is fair to argue that this chapter is not a replacement for those resources, but rather this is a means to highlight some of the more basic mistakes that journalists still make in the course of gathering the news.

It is fair to argue that some readers of this book may not be convinced that math is a vital element of journalism and chose to enter the field with some sense of not having to face a pop quiz on statistics during a given work shift. The problem with that idea is that journalists that do not have a good grasp of math will tend to miss the big picture when it comes to newsworthy stories.

MATH AS A WAY OF GETTING TO THE TRUTH

Eesha Pendharkar told one of the stories that highlight the need for a foundation of math during the 2019 CMA/ACP conference. Pendharkar works at the Bangor (ME) Daily News. She was reporting on the crime rate in Maine dropping for the seventh straight year. The State of Maine Department of Public Safety initially sent out a press release noting a nearly 56% drop in all crimes over the past ten years in the state of Maine. It was a fantastic stat given by the Department of Public Safety. Unfortunately, it was a little off. Pendharker dug into the numbers and discovered that the actual drop in crime was around 44%.

Why were the two numbers different, and how did Eesha catch the mistake?

The table below shows a summary of the numbers as presented by the Department of Public Safety.

Total Crimes in the State of Maine from 2011 to 2018 ^		
Year	Total Crime	Percentage Change from the Previous Year
2011	35615	***
2012	35073	-1.52%
2013	32162	-8.30%
2014	27987	-12.98%
2015	26000	-7.10%
2016	23748	-8.66%
2017	21803	-8.19%
2018	19773	-9.31%
Reported Ten-Year Change by the MDPS ^ ^		-56.06%
Reported Ten-Year Change by Daily News ^ ^ ^		-44.48%
^ Source:	https://www.maine.gov/dps/msp/sites/maine.gov.dps.msp/files/inline-files/Crime%20in%20Maine%202018.pdf	
^ ^ Source:	https://web.archive.org/article/overall-crime-in-maine-drops-homicides-assaults-increase-new-data-shows/29560440	
^ ^ ^ Source:	https://web.archive.org/web/20200628174420/https://bangordailynews.com/2019/10/23/news/crime-in-maine-drops-for-the-seventh-consecutive-year/	

In the grand scheme of things, this statistical error could be considered minor as the end story is essentially the same as the rate in crime over the past seven years has dropped dramatically. The more significant point raised by Pendharker, and the point of this chapter, is that journalists need to go over those types of government documents and spreadsheets to see if the numbers make sense and report the patterns they raise.

WHY PRACTICING MATH IS VITAL FOR JOURNALISTS

There are five ground rules that all students taking my "Data Journalism & Infographics'" course should be comfortable with before producing their first story. The first ground rule is, "Don't drown in the data." There are two ways to read this rule. One way is that the reporter should not be overwhelmed by the number of statistical documents they uncover in the newsgathering process. All aspects of everyday life are documented and analyzed in some manner by either a government agency for making policy decisions, a non-profit organization to help others, or a corporation to make a profit on that information. Journalists need to be able to filter those datasets to tell a story. That is where understanding math helps reporters craft a narrative. The second way to read this ground rule is to ensure that numeral data in the story is not overloading the audience with information. This way to read the first ground rule leads to the second ground rule.

"Tell the narrative by showing your work" is a reminder that the information journalists get from those documents and datasets are assets to a story similar to how quotes and mediated works add to the overall story. A journalist must be transparent on where the information is when using numeral data. Include the archived URL in the article if the dataset is publicly available online. An **archived URL** is a snapshot of a website taken by a service like the Internet Archive's "Wayback Machine" to preserve the site for future reference and protect it from deletion or changes.

Government, organizational, or corporate documents that are not publicly available can be determined to be credible if the journalist explains the process they use to acquire that information. A **Freedom of Information Act request (FOIA)** is a useful tool in the United States to gain access to government datasets. There are state and federal letter templates a reporter can fill out to obtain the information from that government agency even if they do not know the name of the specific document or database file with the information they need to tell the story (Hopkins, 2018). There are versions of this act in various other countries for international coverage (Lagunes & Pocasangre, 2018; Cuillier, 2019). Once the documents and databases are gathered and archived, mathematical principles allow the narrative to appear from the collected information.

The third ground rule we go over is the "Spreadsheets, datasets, and other organizational documents show the priorities of that organization." I consider this one of the more overlooked elements of data journalism as it is one of the simplest of these ground rules. Journalists should pay close attention for three details when looking over a document:

1. the information or categories listed leftmost,

2. the information or categories listed topmost, and

3. the grouping of information or categories in the document.

The leftmost and topmost areas of a document or dataset are worth noting. Those would be the areas where the most critical information would appear as it is the most accessible section on a document, spreadsheet, or dataset. The rationale for this statement is based on a Western reading of text matching how Western society tends to read information from top-down and left to right while placing importance on the information presented in those spaces (Snell & Grainger, 2019). Noting how data is grouped can provide some contextual clues on how to interpret the information in the given file (Gong et al., 2018). For example, if the first column of a spreadsheet had "Last Name," with the next series of columns having the header row containing "First Name," "Street Address," "City," "State," and "ZIP Code," one would rightly assume that the purpose of the spreadsheet was to maintain a mailing list for a specific reason. The reason for acknowledging this ordering and level of importance of the information is directly related to the fourth ground rule for data journalism.

We talk about the "All spreadsheets, datasets, and other documents are created by people" after examining several spreadsheets and datasets in class. This point is also often overlooked. The files in questions typically come from an organization rather than an individual. It is rare to associate a person's face with a given document unless one understands the organization's inner-workings that produce those files. The rationale for remembering this piece of wisdom is that sometimes the records reflect personal agendas rather than an organization's mission statement.

This understanding of how personal influence can impact organizational documents leaves us with the final ground rule for data journalism. "Humans can screw these documents up because people can be fallible, unaware of all of the potential information to add to a record, or trying to hide something by leaving out information/purposefully making the content too hard to analyze." This ground rule gets us back to the Bangor Daily News example. It would be easy to argue the fallible position and assume no malice as it would be easy for those not trained to simply add up the percentages in the right column to come to the answer of -56.06% rather than subtract the total crime of 2018 from the 2011 figure and then divide that result from the 2011 figure to come up with the -44.48%. It comes from understanding how some essential math functions work and what they represent as a means for telling a story. The next section of the module will focus on the four areas of math that journalists should understand to tell better stories. We will start with an area of math with the most broad-reaching impact in storytelling, which would be the use of averages.

AVERAGES: MEANS, MODES, AND THE MEDIANS OF NUMBER SCALES

Averages are useful in journalism as they represent the parts of everyday life that people would consider the norm. The strict definition of **average** is the middle point of a given set of statistical numeral information. The problem is that there are at least three ways this middle point is determined (Godin, 2019). Journalists will deal with sets of numbers regularly as part of newsgathering. One of the first concepts to learn is that a journalist will deal with four types of number sets as those number sets are essentially based on the scale that they use to assign numbers (Stevens, 2010). Numbers will typically be associated with some sort of unit of information (Kille, 2015).

The most basic of these number scales are the nominal or categorical scale. **Nominal scale** refers to the idea that the number is a placeholder for a name. Think of nominal ordering as ordering a meal from a fast-food restaurant. The #1 could be a hamburger, fries, and a drink, #2 could be chicken strips, chips, and a drink, #3 could be a superfood salad, apple slices, and bottled water, and so on. The number is how those meals are classified on the menu. The way to find what meal people usually get is by getting the mode of this set. The **mode** is the most frequently occurring value of a given set of numbers. If ten people get the #3 meal from our previous example, six people get the #2 meal, and four people get the #1 meal, the mode would be the #3 meal of the superfood salad. Nominal sets are also known as **dummy sets**, as this method of analysis is

270

useful for social-scientific research (University of the West of England, Bristol, 2020).

The second type of number set is the one in which people or criteria can rank elements from a given set. This numerical scale is called an **ordinal scale**, as it places the elements in a set into a ranked order. There is no ability in this set to determine the degree of difference to which one item of the set is better than another. Let's extend the previous example, and we look at the bottom of the receipt where we can fill out a survey about our experience at the restaurant. One of the questions that seem to always appear in this type of survey is, "How would you rate the quality of your meal?" The choices for this question are typically, 'very unsatisfied,' 'unsatisfied,' 'neutral,' 'satisfied,' and 'very satisfied.' It is hard to put a numerical value on the differences between 'very unsatisfied' and 'unsatisfied.' The order of the elements is important, but the value of those elements is not important. The average of this set is determined by taking the median of the set. The **median** is the middle point of the data set when the values are taken from lowest to highest. If 15 people took the survey and one person was 'very unsatisfied,' two people were 'unsatisfied,' one person was 'neutral,' five were 'satisfied,' and four were 'very satisfied,' the median would be at the 'satisfied' level.

The last two types of scales both deal with named and ordered information sets with a proportional difference between the elements of the set. An **interval scale** means that a person knows the distance between two points of the scale. An example of this scale is looking at your phone to see the temperature outside. The weather app tells you it's 90 degrees Fahrenheit now and will be 45 degrees tomorrow morning. You know that it is going to be 45 degrees cooler tomorrow. You can't say it's going to be half as warm tomorrow than it is today. That's because zero degrees Fahrenheit is not the absolute zero of the temperature scale when we look at the weather. A **ratio scale** has an absolute zero. A person's height, money in a savings account, or a book's pages use a ratio scale. A textbook can have ten times the pages of a children's novel. It is possible to add, subtract, multiple or divide values on a ratio scale. It is only possible to add or subtract numbers on an interval scale. Knowing if some scale has a baseline allows the journalist to describe the information when comparing two figures.

Typically, the term average refers to the arithmetic mean. An **arithmetic mean** is found by adding up all numbers in a range of numbers and dividing by the total amount of numbers in the field. The arithmetic mean of a range of numbers containing {3,5,7,9} would be solved as:

$$(3+5+7+9)/4$$

$$24/4$$

$$6$$

An arithmetic mean is useful when the numbers you are dealing with either have no dramatic outliers (numbers that are fundamentally larger or smaller than the majority of numbers in the set), or the set of numbers has a **central tendency** towards the middle point of the range of numbers. The idea of a central tendency is also referred to as a **symmetrical data set** as no numbers are skewing the middle point of the range of numbers. It is possible to find the reasonable central location of a range by taking the arithmetic mean of that set (Kille, 2015). A skewed data set can only use a median to come to the average. The weekly average temperature of a city uses the arithmetic mean. Figuring out the average yearly income of a business usually is best served by finding the median. The reason for using the median for the average employee income is that the dataset more likely than not is going to be skewed. The average CEO of a company in the United States earns $15.6 million per year, while the typical worker in the United States earns $58,000 per year (Mishel & Schieder, 2017). The CEO and other executive-level workers are a small percentage of the overall workforce of a given company and would skew the dataset higher than the actual average should be. This breakdown of a given organization gets us to the next set of mathematical terms to be familiar with when reporting stories.

RATIOS: PERCENTAGES, PER CAPITA, AND OTHER RATES

If the average represents the community's norms, then ratios should be considered what part of a community we define ourselves in, based on a given situation. **Ratios** measure out the parts of a whole using easy to understand numbers. Fractions are often the first ratios we come across in school, as it makes it easier to describe how much of a cake or pizza one has taken. This understanding of fractions allows journalists to move to the next related ratio worth adding to stories.

Percentages are the parts per hundred of a given ratio. A percentage on a test notes how much of the hundred parts the student got correct. This fraction of the whole represents a meaningful relationship between a segment and the whole. Let's go back to the first example to clarify this point. The 44% statistic in the story has a couple of levels. The most basic way to interpret the data is the reduction in crime. Reading of the numbers would allow the person to get the impression that the police departments and sheriff's offices reduced in 2018 nine out of the twenty crimes reported in 2011. Another vantage point is what percentage of the population was affected by crime in 2011 and 2018. According to the U.S. Census Bureau, Maine's population was 1.328 million in 2011 and 1.339 million in 2018. These figures mean that crime impacted 2.68% of the people living in Maine in 2011 and 1.48% of the population in 2018. Types of crimes are also worth an examination. There were 23 murders reported in Maine in 2018, which accounts for .11% of all crimes in Maine and impacted .02% of Maine's population. It is worth mentioning that the percentages dealing with populations often use a different ratio.

Social and cultural factors that impact a population are shown using a rate of per 1,000 people for smaller towns, 10,000 for larger cities, 100,000 for states, or per 1,000,000 people for nations. It helps those looking at the numbers to account for population size in a measured way. It is also the standard adopted by organizations like the Federal Bureau of Investigations (n.d.) and the Center for Disease Control and Prevention (2012) to provide easily accessible datasets to the general public. When dealing with the financial information of a nation, one last rate gets used.

Per capita is the figure economists use to measure the average income that a person in a given area earns in a year. It tends to be used to show the strengths of different sections of a location's economy and reflects if the region is going through a recession during a range of years. The problem is that these figures are the arithmetic mean of the economic dataset. The skewing of this economic dataset will not present an accurate description of the area's financial strength.

The next set of math terms moves away from the numbers used by government agencies and non-profit organizations to the statistics produced by media organizations and other corporations.

SURVEYS: SAMPLE SIZES, OBJECTIVITY, AND ANALYZING RESULTS

One of the ways that journalists can present community issues is by asking members of the community their opinions about those issues and report back the results. The most common way to gather views from community members is by using a survey. **Surveys** are a means to gather people's opinions about real-world issues and convert them into numeral data points. Journalists will often use surveys to give the audience an understanding of how community members feel about a subject. However, a great survey can create a new vantage point to approach the issue's underlying factors or introduce the matter to the audience if they are not familiar with it.

It is easy to use surveys produced by outside organizations when reporting on an issue. Newsrooms' emails fill up with press releases from research institutions and non-profit agencies reporting out the latest results from their public polls, political surveys, and other means of gathering people's opinions about the state of the world. Journalists should look carefully at these surveys before including them in any story. Knowing who participated in the study can give the journalists a better sense of if the information presented in the survey results matches the reality of the community addressed in the survey. Doing some background research on who submitted the press release or survey result is useful to get a sense if that group is objective in creating the study and gathering its results (Smith-Frigerio, 2016).

There are a few requirements a survey and researchers need to pass before it is fair to call the survey objective. Reporting out of the survey result should give a detailed, quantifiable description of the **population** that the survey intended to cover and how the researchers ensure that the survey takers represent the diversity of the study population in the form of a **sample pool**. It is fair for the researchers to include the limitations of the survey process (how were the survey takers picked, who could potentially be left out of taking the survey, or any barriers or problems that impacted the ability to perform the study). The survey format must be **standardized** to ensure that everybody gets the same survey, and the survey's presentation does not influence people's answers (Gray, 2018).

The most common way that researchers will get the pool of survey takers is by using random sampling. **Random sampling** occurs when all possible members of a population are accounted for and have an equal chance of participating in the survey. Simple random sampling occurs when a random number generator or some other method to select people for the sample pool. Researchers will use a **stratified random sampling method** to make the sample more representative of the population as people are placed into strata based on demographic, psychographic, or other characteristics.

Another requirement to call a survey objective is that the survey has no loaded questions. **Loaded questions** are written using an underlying assumption that would be considered controversial as the central premise of the question. These types of questions typically violate two critical criteria of objective surveys. Loaded questions include a **priming element** that attempts to lead the survey takers to a specific answer or small subset of responses that they themselves would not usually pick. The example of this type of question is, "where did you hide the body?" If this is the first question of a conversation, it presumes a lot of information.

Loaded questions also use **imprecise language** to confuse the survey taker. A vague question makes it difficult to interpret the meeting of the question and allow the research to influence the survey taker's responses. Including ambiguity to the question by adding words with more than one meaning also enable the researcher to influence the responses. Understanding loaded questions would allow journalists to be more critical in the survey questions. This critical thinking is why researchers must include the wording of their questions when reporting the results of their surveys.

Beyond loaded questions, survey takers may also present an inaccurate representation of reality based on a simple bit of psychology. **Social desirability** can come into play when taking a survey as the survey takers might put down a response that they think is the socially acceptable answer for a given question instead of an honest answer (Wasylkiw, 2007). Issues dealing with taboo subjects like drug use and sexuality are the areas more likely to invoke a socially desirable response from the survey taker.

The last requirement for an objective survey is the process used to analyze the results. For numerically substantial studies, the next section will focus on determining the objective nature of the study. The surveys that have more textual responses are often called **qualitative surveys** or **questionnaires**. Those types of surveys or questionnaires will often require a thematic analysis to provide some conclusions. **Thematic analyses** are conducted by first recording all of the answers given by the survey takers. Those answers are slightly edited to get to the core of their response. This adapted response is called an **artifact** in social-scientific research. The artifacts are groups based on common elements in the responses, which become a series of themes that address the core of the questions posed by the research. The more artifacts that the researchers share to support their ideas means that those themes are more likely to be an objective representation of the sample pool's responses to those questions.

OBJECTIVE NUMERICAL DATA: NORMAL DISTRIBUTION, STANDARD DEVIATION, MARGINS OF ERRORS, AND THE SIGNIFICANCE OF STATISTICAL ANALYSIS

This section of the chapter will be a little more of a deep dive into what makes the data gathering from a survey useful for explaining the community's opinion about the issues they face. To do this section justice, we need to explain what makes central tendency a valuable marker for the norms of a community. The numerical responses for a given question of a survey should follow a **normal distribution pattern** in terms of the answers provided by the survey takers. The shape of this pattern is often a **bell curve**.

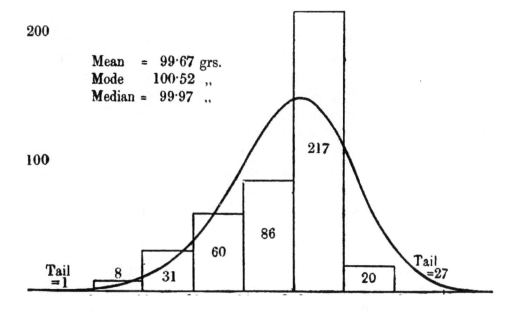

An example of a bell curve on a distribution bar graph with measurements of the averages of the graph from the 1921 book "The Essentials of Mental Measurement" written by William Brown and Sir Godfrey Hilton Thomson.

When a bell curve appears to be the distribution of answers for a survey question, the mean, median, and mode turn out to be very close together, if not the same value. This pattern of answer distribution gives the researchers some knowledge about the sample pool and the population as a whole. The first piece of knowledge that research gains with a bell curve is that they can identify the answers given by 68% of the sample pool. That range of answers is called the standard deviation. **Standard deviation** refers to the subset of answers close to the mean of the curve.

I sense that a little bit of panic is starting to rise in you.

Breathe.

Are you good?

Cool.

Standard deviation can be figured out in programs like Microsoft Excel, OpenOffice, or Google Docs using the STDEV function. Once you have that number, there are some fantastic pieces of knowledge you can learn about the set (Letkowski, 2015). For starters, researchers will note the probability that their distribution actually represented the population and did not occur by random chance. The term for this value is the **significance value** or the **p-score**. Programs like Excel can also determine this value. There is typically a Data tab, which will give you the opinion to select **t-Test for One Sample Mean**. A **Student's t-test** or **t-test** is a statistical tool that helps determine if the distribution of answers follow the bell curve. If the p-value in the t-test is less than or equal to .05, it is fair to say that the graph follows a normal distribution and is significant (Glen, 2019).

Knowing the significance of the distribution of answers can help us know the margin of error. According to Andrew Mercer (2016), the margin of error helps researchers (and the journalists reporting on the research) be a little more precise in their discussions about the issues.

> Because surveys only talk to a sample of the population, we know that the result probably won't exactly match the "true" result that we would get if we interviewed everyone in the population. The margin of sampling error describes how close we can reasonably expect a survey result to fall relative to the true population value. A margin of error of plus or minus 3 percentage points at the 95% confidence level means that if we fielded the same survey 100 times, we would expect the result to be within 3 percentage points of the true population value 95 of those times.

This value is useful as it tells the audience how far away from the mean the researchers expected the "actual" final result to be. This value is referenced during elections to show the general public how close the given races are expected to be. Adding the margin of error to the mean provides the upper range of the confidence interval. Subtracting the margin of error from the mean gives the lower range—those values within the confidence interval shows where the final result should be.

The final term to be familiar with is the trendline. **Trendlines** are estimations of the direction data is going through a graph (Cameron, 2005). These models of behavior are developed by plotting out the relationship between two variables on a chart using regression analysis. **Regression analysis** examines the impact an independent variable has on a dependent variable (Gallo, 2015). The relationship graphed by the trendline can be positive, negative, neutral, or no relationship at all.

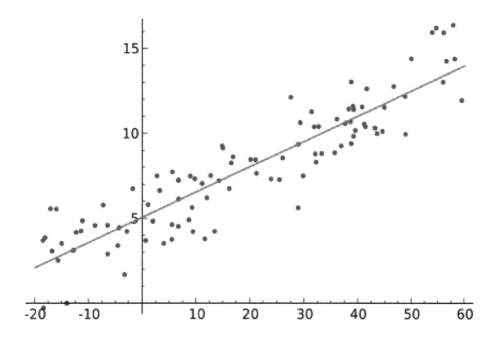

Data points placed in a regression analysis to show a positive trendline between the two variables. Created on Wikimedia by Sewaqu

CONCLUSION

It is fair to argue that most journalists still do not enjoy using math as part of their storytelling. The problem with that line of thinking is that many stories can be found by digging through the data. Surveys help clarify the community's position about issues of local importance. Datasets can explain the way that an organization operates. Governments can be the most transparent on spreadsheets even if the reports on those spreadsheets can misrepresent the issue's critical facts.

This chapter might not change your opinion on math. If you are one of the select few that were okay with math in high school, this chapter should be seen as a reminder of how to use math as part of a journalistic narrative. Those that are less than comfortable with math, hopefully you can use this chapter to help make sense of the statistical data that is out there in the real world.

BOOTCAMP EXERCISE

Pick an accessible public dataset from a government agency. Pick one variable from that dataset to create a distribution bar graph. Show the mean, median, and mode of that dataset.

ASSESSMENT OF THE MODULE

Basic: Find a story that uses an opinion poll as part of its narrative. How is the journalist using the data to enhance the narrative?

Intermediate: Using the distribution bar graph from the bootcamp, write a progression based on the chart's trendline.

Advanced: Write an article using the intermediate progression. Explain what those datapoints mean in your story and support those claims.

WORKS CITED

Cameron, S. (2005). Making Regression Analysis More Useful, II. In *Econometrics* (pp. 171–198). McGraw-Hill.

Centers for Disease Control and Prevention. (2012, May 18). *Principles of Epidemiology*. https://www.cdc.gov/csels/dsepd/ss1978/lesson3/section3.html.

Cuillier, D. (2019). Scandals and Freedom of Information. In H. Tumber & S. Waisbord (Eds.), *The Routledge Companion to Media and Scandal* (pp. 215–225). Routledge.

De Neve, J. E., Ward, G., De Keulenaer, F., Van Landeghem, B., Kavetsos, G., & Norton, M. I. (2018). The Asymmetric Experience of Positive and Negative Economic Growth: Global evidence using subjective well-being data. *The Review of Economics and Statistics, 100*(2), 362–375. https://doi.org/10.1162/rest_a_00697

Federal Bureau of Investigations. *The Nation's Two Crime Measures*. Retrieved June 30, 2020 from https://www.ucrdatatool.gov/twomeasures.cfm.

Gallo, A. (2015, November 4). *A Refresher on Regression Analysis*. Retrieved June 30, 2020 from https://hbr.org/2015/11/a-refresher-on-regression-analysis.

Glen, S. (2019, September 30). *Significance Level vs Confidence level vs Confidence Interval*. Retrieved June 30, 2020 from https://www.datasciencecentral.com/profiles/blogs/significance-level-vs-confidence-level-vs-confidence-interval.

Godin, S. (2019). What's the Problem?: Messing with mean, median, and mode. *Gazette: Ontario Association for Mathematics, 58*(1), 44–46.

Gong, K., Liang, X., Li, Y., Chen, Y., Yang, M., & Lin, L. (2018). Instance-Level Human Parsing via Part Grouping Network. *Computer Vision – ECCV 2018 Lecture Notes in Computer Science*, 805–822. https://doi.org/10.1007/978-3-030-01225-0_47

Gray, D. E. (2018). *Doing Research in the Real World*. SAGE.

Hopkins, W. W. (2018). *The U.S. Freedom of Information Act at 50*. Routledge.

Kille, L. W. (2015, March 16). *Math basics for journalists: Working with averages and percentages*. Retrieved June 30, 2020 from https://journalistsresource.org/tip-sheets/foundations/math-for-journalists/.

Lagunes, P., & Pocasangre, O. (2018). Dynamic Transparency: An audit of Mexico's Freedom of Information Act. *Public Administration, 97*(1), 162–176. https://doi.org/10.1111/padm.12553

Letkowski, J. (2015). *Doing Statistical Analysis with Spreadsheets*. Retrieved June 30, 2020 from https://www.una.edu/sobie/proc2015.pdf#page=10.

Mercer, A. (2016, September 8). *Understanding the Margin of Error in Election Polls*. Retrieved June 30, 2020 from https://www.pewresearch.org/fact-tank/2016/09/08/understanding-the-margin-of-error-in-election-polls/.

Mishel, L., & Schieder, J. (2017, July 20). *CEO Pay Remains High Relative to the Pay of Typical Workers and High-wage Earners*. Retrieved June 30, 2020 from https://www.epi.org/publication/ceo-pay-remains-high-relative-to-the-pay-of-typical-workers-and-high-wage-earners/.

Ricker, W. E. (1984). Computation and Uses of Central Trend lines. *Canadian Journal of Zoology, 62*(10), 1897–1905. https://doi.org/10.1139/z84-279

Robinson, S. B., & Leonard, K. F. (2019). *Designing Quality Survey Questions*. SAGE Publications, Inc.

Smith-Frigerio, S. (2016). *Polls & Survey Training*. Retrieved June 30, 2020 from https://www.schooljournalism.org/polls-survey-training/.

Snell, J., & Grainger, J. (2019). Word Position Coding in Reading is Noisy. *Psychonomic Bulletin & Review, 26*(2), 609–615. https://doi.org/10.3758/s13423-019-01574-0

Stevens, S. S. (2010). On the Theory of Scales of Measurement. In N. J. Salkind (Ed.), *Encyclopedia of Research Design* (pp. 971–973). essay, SAGE.

The University of the West of England, Bristol. (2020). *Data Analysis*. Retrieved June 30, 2020 from http://learntech.uwe.ac.uk/da/Default.aspx?pageid=1440.

Wasylkiw, L. (2007). Social Desirability Bias. *Encyclopedia of Social Psychology, 1*, 891–892. https://doi.org/10.4135/9781412956253.n527

CHAPTER 18: INFOGRAPHICS

Applying the mathematical information from the previous chapter in the structure of an article can be complicated as using text to explain the relationships discovered in the spreadsheets, organizational documents, and databases between Elements can create more confusion. Narratives on journalistic platforms are the most effective at being compelling when the text and media drive the underlying narrative of the topic, issue, point of interest, or event without being weighed down by getting into the technical side refinement that drives most explanations of numbers within a story. Numbers are vital in journalism as they provide essential relevance of the bonds explained in the story. Those numbers must be presented to amplify critical truths rather than confuse or repeat information. It is this necessity to include numeral and relationship data in a story that makes infographics an attractive asset for many articles.

These types of graphics were discussed in some detail in the fifth chapter of this book. It is fair to understand infographics as the visuals designed to clarify data. These graphics make information more accessible to the audience through understanding relationships between key points addressed in the graphic. One of the tangent benefits of using these assets is that they add a creative element to the telling of the narrative that enhances the story's aesthetics. Infographics' effective use transforms basic charts and spreadsheets into exciting works of art and reveals a central truth beneath the numeral content of datasets. The issue with this form of an asset is the artistic expertise it can take to craft such a work. This chapter will go over the rules for creating a quality infographic and some tools that can help a journalist design one.

INFOGRAPHICS AS PART OF MULTIMEDIA JOURNALISM STORYTELLING

In the fifth chapter, infographics were briefly covered in our discussion about graphics as a media enhancement. That discussion left out the rationale for their increased use in journalism. Benjamin Wiederkehr (2011), the editor of Data

Visualization, noted that infographics are useful as they are "visual representations of information, data or knowledge often used to support information, strengthen it and present it within a sensitive context. They are specific, context-sensitive and often times hand-crafted." This ability to represent information visually allows journalists to be thoughtful in the expression of vital numeral points that drive parts of the narrative.

It is fair to point out that the infographics are more natural to add to articles in the era of Disruptive Journalism as the tools of image visualization allow even those with limited artistic training to craft infographics that look reasonably good. Services like Canva, Piktochart, Venngage, and other services have basic templates that are commonly used in journalism with icons that readers can understand and connect with concepts in the story. The infographics can be arranged in short order as long as the journalist understands the relationships that they want to show off in the infographic. This understanding also means understanding how the audience needs this information to communicate with them.

Three journalism organizations are the models for infographic communication. Even though it is fair to argue that infographics have been around since the history of the human race. Rebecca Hagan & Kim Golombisky (2013) noted this use of graphics,

> The earliest humans on the planet shared information in pictures carved and painted on rocks and caves, not to mention tattooed on bodies. All over the globe, ancient peoples documented themselves and the world around them in pictographs from Japanese Kanji derived from Chinese ideographs to Egyptian hieroglyphics.

The visuals themselves were the mode of communication that was the most understood by the average citizen. *USA Today* took those hallmarks of communication and turned them into a compelling snapshot of reality at the bottom of every section's first page. Those creative graphics communicate to the audience an essential story from every section quickly and clearly.

Before *USA Today, National Geographic* would lay out dual-page maps that would explain the current geopolitical state of the world and diagrams that would highlight cultural interactions between people or natural movements of animals in the wild. These journalistic assets were pieces of art collected by fans of the magazine that would go above and beyond the work found in any textbook on the subject of anthropology, biology, or sociology. Those graphics provided clarity on the messy subject of living on Earth.

The last example to consider isn't a traditional news organization as the Pew Research Center is able to take their various research polls and turn them into short infographics that add contextual information about the issue they are discussing. These infographics can be used by a news organization to address the community's more substantial social and cultural issues.

Infographics work for professional news organizations as they have professional graphic designers that have access to an archive of artistic elements and software programs that allow the crafting of visual representation of Elements that can be understood by the audience. Professional infographic designers that work for those organizations rely primarily on graphic design programs to create their infographics works. However, practicing on any graphic design program (even a free one like Canva, Pixlr, GIMP, or Vectr) allows the journalists to find their creative voice in the software.

The issue comes up that a journalist can use the software but do not know what to say via the program. This writer's block happens when the journalist can not effectively communicate the complex concepts behind a story effectively enough to channel that information into the visual. Journalists need to feel comfortable mashing up the data with the design elements crafted in the software and the narrative already advanced by the journalist via the Writing Progression.

Therefore, the first bit of wisdom about infographics is to draw it out on a piece of paper. The infographic content will come from answering the following question: "What is the one relationship in my story that has the most connections with other Elements?" I try to answer this question with the same focus I would answer the primary truth question in a Writing Progression. The answer must be one or two declarative sentences long. The information in those sentences allows me to think about the icons and logos that might help me get that information across. **Logos** are the distinctive symbols that companies, publications, or other organizations use to identify themselves to the general public. At the same time, **icons** are the images that the audience can easily interpret for the image, as they closely mirror the real-world representation of the object in question (Lester, 2019). I will generally underline the parts of the sentences that lead to logos or icons that can be used in an infographic. Highlighting those critical elements in the sentence leads me to the next step in sketching out the work.

SKETCHING OUT AN INFOGRAPHIC

I borrow the next step in this process from Rebecca Hagan & Kim Golombisky's (2013) excellent text on graphic design and visual communication, *White Space is Not Your Enemy*. The model that helps me work on my design is the **Works-Every-Time model** they propose in their book. The model is adjusted to better serve the process for creating infographics.

Drawing out a general template on a sheet of paper (graph paper works the best for this practice) as a foundation for this graphic is often the first step. It seems that I always use a 5" x 7" rectangle with a 1/2" margin around the inside edge. This template gives me a 4" x 6" space to work. I will add a small 1/2" gutter in the middle of the rectangle from the top-down. This addition gives me two 1.75" x 6" rectangles to work within my design.

My choice of **central visual** will depend on the nature of the story. Pie, bar, or line charts work well if the critical relationship depends on introducing a significant amount of numbers into the story. **Line charts** are useful when explaining those relationships over time. **Pie charts** have their place when the ratios tell the story. Stories that involve several groups or factors within the community might need a **bar graph** as the infographic. Most spreadsheet programs can produce those charts quickly.

Factoid boxes use three to five facts in bullet point form to highlight the central pieces of information that the audience needs to know about the story. These infographics are the most effective when it is supplemented with a strong visual that the audience can identify with the facts in the box. For example, a dollar bill tends to be an excellent visual when the facts are about money.

Data maps are a reasonable way to approach the central visual for relationships based on the connection between numeral information and a given location. The best example of a data map is a weather map that uses numbers and colors to represent temperatures and icons to describe the overall weather that a given area will experience today, tomorrow, or sometime soon.

Diagrams are the most artistically demanding central visual as they offer details about objects, events, or locations to give the audience a sense of how the parts interact with the whole. These visuals only work if the audience can clearly identify the parts, and the audience easily understands the nature of their relationship. The IKEA instruction guide mentioned earlier in this book is a compelling example of a diagram as it shows how to put furniture together without the use of text (Lester, 2019).

Sketching out the central visual in the middle of the template is the next step. There needs to be enough room toward the top and the bottom of the visual to add necessary contextual information about the visual. The sketch will be rough, and that's fine. It does not need to be a perfect version of the visual as long as you get a sense of how it will appear within the space allotted.

Captioning the visual must be the next part of this process as the visual will need, at a minimum, three additional pieces of information to complete the work. An infographic must state all of the sources that the journalist used to get their data. This credit provides transparency to the process. It is also vital to include a simple description of the central visual to help the audience interpret the image. The last part is a brief explanation of how this visual fits the overall context of the story. I find that explanation the most useful element of the caption as it is important to remember that an infographic must be self-contained. All the information that the audience needs to make sense of the story must be included in the graphic. An infographic can get shared on social media without the rest of the story attached to it.

Captions appear as a rectangle near the central visual with an arrow pointing to a blank spot on the paper. That bare spot is where to write the three parts of the caption. The rectangle can be made larger if more information is needed.

Headlining the infographic means write five to ten words that hit the primary purpose of the infographic. This area is where journalists must summarize the answer to the question that kicked off this design. It must follow the practice of good journalism headlines by being a truthful representation of the reality presented in the visual and use short, active language to get the message across about the purpose of this graphic.

The last part of the infographic design includes any additional text about the graphic that can be beneficial to know while fitting into the template's space requirements. This **copy text** acts as the one or two final points about the story that are independent of the visual, headline, or caption elements but add value to the overall infographic. The infographic is finished with the inclusion of the brand's logo and/or some other form of **identification tag** to show the audience who created the infographic. Both the copy and the tag are sketched out as rectangles with an arrow pointing to the information those rectangles will include.

Congratulations, you have sketched out your first infographic. The next step is to fine-tune that sketch by going over the form and function of this journalism format.

THE FORM AND FUNCTION OF JOURNALISTIC INFOGRAPHICS

Benjamin Wiederkehr (2011) describing infographics as "visual representations of information, data or knowledge often used to support information, strengthen it and present it within a sensitive context" gets to the real power of infographics. They are most compelling when they are an aesthetically pleasing piece of graphic design (**the form of the infographic**) that communicates a central truth about a newsworthy topic, issue, point of interest, or event to a given audience (**the function of an infographic**). As described before, infographics are an asset to journalistic work. They are easily shared with others via social media, other electronic forms of communication, or face-to-face exchanges. Those graphics become the means that others use to support positions about issues affecting their community, point out reasons to care about a given topic, explain what a community point of interest is an area of local pride, or learn useful information about an event. Journalists should understand the rules of form and function to engage in that area of conversation with your audience.

THE INFOGRAPHIC RULES OF FORM

Infographics follow an aesthetic code from the previously listed examples in the chapter. Journalists do not need to be professional graphic designers but rather need an awareness of the styles and techniques used by past multimedia journalists to tell the story in the data. This style awareness means that journalists need to be more in turn with visual literacy. Visual literacy is not the same as practicing artistic techniques. Instead, this literacy type means knowing how to communicate with visual content as one would communicate using text effectively. Being visually literate means following these six rules.

1. **Conciseness is key.** Infographics should make one central point be the driving element within the visual. This one main point only works if the concept is both simple enough to be understood clearly without text, yet explains the complexity of the relationships within the main story. The conciseness level means that the visualization should describe the data with the text, providing a minimal amount of clarification.

2. **CRAPpy design is okay.** Robin Williams (2014) notes that four **Principles of Design** help maintain excellent aesthetic form. **Contrasting visuals** can help attract the audience's attention as long as those elements are not used to the point of losing meaning. **Repeating elements** are useful as those elements help viewers understand how to interpret the content on the screen. Audiences are trained by past media experience to learn the meaning of those elements. Those viewers are also looking at the way that visuals are **aligned** to determine what visual elements contain similar pieces of information. The **proximity** of the visual elements also informs the viewers which parts of the design are contextually related.

3. **Using the "Rule of Three" makes the message clearer to me.** The **Rule of Three** refers to a basic design concept that any well-crafted visual shall not here more than three different colors, different visual elements, or typefaces in the design (Buley, 2013). **Typefaces** refer to the family of related fontfaces. 12-point bold Times New Roman is a fontface, while Times New Roman is the typeface. There is a tangent rule called the Rule of Thirds that states dividing a space into three equally sized vertical and horizontal sections allows the designer the best spots to place visuals in the area. Namely, it's the space where two section lines intersect with one another.

4. **The typeface selected for the headline will amplify to the tone of the infographic.** One of the quotes I often say in class that came from a source that I can no longer remember their name or even find on Google is "Typefaces are the emotional tone of the written word." This quote is useful to remember as Times New Roman, Ariel, or Helvetic for the headline have been overused in most infographics. It is okay to search for a typeface on the graphic design program that you feel matches the tone stated in the headline. Graphic designers do it all the time.

5. **The infographic must use visuals that are relevant to the subject at hand.** It is vital to use images and graphics whose meanings are in line with the topic, issue, point of interest, or event being communicated about in the infographic while being timely to the discussion points raised by the visual.

6. **Visuals are more compelling if they give the audience a creative insight into the data that the audience hadn't considered.** Appealing graphics change the vantage point that the viewer has of the world.

The rules of form are not a complete education of all design practices. However, these six represent a good start toward approaching the design of the infographic. The next set of rules deal with the underlying communication functionality of the infographic.

THE INFOGRAPHIC RULES OF FUNCTION

Infographics in journalism must speak similarly to the other means that journalists use to communicate the news. We practice short, clear, and concise writing in most of the content we produce. The aspects of functional communication practiced by journalists are applied in infographics when the journalist recognizes what Elements are needed to tell the story. There are five rules of function that multimedia journalists must follow for the infographic to tell the data.

1. **Infographics must be transparent about which sources were used to craft the data in the graphic.** Journalists must double and triple the accuracy of the data within a given source. Audiences are less likely to

trust journalists when they use false or misleading data sources. The transparency that happens when the sources give the audience more comfort about the reliability of the infographic.

2. **Do not drown the audience in the data.** The only way an infographic is a useful asset is if it breaks the data down into manageable chunks of knowledge and simplifies the answers that come for the questions within the dataset.

3. **Restate the central conclusion raised by the data.** If the infographic follows the first rule of function, the journalist is allowed to explain why this infographic is essential to the audience. The headline and the copy can help with this restating.

4. **Incorporate more than one dataset if it's needed to explain a complicated relationship between Elements.** Some of the best infographics use multiple datasets together to finding a truthful narrative thread that can not be crafted from a single source.

5. **Infographics are still assets to tell a story.** It is up to the multimedia journalist to figure out the best use of the infographic for a given story. Sometimes, it is sharing in on social media to attract attention towards the bigger story.

Functional infographics follow the practices of excellent visual communication. Paul Martin Lester (2019) explained that visual communication depends on the audience seeing the central message within the observed content. The best visual communication messaging occurs when the designer makes it easy for the audience to sense the critical information within a given visual for them to select those details and perceive the underlying message from the optical data in front of them. Following these rules allows the audience to see the central message of the infographic clearly.

THE PROCESS OF DESIGN

Using a graphic design program only happens after a journalist knows that their sketch follows the rules of form and function. This point should make them more comfortable that they are effectively using the visual to tell the story. This part of the process will not be a tutorial of using graphic design program. As stated in the previous modules, the software developers will typically have access to better tools for instructing journalists on how to use the software. This section is more of a broad set of ground rules when using any software for this purpose.

- **Follow good naming conventions.** Most news organizations will have a system that journalists use to save their work. Learn it early and follow it. The system that I teach students to use is one that I learned while working video production when we did the transition from analog, linear editing to digital, non-linear editing in the early part of the 21st century. It starts with eight digits. This code represents the day of creation or editing a media asset. The first four digits are the year, followed by two digits for the month and two digits for the day. For example, July 4, 2020, would be coded as 20200704. I follow this naming convention because it is harder for me to lose files if I generally know what month they were created. The date is followed by an underscore (_), and the slug of the file. Slugs are two to four-word short descriptions about the content with each of the words separated by an underscore. Another underscore and your last name follow that slug. I can know everything I need to know about a file if it follows this naming convention. Use the one your organization mandate in their guide, otherwise use this one.

- **Save your work early and often.**

- **Every new element you add to the graphic should be on a new layer, if possible.** This practice minimizes mistakes in the design. **Layers** are the levels of a graphic file that design can use to focus on one aspect of the design. Most programs will support locking layers to prevent erasing or adding parts of the design by accident. Hiding layers is also common to give the designer a better sense of how elements are working together. These levels might have additional functions depending on the program.

- **Zoom in to at least 300% when working on a design.** This zoom level allows designers to hide some of their less-than-quality parts of the drawing.

- **Refer back to the sketch and make changes as needed.** The sketch is supposed to be a model to follow. It is not the final design. Work between the sketch and the computer to find the final design.

CONCLUSION

Being a proficient infographic designer does not mean being a great artist. It means knowing what makes for functional visual communication with the limitations of the design. Designers recognize the most effective means and modes of telling a story via the mediums of communication. Specifically, they know how to combine assets to tell the narrative in the data. Assets that graphic designers use do not need to be perfect, but they should fit the message's context and overall design perfectly.

BOOTCAMP PRACTICE

Find a publicly accessible dataset. What is the one relationship in that dataset that tells a story but is too complex to say with words alone? Sketch out an infographic and design it using a graphic design program.

ASSESSMENT OF THE MODULE

Basic: Find a story that uses an infographic as part of its narrative. How is the journalist using the infographic to enhance that narrative?

Intermediate: Create two to four infographics about the same topic, issue, point of interest, or event. How do those infographics enhance the audience's understanding of that subject?

Advanced: Write an article using two infographics that you created. Do an executive review of the story.

WORKS CITED

Buley, L. (2013). *The User Experience Team of One: A research and design survival guide*. Rosenfeld Media.

Hagen, R., & Golombisky, K. (2017). *White Space is not Your Enemy: A beginner's guide to communicating visually through graphic, web, and multimedia design*. CRC Press.

Lester, P. M. (2019). *Visual Communication: Images with messages (8th ed.)*. Lex Publishing.

Wiederkehr, B. (2011, February 21). *Visualizing the World's Well-being*. Retrieved July 5, 2020 from https://datavisualization.ch/opinions/visualizing-the-worlds-well-being/.

Williams, R. (2014). *The Non-Designer's Design Book*. Peachpit Press.

CHAPTER 19: CONTENT MANAGEMENT SYSTEMS

The foundation of all writing journalists produce comes from the understanding of the basics of the journalistic style of writing. This book, up to this point, has hopefully helped you improve in this area. Understanding this fundamental technique is just the first step in becoming an effective multimedia journalist. Multimedia journalists should be proficient in taking pictures, capturing audio, and using video to tell the full story. The expectation is not to master all of the skills. A journalist who has mastery in all of the above skills working in a community with a rich tapestry of stories to tell will find success in the industry. One of the last steps to go over is putting those pieces of media together to tell the story and publish the work so that the audience can experience those works. It is here that we will begin one of the last modules for the book through the discussion of content management systems.

This bootcamp is the most technical-driven of the module chapters. It will dive into the elements that help journalists and media organizations get their content out to the general public. Content management systems change as there are new web and communication technologies that keep the general public connected. This evolution of content management system software will continue as long as the Internet gives users new abilities to view the world and learn more about it.

DEFINING CONTENT MANAGEMENT SYSTEMS

Content management systems (CMS) act as the backbone of a media organization's online platform. This type of system is software (or a suite of software) that works by creating a database of stories where each part of the story is separated and organized on the platform's site. For example, the headline, summary of the story, pictures, the reporter byline credit, and the story itself are four separate parts of one story. The CMS can place the headline and summary of the story on the front page of the site. The audience can then click on the headline or summary to see the full story fit into the template designed by the platform to maintain its style. All of these pieces of the story are nothing more than pieces of data. We need to discuss metadata, as it is the language that CMS speaks to construct the site that the audience uses. **Metadata** is a subset of data that tells the CMS how to format other data, make it appear on the site, add additional information that other services can use to repurpose the data, and gives the actual content of the site the essence of an "actual message or information" (Mauthe & Thomas, 2007, p. 4) useful to the audience.

CMS gives the brand more control of the presentation of content by changing the themes and functionality of the system. In this context, **CMS themes** refer to the aesthetic look of the site and the underlying functionality that comes for work outside the customarily published content on the website. The files used to create the themes incorporate metadata in the form of a style sheet to tell the CMS how to look and where to grab assets to display. These sheets, known as **cascading style sheets (CSS)**, are responsible for all aspects of presentations. CSS controls the colors that appear on the screen, the fonts used for the text, how much space appears between stories, how big images must be on the page, and hundreds of other visual controls for the site (Clark, 2007). These sheets are robust as a designer can change those visible details of the website by typing a few words in the CSS instead of manually changing all of the visual components page-by-page.

CMS also maintains the organization's workflow as the system gives certain people the ability to publish a story. Editors and publishers are two of the roles within the CMS. **Roles** are assigned to the different accounts to give people more functionality on the site to publish stories, change the template to provide the site with a new theme, or other actions that help maintain the site's flow.

Three different CMS companies account for more than 40% of the websites online. WordPress is the most popular with three out of every ten sites using it as their content management system (Sawers, 2018). The reason for its popularity is that it is relatively easy to set up with user-friendly tutorials and thousands of programs known as **widgets** that can change the site's functionality to fulfill many different purposes. The other two CMS used often by journalistic organizations are Joomla and Drupal (W3Techs, 2020). Those three listed CMS are **server-side options**, which refers to the concept that a company can install the CMS on a server that can control most, if not all, of the performance (So, 2019). Companies like SquareSpace, Wix, and Blogger offer a journalistic organization a full-service set up of their site. Those companies do that by maintaining the servers that the site is hosted on, updating critical

,ecurity protections, and backing up the content from the site. These types of CMS are called **software-as-a-service or SaaS**. The journalistic organizations do virtually none of the technical support for the site (Barker, 2017). There are other sites like Medium that act as a journalistic CMS, but are more in line with the functionality of a social media service, giving them the moniker of **social journalism** (Hirst, 2018).

It is important to note that all of the CMS listed above are general-purpose solutions. They are not specifically for journalistic organizations. Tassos Morfis (2018) highlighted six criteria that would define the perfect CMS for journalists.

1. A CMS that enables journalists to easily create multimedia stories and follow them up because they matter to the community.

2. A CMS that enables journalists to easily create, share, pursue and monetize multimedia stories that matter, globally.

3. A CMS that enables journalists to find out at a glance which stories have the most impact with the audience in terms of being shared and the greatest amount of dialogue between verified community members via comments.

4. A CMS that enables journalists to fix problems with the site quickly and easily.

5. A CMS that enables journalists to follow up on important stories that maintain the thread of information between stories dealing with a similar subject.

6. A CMS that enables journalists to secure a steady income for their labors.

Most national and international news organizations have built their own CMS to hit those six criteria. This building of a bespoke solution for a journalism organization is called **home-brewed** (Loukissas, 2019).

A CMS is useful for keeping the news organization in control of the content coming into the newsroom. Newsrooms are only as good as their content. The next part of the analysis will focus on how the content gets from the fingers of the journalist to be published on the site in the era of CMS. This process means understanding the two workflows that are occurring at the same time.

PERSONAL AND PLATFORM WORKFLOWS

A **workflow** is how content makes its way from the journalist to publication. The first of the two workflows that drive most news organizations is how all journalists within the newsroom connect to publish their content. This level of workflow is platform-level. **Platform-level workflows** are programs that keep track of the stories that everybody is working on in the newsroom and their current status. For example, even a smaller newsroom uses a platform-level workflow. Airtable is a site that the Northern Review journalists use to manage the editors' day-to-day activities and the rest of the staff. It is a cloud database that has fields for:

- story slug,

- date of the event,

- the story status (in progress, first draft submitted, final draft submitted, published, or archived)

- the reporter responsible for the story,

- the editor that the story needs to be turned in,

- the date the article was assigned,

- rough draft deadline,

- final draft deadline,

- publishing deadline,

- who's responsible for promoting the story on social media,

- when the article will be published on social media,

- the section/categories the article will be published under,

- photos for the story,

- the URL of the story, and

- any other notes about the story.

This information is the lifeline of our paper. It keeps all of the journalists on the same page regarding who is doing what across the organization. Professional news organizations will use the systems either use:

- ENPS from the Associated Press,

- a system created by a central office (e.g., Presto for Gannett),

- a workflow package of software specifically designed for newsroom (e.g., K2 or Desk-Net),

- a widget embedded in the CMS (e.g., jetFlow), or

- a more simple cloud-based database (e.g., like our use of Airtable).

Journalists must be familiar with whatever system your organization implements and stay on top of what is happening in the workflow. There is still a trend to have a pitch meeting work in line with the platform-level workflow. A **pitch meeting** occurs anywhere from once a month for magazines to three-times-a-day for international news organizations. The editorial staff will highlight the stories and assign them or let reporters pick the story they want. Those assignments get placed in the workflow, and life in the newsroom continues.

The next level of workflow is interconnected with the platform-level workflow. **Personal workflows** act as an accountable sheet for the stories that one has in the pipeline at any given time. These types of sheets tend to work well as a spreadsheet. My personal workflow is called "Story Rundown." I use a Google sheet that has the following columns:

- Title,

- Post #,

- Original Post #,

- Date,

- Status (Title, Draft, Published, Archive),

- Category,

- Feature Pic (600x600) (yes or no)

- Banner Pic (1800x500)

- Strata,

- Work,

- URLs, and

- Notes

It looks like the platform-level workflow but allows me to direct my time, attention, and focus on the next story. The first step in creating a new article for my site is to give the story a temporary title and a one-paragraph description of what I want the story to be about. This stub is given the "title" status. My CMS generates a post number for the article, and I put that information in the spreadsheet. I had to rebuild my site several years ago. This rebuilding process forced me to use new numbers for some of my articles, thus requiring an original post number column. The story becomes a "draft" once I've got several paragraphs for the essay. Date refers to when the post was added to the site either in draft form or the final publication. Every story that I write must have a feature and banner pic to work well with my theme.

A personal workflow should fit the needs of the writer. For example, I include the Strata column to explain what version of the site the story originally _ared online. There have been ten versions of my website. Finally, I like to know where I was working during the time I published the article. All of this information is useful to me but probably would have no use to you. Design a personal workflow that allows you to be as productive as you need to be. If I've finished the first story in the rundown, I will work on the first draft in the sheet. If all of the drafts are done, I work on any articles that are just the titles and brainstorm some new articles.

Understanding good workflow practices will allow you to take the next step in the process. Journalists need to transfer their stories from the workflow and add them to the CMS.

BREAKING DOWN CMS FUNCTIONALITY

There are other guides out in the world that will help you more in terms of setting up a CMS "out of the box." This chapter will not cover that part of the process as the company that produces those CMS will do a far better job supporting you in developing your new site. The technical aspects of setting up and maintaining a website using a CMS would fill a whole book. The rest of the chapter's focus is on how to put a story into a CMS.

This point of the module is the area that my students are trained on the "Tilton's Laws of the Academic Universe." Specifically, we discuss the second rule, "Technology especially fails when you especially need it." It is better to write out the story using Microsoft Word or OpenOffice and save the document every ten minutes and anytime you remember to save your work. Another option is to use a service like Google Docs or Grammarly to write as it tends to back up the writing automatically in the cloud. It is a bad idea to start writing a story in a CMS as it can crash, and the story would be lost. CMS are great for publishing stories and not great being the place to start writing them. This reference to losing a story brings up rule #32, "You must remember to back up correctly or else." Backing up correctly means having three copies of the same file in two different formats, with one of those copies being in the cloud. This process is referred to as the **3:2:1 rule** (Ruggiero & Heckathorn, 2012).

Completing the story and knowing where all of the mediated elements should appear in the content means you are ready to upload that article to the CMS. The next series of sections will treat that content as the first story you have published for the platform.

CREATING AN ACCOUNT

There are three pieces of wisdom I can offer about creating an account for a journalistic CMS.

1. **Make sure the name you want to be known by is placed early on in the system.** Drupal will assign a name based on the email address used to open up the account. The longer that email name remains associated with your account, the more problems come up (security, finding older articles, identifying the author, etc.). Using a standard name allows you to build your reputation early on the platform.

2. **Take a picture of yourself that matches the mood of the platform.** This advice is not the same as taking a professional headshot with business attire. Instead, it is helpful to see the photos other journalists use for their bios and adopt elements of the writing staff's collective style. Choosing the style of the writing staff should not seem fake. If you can not pull it off, go with the professional headshot in business attire. It is better to dress up to maintain a sense of journalistic ethos.

3. **Write a short bio.** Writing 100-to-200 words about you as a journalist and how you fit into the platform's overall scheme is one of the first steps in finding your voice on the platform. The bio is what makes you unique as a journalist but shows why you are a credible journalist for the platform. Once again, look at your colleagues' bio to see the acceptable style for the platform.

Once those bits of housekeeping are done, you can start putting the story together for the website.

DRAFTING A STORY

Every CMS starts the process of drafting a story differently with the preface that you have the correct role or set of permissions to add a story to the CMS. Drupal will give you several options, including article, basic page, blog post, event, slideshow entry, webform, and others, depending on the modules added to the CMS. WordPress has options for posts, pages, media, and other content, depending on the widgets added to the site. Joomla allows users to upload stories and other content.

Most media organizations have a guide for using their CMS. Follow that guide when possible. The rest of the sections on CMS can be used if there is no guidance from the organization on how to add elements to the CMS.

TITLE/HEADLINE

Headlines are the first component that a journalist crafts to gain the interest of the audience. A compelling **headline** must be factually correct regarding what it implies and connect with the audience through easy-to-understand and selecting language that sets the tone of the rest of the article (Mann, 2004). The tough part of hitting all of those marks is making the headline 6 to 12 words. This limit is reached by not using articles, conjunctions, or unidentified pronouns in the headline's construction while creating a sense of urgency in the brevity of the title (Taylor, 2020).

There are five additional questions I use to determine the quality of the headline. The first question is, "Does the headline end with a question mark?" A headline framed as a question violates **Betteridge's Law of Headlines**, "Any headline that ends in a question mark can be answered by the word no" (Betteridge, 2009). The law tells you it is the waste of a headline to frame it as a question. The other four groups of questions come from Dr. Merlin R. Mann (2004):

1. Is it in good **taste** (using precise language to get the message across to the audience and not offensive in any way)?

2. Does it **attract** the reader's attention?

3. Does it clearly and quickly **communicate** the central theme of the story (no confusion through the use of odd words or double meanings)?

4. Is it presenting an accurate **truth** (both in the proper terms for the situation and "the thrust of subject-verb")?

Mann refers to this as the "TACT Test." The headline must be rewritten if any of those questions can be answered with a "no."

SUMMARY

A **summary** is a short description of the article that is accessible to the audience. It is important to add two or three tags from the story as those act as the keywords for the article. **Keywords** are words that attract the attention of social engines to help people find your story. They pop up on a search engine when they are looking for similar subjects to the ones addressed in your story. Knowing the right keywords comes down to what you would use to find this story on a search engine.

BODY

The story will simply need to be plugged into this section of the CMS at this point in the process. The only elements to be careful of are those elements that are embedded in your story. Most professional CMS allows journalists to upload audio and video content and maintain the style of the website. CMS can format media content to fit the context of a platform. This formatting is called adding a **wrapper** to the content. Wrappers are simply pieces of code that inform the CMS on how to use a piece of media on the site.

Most of the newer versions can auto-generate the embedded media from many services. We use SoundCloud to upload audio to the web. The previous method of including an embedded audio file from SoundCloud was changing the text in the body to plain text and copying the embedding code from SoundCloud. The current version of WordPress, Drupal, Joomla, and other CMS can simply take the URL of the embedded file and turn it into embedded content.

The last bit of wisdom is to use the preview button before uploading the story. This information is useful for two reasons. It helps make sure that your format of the story looks right. There are times that the CMS can add extra spaces, change the formatting of images, or other quirky things that impact the look of your story. The other reason is that you want to make sure that the embedded links in the story are visible. Some CMS will not natively underline links. It is vital to give embedded links contrast compared to the standard body text in the story.

PHOTO

Most of the information dealing with photos was addressed in the photojournalism chapter of this book. The only additional wisdom to add is to be aware of how the CMS formats images. This formatting can stretch out images, skew the focus, or crop it in a way that loses vital visual information from the photo. Previewing the pictures before they are published will inform you if you need to edit the image to have it fit in the story.

Adding the right metadata is critical when dealing with images. There are three different fields that most CMS use. **Title** or **Caption** fields should be the photo caption, as described in the chapter on photojournalism. **Alternate Text** is the straightforward description of the image that the visually impaired get in their screen reader programs and the information that search engines use in the search queries for images. There might also be an **Image Theme Text** or some language similar to that. This field is where additional information about the image goes. Typically, these fields are addressed in the media organization's CMS style guides.

CATEGORY

These next two sections get into the organization of the CMS. **Categories**, like the sections of Legacy Journalism publications, represent the different areas of a site that still fit into the overall purpose of that given platform. They represent a top-down view of how the story fits into the platform's overall context as it is the editorial staff of the platform that defines these categories.

Each category on a website must have a discrete definition for every story to be put in a unique category. It is beneficial to see the description to make sure that your article fits into the context of the category. The next best opinion is to look over thirty or more stories in each category to see how each of the categories is different for one another.

TAGS

Tags are the keywords that journalists use to define how their story fits the rest of the site's context. These keywords are useful as they allow search engines to find your article based on the search queries that the user of the search engine put into it. All tags are based on existing words and concepts. It is fair to examine other stories on the website covering similar subjects to see which tags make the most sense to add to your story.

Multimedia journalists need to be aware of the tags that are commonly used on the site. A good rule of thumb is that an article should have a minimum of six tags and a maximum of eight with at least one of those tags being one of the twenty most popular tags used on the site. Three of the five to seven remaining tags must have been used at least three other times on the website, with the last two to four tags either being new keywords or hashtags associated with the topic, issue, point of interest, or the event. Those original tags can be the key actors, locations, or essential aspects of the story.

OTHER METADATA

It is fair to let any other field on the screen blank unless you are explicitly told to fill it in with some information. CMS style guides should guide you in this area.

CONCLUSION

CMS are the means of distribution of multimedia journalists to get their stories out to the public. These flexible software packages allow media organizations to place stories into various platforms and allow for community interactions to shape the direction of the conversation. Systems like Drupal, WordPress, Joomla, Medium, SquareSpace, Wix, and Blogger still require great multimedia journalists to tell the community's stories by formatting their work in the CMS for the audience to see it once it is published.

BOOTCAMP EXERCISE

Open an account on a CMS. Fill out all of the account information, including the name you want to use on the account, a picture representing you, and your journalism bio.

Practice creating a story on the site using a story that has been covered by a national news organization. Include at least one picture, one YouTube video, and one embedded Tweet with a caption for each of these elements. Use three embedded links in the story from credible sources. Add six tags to the story that fits a news organization CMS standards for tags. Write the headline and summary based on the suggestion given in this chapter.

ASSESSMENT OF THE MODULE

Basic: Write ten new headlines for stories that are already published. Review the work that you did.

Intermediate: Practice using a service like SoundCloud to upload media. Fill out the fields when you are uploading the media in order to provide a detailed description of the content that was uploaded.

Advanced: Produce five stories using a CMS. Review the work that you did.

WORKS CITED

Barker, D. (2017, February 1). *An Unofficial Guide to Whatever-as-a-Service*. Retrieved July 1, 2020 from https://gadgetopia.com/post/9981/.

Betteridge, I. (2009, February 23). *TechCrunch: Irresponsible journalism*. Retrieved July 1, 2020 from https://web.archive.org/web/20090226202006/http://www.technovia.co.uk/2009/02/techcrunch-irresponsible-journalism.html.

Cabot, J. (2018). WordPress: A content management system to democratize publishing. *IEEE Software, 35*(3), 89–92. https://doi.org/10.1109/ms.2018.2141016

Clark, D. (2007). Content Management and the Separation of Presentation and Content. *Technical Communication Quarterly, 17*(1), 35–60. https://doi.org/10.1080/10572250701588624

Hirst, M. (2019). *Navigating Social Journalism: A handbook for media literacy and citizen journalism*. Routledge.

Loukissas, Y. A. (2019). *All Data Are Local: Thinking critically in a data-driven society*. MIT Press.

Mann, M. R. (2004). *Headlines*. Retrieved July 1, 2020 from https://web.archive.org/web/20041108032317/http://www.columbia.edu/itc/journalism/isaacs/client_edit/Headlines.html.

Mauthe, A., & Thomas, P. (2007). *Professional Content Management Systems: Handling digital media assets*. Wiley.

Morfis, T. (2018, May 9). *Is a CMS Out there that Journalists Actually Love?* Retrieved July 1, 2020 from https://medium.com/journalism-innovation/is-a-cms-out-there-that-journalists-actually-love-5c7f707e2173.

Ruggiero, P., & Heckathorn, M. A. (2012). *Data Backup Options*. Retrieved July 1, 2020 from https://www.us-cert.gov/sites/default/files/publications/ data_backup_options.pdf.

Sawers, P. (2018, March 5). *WordPress now powers 30% of websites*. Retrieved July 1, 2020 from https://venturebeat.com/2018/03/05/wordpress-now-powers-30-of-websites/.

So, P. (2019). The Server Side: From Monolithic to Decoupled CMS. In *Decoupled Drupal in Practice* (pp. 11–20). Apress.

Taylor, M. (2020, June 17). *Headline Writing: 19 ways to write irresistible headlines*. Retrieved July 1, 2020 from https://www.ventureharbour.com/writing-great-headlines/.

Tilton, S. (2020). *Tilton's Laws of Academic Universe*. Createspace.

W3Techs. (2020, July 1). *Usage Statistics and Market Share of Drupal*. Retrieved July 1, 2020 from https://w3techs.com/technologies/details/cm-drupal.

W3Techs. (2020, July 1). *Usage Statistics and Market Share of Joomla*. Retrieved July 1, 2020 from https://w3techs.com/technologies/details/cm-joomla.

CHAPTER 20: CRAFTING EXECUTIVE SUMMARIES

The last of these modules is less about the craft of journalism but instead teaches a template to create a media project that fits within a given brand. This module is typically completed by those that want to create a podcast, online show, or some form of limited series. An executive summary acts as an elevator pitch for the content and the starting place of a "proof-of-concept" pilot for a show. The ultimate purpose of this document is that the person responsible for creating this work should feel more comfortable discussing the project with others and have a clearer vision of the shape of the project after the completion of all of the work listed in the executive summary.

EXECUTIVE SUMMARY

An **executive summary** is a document created before any work begins on a mediated project. It gives a framework to the content creator for all actions and resources needed to complete a project before a deadline. Logically, this document is part of the pre-production process discussed earlier in this book. Executive summaries are a vital part of media production as it will save time, money, and personal planning out if the project is feasible. The more specific and clearly written the executive summary is for the people responsible for approving content, the more likely the project will be accepted.

The version of the executive summary I use in class is one I learned from Michael Williams when he taught at Ohio University. I found this form was one of the more straightforward means of getting the core details of a given media project and was flexible enough to work for a variety of communication projects. We used this model of summary for interactive media projects to show a client all of the work necessary to craft a final product that would meet the client's standard and fit the primary purpose of the given project.

PURPOSE

Clearly presenting the purpose in the first several paragraphs of the document allows all parties to have a deep understanding of the overall media work required to complete the project. **Purpose** for an Executive Summary is the rationale for creating this work. This rationale goes beyond the motivation of crafting this idea. It provides a broad stroke of the subject areas being covered in the project. This level of detail should also show the connection with the people responsible for creating this project. It is beneficial to include in this section to describe what the talent, location, or even occasion adds to this particular project.

The purpose section of the proposal must clearly define the expected objectives of the project. The minimum requirement for this section is a full paragraph (3 to 5 sentences) and must be coherent enough for a layperson to understand the rationale. If this was the only information given to a prospective client, they should have a simple understanding of what will be in the project. These objectives should also not be too narrowly defined as it may limit what you can place in the project and should not be too abstract to confuse.

For example:

> The purpose of this project is to create an interactive catalog for the Dairy Barn in Athens, OH, for their annual "Bead Show." The catalog should showcase the feature pieces of the show and allow the user to see the different aspects of the show through a series of pictures and informative content explaining the pieces of art. By viewing this multimedia catalog, the user should have a more in-depth understanding of the show and the artist's work. Fallout Shelter Productions, LLC is able to craft this interactive catalog due to their past work in both interactive technologies and their previous work with museums and other artistic arenas. Scott Alexander and Liesi Lambert are the perfect selections for the hosts of this catalog. They both have worked with the Dairy Barn in the past. Their knowledge in beadwork will give the audience a keen insight into the amount of talent needed and creative expressions embedded in each of the pieces on display.

Purpose sections divide up into two parts: the clients' objectives and the expectations of the audience. The better this section is fleshed out, the less time you will spend designing your project's skeleton. The clients' objectives usually sound like an elevator pitch, where the clients learn about the benefits of this project. Talking about the audience's expectations allows the content creator to go over the project's general takeaways.

One of the last elements to include for a purpose section is to explain what shows are already out there, covering areas similar to those mentioned previously. An excellent purpose section must tell why the show presented in this document is fundamentally different from those that are already being broadcasted or published. This defense of the show must be more than describe what the show's talent brings to the subject matter or even the slight differences in the format structure. It must be a deep dive into why this show will find an audience.

AUDIENCE

The first chapter introduced a simple definition of the audience. Audiences being "the people that read, see, or listen to the work that the journalist produces" need some more refinement to fit the executive summary concept better. A reasonable audience section has three parts to flesh out the requirement for this section.

The first part of the audience section must have a general definition of who would be interested in the proposed project. Writing this part requires understanding the demographic characteristics of people interested in the subject matter, as listed in the purpose section of this summary and those that would spend the time watching, reading, or listening to the project. The center of this Venn Diagram is the group that makes this section of the summary.

Demographics are the identifiable elements that researchers and media professionals use to group segments of a given population. The most common recognizable features used for this purpose are age, gender, income, level of education, marital status, employment, homeownership, geographical location, household languages, disabilities, household size, race, and ethnicity (Pollock, 2014). The style of demographics uses in this type of document relates to the various demographic elements being "more likely" or "less likely" to be interested, be willing to watch (or listen to or read), be a financial supporter, or be a fan of the project proposed in this summary (Chekima et al., 2015).

The next level of audience analysis is a little tricky as it addresses the needs, wants, and desires of those demographic groupings. **Psychographics** refers to studying people's attitudes and aspirations for market research (Walls, 1975). It is fair to focus on hobbies, interests, and other tangible actions that people in those demographic groupings highlighted in the first part of the audience section. This section's critical component is tying those hobbies, interests, and actions to the purpose section and explaining why those activities would connect the people to the show (Kahle, 2018).

An audience section of an executive summary should conclude with a hypothetical example of an audience member who would be interested in reading, listening, or watching the project. An **ideal audience member** is a character sketch of an imagined person that would be a fan of the work. This write-up must name this individual, the demographic characteristics that define that person, the psychographic elements that drive their personality, and their rationale for being a fan of the project.

Each of the three parts of this section must be at a minimum of one full paragraph containing four to five sentences. It must be coherent enough that if this were the only information given to a prospective client, they would have a simple understanding of the basic demographics of this project and the demographics of the topic covered in this project.

For example:

> The audience of this catalog would more likely be to skew toward females over 35-years-old, live in Athens county, and be middle to the upper class. This demographic would be less likely to be computer literate than the rest of the United States' general population. Based on public data of the area, this group would also be more likely to own computers five to seven years old and would be less likely to have new computers in their homes.

Fans of this type of work should enjoy the local culture and the artistic works of the Appalachian region of the United States. They would most likely be open to newer creative experiences that are not traditionally found in art museums. They would be interested in quirky and original exhibits that speak to the human condition.

Betty Beadlin, a 52-year-old female who has lived in The Plains all of her life, is an imagined ideal audience member. She loves attending various student shows at the Ohio University School of Fine Arts in the Trisolini Gallery and the Department of Visual Communication student exhibits in Studio 4. Betty goes to several of the "Uptown Athens" events throughout the year and goes on the "30 Mile Dine" tour once a year.

A proper audience analysis allows those responsible for signing off on the project to feel comfortable that the content creator has a keen understanding of the audience, which signifies that the project can be successful.

RESOURCES

Discussing resources in an executive summary is vital for this type of document. It shows those in the industry that the content creator can be efficient in their use of outside support. **Resources** are the assets that a content creator has direct control of in order to craft a given piece of content. The general categories of resources are money, time, equipment, personal, locations, and other pieces of content (Blaschke & Hase, 2019).

The resources section of the proposal must have a general description of what content you have to put into this project, who will be needed to finish this project, how much money is required to complete this project, and should have a preliminary timeline for the project. Usually, this section has several full paragraphs (3 to 5 sentences) or a series of laid out bullet points along with a couple of resource charts. This information must be coherent enough that if this were the only information given to a prospective client, they would have a clear understanding of what will be needed to finish the project.

For example:

> As of right now, we have every piece of art as a jpeg file, with a description of each art piece (title, date of creation, etc.) and a bio of each of the artists. We also have the history of this art show as a text file and pictures from the previous "Bead Show." We also have the PR media packet from the Dairy Barn. What we are going to need is some interviews from some of the key artists, the director of the Dairy Barn, and a couple of days to shoot in the inside of the Dairy Barn after the show is set up.

SAMPLE PROJECT BUDGET

Description	Quantity	Unit Price	Total Cost
Blank DVDs	650	$0.50	$325
Authoring Cost (per hour)	10	$90	$900
Videography Production Crew (per member per hour)	48	$40	$1,920
Studio Time (per hour)	8	$50	$400
Editing (per hour)	10	$50	$500
Digital Rights: Background Music #8B1	1	$550	$550
Color Correction & Final DVD Production (per hour)	10	$40	$400
Catering and Other Misc. Crew Expenses	****	$1,500	$1,500
Final Budget			$6,495

SAMPLE PROJECT SCHEDULE

Date	Task
January 15th	Begin compiling all of the digital assets (jpegs of artwork, text files, archive videos) into a file structure.
January 18th	Compiling is finished, the Bead Show is being set up
January 20th	Bead Show is set up, and video crew shoots the inside of the Dairy Show
January 21st	Shot tear down, beginning to edit together footage
January 22nd	Editing continues, begin interviews in Studio C, WOUB, 5th Floor
January 23rd	Second day of interviews, Dairy Show footage edited into packages for the catalog
January 24th	Last day of interviews, the graphics team creates backgrounds, the rest of the team works on the code and structure of the catalog
January 25th	Interviews are edited, the final catalog is fully edited and is hard storage on-site, and the test DVD is shown to the client.
January 27th	Any last-minute edits are finished as per client wishes.

January 30th	Artwork for the outside of the DVD case and on the DVD is finished and approved by the client. Final prints are delivered in the evening
February 1st	Final approved DVD is copied onto the DVDs for distribution
February 2nd	Catalogs are ready for distribution in the morning, and Bead Show opens at 6 PM.

The classic adage about a project is vital to remember as a project isn't a project until it has a series of defined actions, a person responsible for overseeing the completion of those actions, resources to help achieve those actions, and a deadline to get those actions done. The purpose section of the Executive Summary explains the first two parts, while the resource section explains the last two.

SUPPORT STRUCTURE OR SYSTEM OF SERVICE

The last actual part of the pre-production planning is explaining what is going to happen to that piece of content after production work is done. This discussion is framed in one of two ways. If the content is a one-shot project, we use the term system of service. An ongoing series or long-term work arrangement will discuss the support structure for the project's continuing progress. The reason for the different languages is the expectations the content creator should set for the post-production process.

A **support structure** section of the proposal must clearly define what you will need:

- to maintain the quality of the project,

- in terms of the system of distribution after each episode or segment is finished,

- in place to continue supporting this project in terms of revenue and, most importantly,

- after the initial set-up/creation of the project.

Writing up a support structure section requires a full paragraph (3 to 5 sentences) for each of the bullet points listed above. This section of the Executive Summary must be coherent enough that a prospective client should have a simple understanding of what will need to keep the project continuing throughout the run of the project.

A **system of service** section of the proposal must clearly define:

- the responsibilities of all parties at the end of production,

- how the final work will be distributed,

- licensing rights,

- revenue sharing and, most importantly,

- services provided after the completion of production work.

Writing up a system of service section requires a full paragraph (3 to 5 sentences) for each of the bullet points listed above. This section of the Executive Summary must be coherent enough that a prospective client should have a simple understanding of what the results will be at the end of this project.

One small sample of a system of service section might look like this:

> This catalog will be created through a combination of video editing software (Final Cut Pro), multimedia production software (Flash), and a DVD authoring software (DVD Authoring Pro). We will also need access to a DVD production

house or a DVD multi-burner. Since the format of this project will be DVDs, we will give the final DVDs to the Dairy Barn, and they will be responsible for their distribution and act as the system that will be supporting the DVD storage on-site. Once the DVD has been created, handed to the Dairy Barn, and proven that the run correctly will end our interactions with the Dairy Barn. The Dairy Barn will own all of the primary rights for this project once the total cost of $8,000 has been paid to Fallout Shelter Productions, LLC.

It can be beneficial to outline as part of this section of the Executive Summary and the resource section the minimum requirements to complete a project of this nature and a hypothetical sample of what a low-quality version of the project would look like. It is also useful to provide an upper-level estimate of what would cost a professional-level version of the project and an example of what would be included in that quality of work. The rationale for including that information is that your Executive Summary should be considered a "middle-of-the-road" approach to creating the project. Most agencies and organizations one will work with during their career will pick the middle choice, which should be the one outlined in the Executive Summary (Porcheddu, 2011).

SUMMARY

In some cases, it may be required to summarize the highlights and bullet points of the proposal. The **summary** must be effective and simply explain all of the expectations regarding the project. It should act as either the contract or begin the progress of creating a contract. This summary is especially needed if the plan is longer than ten pages (with a budget, schedule, and other important information required to complete the plan). This section should have no more than three parts.

For example:

BEFORE THE PROJECT

It will be required to have access to all digital assets or delay the completion of the catalog. Any delays from the Dairy Barn may require an additional fee to compensate Fallout Shelter Productions, LLC.

RESOURCES AND TIMELINE

To meet the required datelines, it will also be important:

- to have access to the required personal,

- to have the approval of the materials completed in a timely manner, and

- to pay the agreed amount on time in order for Fallout Shelter Productions, LLC, to have access to the required facilities and materials.

DUE NOTICE

All of these must be met, or it will delay the completion of the catalog. Any delays from the Dairy Barn may require an additional fee to compensate Fallout Shelter Productions, LLC.

CONCLUSION

This module is not strictly about journalism, as mentioned in the introduction to this chapter. The rationale for including this information is to prepare journalists to take ownership of their work outside the typical news organization structure. The executive summary concept is a suitable means to flesh out a design for a show or a long-form piece of journalism and see if the plan survives a critical analysis of the concept. Completing the step in this chapter should give you a better sense of if the work can be feasible.

BOOTCAMP EXERCISE

Take a day or two to study one journalism show, series, or YouTube channel. Create an executive summary based on watching the content and analysis of the audience for that work. Discuss what makes that concept good based solely on the Executive Summary you have written.

ASSESSMENT OF THE MODULE

Basic: Perform a fundamental audience analysis of one media platform you use regularly.

Intermediate: Create an executive summary for a show you would want to work on. Do the basic audience research and analysis of other shows of a similar nature already out there. Pitch the show idea to your professor or a colleague.

Advanced: Create a pilot for the show outlined in the Executive Summary you developed in the intermediate assessment.

WORKS CITED

Chekima, B., Chekima, S., Wafa, S. A., Wafa, S. K., Igau, O. A., & Sondoh, S. L. (2015). Sustainable Consumption: The effects of knowledge, cultural values, environmental advertising, and demographics. *International Journal of Sustainable Development & World Ecology, 23*(2), 210–220. https://doi.org/10.1080/13504509.2015.1114043

Frick, T. (2008). *Managing Interactive Media Projects*. Thomson Delmar Learning.

Kahle, L. R. (2018). *Cross-national Consumer Psychographics*. Routledge.

Pollock, J. C. (2014). Illuminating Human Rights: How demographics drive media coverage. *Atlantic Journal of Communication, 22*(3-4) 141–159. https://doi.org/10.1080/15456870.2014.916292

Porcheddu, D. (2011). Choices from Identical Options in a Virtual Shopping Aisle. *The Open Business Journal, 4*(1), 36–45. https://doi.org/10.2174/1874915101104010036

Wells, W. D. (1975). Psychographics: A Critical Review. *Journal of Marketing Research, 12*(2), 196–213. https://doi.org/10.1177/002224377501200210

PART 2: CONCLUSION

August 25, 2014

The Northern Review had the first staff meeting of the academic year with me as the adviser. I remember looking at these wonderful student journalists that I inherited from the previous advisors (Bill O'Connell and Druann Bauer) and feeling nervous. Ohio Northern is the stalwart of college journalism. The university founded one of the first collegiate honoraries to acknowledge the hard work those students did in service of reporting the truth about college life. What they learned here would provide a foundation for future journalism, and I didn't want to screw that up.

I sat down with Dr. Bauer and Dr. O'Connell the week before school started to get their advice about running the newspaper. I ran an academic program before for four years, but we had limited student media on campus. My creative students at Ohio University Lancaster worked out an agreement with the local radio station to produce a weekly show with the feel of college radio. Reid Dillashaw, Jamie Polling, and Josh Mogan took what they learned in class and made something amazing. I told O'Connell and Bauer. They nodded as I told the story and came back with the only wisdom they had to offer.

"Listen to your students."

It was with this wisdom that I listened to the students to do the first pitch meeting. Sam Ventrella (my Editor-in-Chief) explained the process they used to write the paper. This process changed from the past as they came from a weekly print edition to an exclusively digital publication format. I spent all summer getting the site ready by transferring about two years of past content on the server.

One of the problems I noticed by the last two years was the number of stories not produced by students at Ohio Northern. Many stories were coming from wire services that the students used to fill the weekly edition pages. The Northern Review was less an expression of the student body on campus and more about the news of the world. It was a little disappointing but it made uploading previous editions quick as there were few stories in each edition written by ONU students.

I explained that this would change. We needed stories of local importance. I told the staff that there was not a hard deadline that all stories needed to be done to be published, as we were going with a rolling deadline format. This change in deadlines gave the editors more flexibility in the approaches to get news published. I explained to those gathered in the McIntosh Center's basement that we need to tell the ONU's story.

The discussion turned to how I would help them get more content for the site. There was a whiteboard in the room. I asked everybody in the room to write down anything that I could do as the advisor to improve the Northern Review quality. This level of discussion led to the development of the Practicum course. ONU already had a Practicum course for the Northern Review. The course was changed to be more a discussion with the students about the craft of journalism. The formal elements presented in this book were designed to supplement the informal conversation in the newsroom and my office.

There were several parts to the new Practicum. Students were now required to meet with me once a week for at least 15 minutes. They would either need to:

1. go over a story they just got published for the site in the form of executive review (which was borrowed for the conversations I had with media professionals and journalists I worked with in the past), using the ethical feedback model, and writing down in the student's journal in the form of reflective analysis, or

2. complete a training module if a story was not ready for review.

This time was useful as both of us (me and the student) looked for ways to improve. Practicum had six training modules that were required at the beginning (Journalism Breakdown, ethics, audio, video, photojournalism, and the CMS). Those topics evolved to the ones you see in this book. Discussion about articles would always begin with "What did you find to be the most difficult part in finishing the story?" This insight allowed me to get a better sense of how I could help the students.

I finished explaining the new Practicum format to the gathered student and added one final point. "This year is going to be a little weird. I'm new. Y'all have a system and way of doing things. We need to change that. My goal is to make you better journalists and be more engaged with the campus."

We ended the meeting. I asked Sam to stick around. Everybody else left. I asked Sam, "How do you think it went?" She told me that it was different, but she thought they were up for the challenge.

I was very proud of the work my first Northern Review staff produced over that year and continue to be impressed with their abilities. This part of the book is my way of listening to the students to find ways to help them.

POSTSCRIPT: THE FUTURE OF JOURNALISM IN SOCIETY

One of the concerns I often heard from colleagues (and some reviewers of this book) is that all of this training improves the journalists' technical skills by getting in the way of the journalist telling the story. One fellow journalist questioned the need for this application of communication practices into the process of the "rather simple craft" of journalism. It is fair to argue that this is a Legacy Journalism position. Journalists entering the industry need to understand how to construct a narrative to explain what is happening in the community to the broader audience by applying underlying theories into the newsgathering practice.

The primary reason I am a big proponent of this application of theory is based on discussions for friends and colleagues when journalists interview them. Most of them refuse to have those conversations because, as several of my colleagues have told me, journalists want the interviewees to parrot and add quotes to the story that has already been written.

These practices listed in the book are not an overt checklist that every editor needs to follow. It should be a grounding for a better conversation about how to improve the quality of the work. The complexity found in the Journalism Breakdown is designed to be simpler the more times the journalist practices this system. Writing Progressions becomes an easy way to get to the truth of the story. Understanding what facts need to be addressed in the story allows a journalist to interview the correct people by posing them unanswered questions in the progression. The article needs the interview quotes presented in their proper context. Other media content should follow the practices gained from completing the modules. The article is finalized when it meets the standards of journalism and passes an editorial review. I compare this technique to getting a piece of furniture from Ikea. This book is the instructions of putting the article together (without the funny-looking figures giving you the dos and don'ts). The process defines the work built on the standards and practices of Legacy Journalism while recognizing how Disruptive Journalism has impacted the industry.

One of the main critiques of this work is that it is built on the foundations of "backpack journalism." **Backpack journalism** is a set of beliefs that the journalist must take on all roles associated with the Legacy Journalism process and workflow, as that is where the industry is going. Bill Gentile (2010) takes this definition farther as "Backpack journalism is the craft of one properly trained professional using a hand-held digital video camera to tell stories in a more immediate, more intimate fashion than is achievable using a team that includes camera person, sound person, correspondent and producer." His focus on the individual storyteller is a good beginning as many communities might be less likely to trust a news crew or a member of the "mainstream media" to report on a community, but a single person who is trying to the tell the story of the action of others within a community is more likely to be accepted.

Gentile argues that the practice of backpack journalism methodologies is "built on the foundation of still photography. More specifically, documentary still photography, in which the practitioner has the luxury of time to document character and story development while altering the dynamics of character and story as little as possible." My background is in television news and documentary videography. Those experiences forced me to quickly understand how different media production tools should help the content creator present a reality based on the objective facts of the situation. It is that fundamental understanding that helps journalists find success in creating multimedia journalism content in an era of changing media systems and economic models. Telling a compelling story will attract an audience. Finding a system that will publish those compelling stories regularly will maintain an audience.

Compelling stories requires actively listening to others and incorporating those shared experiences into one overall narrative that clearly explains the interactions that are happening within a given community. This explanation does require a little bit of an understanding of sociological and psychological theory, which was baked into the previous chapters.

The final goal of working on this system and turning that information into a textbook is for journalists to become more thoughtful in their approach when covering the events of the day and use the tools of media production to craft truthful, compelling narratives that the audience has a reason to care about.

INDEX

academic research — 14
acoustics — 194
actor — 8
agenda — 72
...building — 73
...setting — 72
alert — 233
archived URL — 268
arithmetic mean — 271
artifacts — 276
artistic — 142
atmos — 195
Audacity — 204
audience — 8, 9, 141, 314
...of convenience — 9
...of interest — 9
...local — 9
...professional — 9
audio — 90, 194
...production — 194
authenticity — 122
averages — 270

backpack journalism — 330
balanced position — 199
bar graph — 287
bell curve — 276
Betteridge's Law of Headlines — 304
bias — 69
bit — 200
bootcamp — 174
brand — 82
breakdown session — 150
bridging transitions — 164
broadcast clip — 92

caption — 306
...the visual — 288
categories — 307
central tendency — 272
central visual — 287
channel — 82
chart — 287
...bar — 287
...line — 287
...pie — 287
Chiaroscuro — 220
clickbait — 75
CMS — 296
...content management system
...themes — 297
collective nouns — 160
comic journalism — 87
communication — 124
communicators — 141
community — 8, 9
...member — 111
...of convenience — 9
...of interest — 9
...of location — 9
...of professions — 9
compelling — 98
complicated situation — 100
confronting — 100
context — 148
contextual denseness — 39
continuing coverage — 233
copy editing — 164
CRAAP Test — 16, 162, 235
...accuracy — 16
...authority — 16
...currency — 16

...relevance	16	executive review	152
...purpose	16	executive summary	312
CRAP Principles	290	...audience	314
...alignment of elements	290	...budget	317
...contrast	290	...purpose	313
...repeating elements	290	...resources	316
...proximity	290	...schedule	318
critical mass of users	227	...summary	313
cross-examining	52	...support structure	319
		...system of service	320
data map	288	expert	110
deliberative	141	expertise	13
deliberate practice	154	explainer	92
demographics	314		
depth of field	93	fact-checking	121
developing story	233	factoid box	287
diagram	288	factors	15
digital audio recorders	199	feature writing	240
Disruptive Journalism	20	...how-to	241
diversity of experiences	227	...human-interest	240
drop quote	30	...informational	241
dropshipping	112	...news	241
DSLR camera	177	...past events	242
...Digital Single Lens Reflex camera		...personality	241
dummy sets	270	..."The Best"	242
		fidelity	194
echo chamber	227	field camera	221
editorial content	74	Five Criteria	138
editorial review	152	...contextual	148
Elements	8	...mechanical	139
empathy	100	...mediation	143
epideictic	142	...rhetorical	140
equipment kit	56	...voice	149
Essential Questions	15	flow	9
essential aesthetics	127	focal length	179
ethics	253	fontface	290
ethical feedback model	138	forensic	141
ethos	10, 143	Fourth Estate	253
event	8	free marketplace of ideas	228
evergreen subject	51	FOIA request	268

...Freedom Of Information Act

Freewriting 16

frequency 194

Fundamental Research 14

gatekeeper 189

gatekeeping 76

GIS 93

...geographic information system

Goldielocks' effect 35

Gonzo Journalism 16

grafs 20

...one-sentence 27

graphics 87, 163

hard news stories 214

headline 304

hedcut drawing 87

HEIF/HEVC format 178

Hertzs 194

home-brewed 298

hooks, hook graf 27

...journalistic hooks 28

...narrative hooks 28

...one-sentence graf 28

...whammy 29

icons 281

ideal audience member 315

ideologies 70

...framing 71

...narrative 70

illustrations 163

immersive technologies 82

imprecise language 275

inartistic 141

indefinite pronouns 157

infographics 88, 284

...form of the 289

...function of the 289

...headlining 288

interactive content 93

interactivity 228

interviews 47

...email 56

...face-to-face 55

...format of the 56

...Ground Rules 59

...group 56

...individual 56

...journalistic 47

...medium of the 55

...panel 56

...protocols 48

...raw 90

...scheduling of the 56

...semi-structured 57

...structured 56

...telephone 55

...unstructured 57

introductory 156

...clauses 156

...phrases 156

...words 156

inverted pyramid 25

issue 8

...cultural 14

...social 14

Journalism Breakdown 10, 132

journalistic organization 10

keywords 305

Kuleshov Effect 220

landscapes 183

lede, lede graf 25

...boring lede 26

...descriptive lede 27

...informative lede 26

Legacy Journalism	20	mode	270
Lego Journalism	76	modifiers	159
lenses	178	...compound	159
...fisheye	180	...dangling	159
...macro	180	module (bootcamp)	174
...portrait	180	modules (CMS)	297
...standard	179	momentum	102
...super telephoto	180	morality	254
...telephoto	180	mpeg4 video format	204
...ultra-wide	180	mp3 audio format	204
...wide	180		
LETTER	67	narrative	7
logos (graphic)	280	...conflicts of literature	240
logos (logic)	142	...filters	126
lossless formats	199	...journalism	71
lossy formats	199	natural sounds	193
		news	10
Maddow Method	54	...breaking	229
mediated work	7	...deserts	112
media	82	...flash	233
median	271	...live	229
medium	82	...organization	10
...electronic	84	newscast	91
...traditional	84	non-linear editing	204
message	141	normal distribution pattern	276
metadata	298	novel subject	51
microphone	200	nuts, nut graf	31
...bidirectional	202	...chronological	32
...cardioid	201	...humanistic	33
...handheld	218	...institutional	32
...hypercardioid	201		
...lapel	218	observational reporting	14
...Lobar	202	observers	112
...omnidirectional	200	...active	113
...pickup	200	...casual	113
...shotgun	218	on the record	59
...supercardioid	202		
mindmapping	17	p-score	272
mirroring	53	paragraphs	20
modal writing	36	parallel construction	160

parts of speech 160
pass-through 218
passive voice 157
pathos 142
per capita 273
percentage 273
performances 70
personal code of ethics 254
photos 163, 306
photojournalism 89
pitch meeting 300
platform 82
podcast 91
point of interest 8
population 274
primacy effect 221
priming elements 275
production stages 210
...post-production 211
...pre-production 210
...production 210
professional code of conduct 254
pronoun confusion 158
psychoacoustics 197
psychographics 315
purpose 141, 313

questions 52
...clarifying 61
...closed-ended 53
...GOSS 61
...leading 52
...loaded 275
...open-ended 53
...probing 53
..."so what" 108
questionnaires 276

radio package 91
random sampling 275

...stratified 275
ratios 272
recency effect 221
reality 122
red flags 63
reflective analysis 173
regression analysis 279
reviews 154
...editorial 155
...executive 155
rhetorical construction 75
rhetorical pivot and shift 29
roles 297
Rule of Thirds 290
Rule of Three 290

SaaS 298
...software-as-a-service
sample pool 274
sampling 199
scale 270
...interval 271
...nominal 270
...ordinal 271
...ratio 271
scribe 114
sentences 20
serial-position effect 221
server-side options 297
setting 141
shots 182, 212
...action 185
...candid 187
...closeup (CU) 217
...extra long (XLS) 216
...extreme closeup (XCU) 217
...extreme wide (EWS) 216
...eye-level 220
...high angle 220
...high-quality 212

...low angle 220
...medium (MS) 216
...mug 187
...slice-of-life 187
...staged 186
...wide (WS) 216
significance value 278
single lens reflex (SLR) 177
skewed data set 272
Skype 203
slug 218
smurf term 99
social desirability theory 275
social journalism 298
social media 226
soft news stories 214
solving 100
sound 194
soundbytes 90, 193
spirit of journalism 10
staged shots 183
standard deviation 261
standardized 274
standards and practices 255
storytelling 84
stream of consciousness 17
structure 238
...Christmas tree 246
...dollar sign 243
...mini-vignettes 248
...traditional 242
Student's t-test 278
subject-verb agreement 160
summary 305, 321
surveys 274
...qualitative 276
symmetrical data set 272
sympathy 100
syndicated works 87

t-Test for One Sample Mean 278
TACT Test 305
tags 307
...identification 289
text 85
...alternate 306
...image theme 306
themes
...CMS 297
...contextual 69
thematic analysis 276
theory of the story 110
thoughtful engagement 228
three-beat timing 209
three-column system 222
title 306
topic 8
train of thought 17
trendlines 278
trends 73
typefaces 290, 291

underlying value 228

verification 123
video 92
...documentary 92
...feature 92
...raw 92
video conferencing 55

WAV 199
...WAVeform audio file format
websites 37
...community-driven 38
...ephemeral 41
...media-driven 40
...microblogging 39
...professional networking 42
whammy 27

widgets	297
witness	113
workflow	299
...personal	300
...platform-level	299
Works-Every-Time model	287
wrapper	305
Writing Progression	34
writing in the round	35
zoom	178
...digital	178
...optical	178
3:2:1 Rule for Backups	222, 302
24-bit depth	200
60 Minutes echo	53
192kHz sample rate	200

CPSIA information can be obtained
at www.ICGtesting.com
Printed in the USA
LVHW062221110723
752151LV00005B/220